South-South Migration

T0382794

South-South migration contributes significantly to the development of the emerging economies, the migration of receiving countries and, at the same time, generates a major share of remittance income flowing into the sending countries.

By capturing field experience and observations from a number of research studies, this book provides a robust catalogue of data, practical experience and analysis focused on the significant issues, risks and challenges that are associated with this evolving phenomenon in international migration. The book also critically explores new theoretical perspectives by highlighting new policy directions for both sending and receiving countries relevant to making South-South migration more efficient, attractive and mutually beneficial.

Patricia Short is an Honorary Associate Professor of Sociology and former senior teaching and research academic in the School of Social Science, The University of Queensland, Australia. Her research and publications on gender and household vulnerabilities have focused on housing access in Australia; microcredit, migration and livelihood strategies in the developing world; and mixed economies of welfare.

Moazzem Hossain is an Adjunct Associate Professor in the Department of International Business and Asian Studies at Griffith University, Australia, and former senior research officer of the Australian Bureau of Agricultural and Resource Economics (ABARE). Over the last three decades, his research has covered forestry economics, economic development in South Asia, telecommunications regulation, and climate change and growth in Asia.

M. Adil Khan is an Adjunct Professor in the field of Development Practice in the School of Social Science, The University of Queensland, Australia, and former senior policy manager at the United Nations, promoting the work of civic engagement in public governance.

Routledge Studies in Development, Mobilities and Migration

This series is dedicated to the growing and important area of mobilities and migration within Development Studies. It promotes innovative and interdisciplinary research targeted at a global readership.

The series welcomes submissions from established and junior authors on cutting-edge and high-level research on key topics that feature in global news and public debate.

These include the Arab spring; famine in the Horn of Africa; riots; environmental migration; development-induced displacement and resettlement; livelihood transformations; people-trafficking; health and infectious diseases; employment; South-South migration; population growth; children's wellbeing; marriage and family; food security; the global financial crisis; drugs wars; and other contemporary crisis.

For a full list of titles in this series, please visit www.routledge.com/series/RSDM

South-South Migration
Emerging Patterns, Opportunities and Risks

**Edited by Patricia Short,
Moazzem Hossain and M. Adil Khan**

Routledge
Taylor & Francis Group

LONDON AND NEW YORK

First published 2017
by Routledge
2 Park Square, Milton Park, Abingdon, Oxon OX14 4RN

and by Routledge
605 Third Avenue, New York, NY 10017

First issued in paperback 2020

Routledge is an imprint of the Taylor & Francis Group, an informa business

British Library Cataloguing-in-Publication Data
A catalogue record for this book is available from the British Library

Library of Congress Cataloging-in-Publication Data
A catalog record for this book has been requested

ISBN 13: 978-0-367-85962-6 (pbk)
ISBN 13: 978-1-138-93480-1 (hbk)

Typeset in Galliard
by Apex CoVantage, LLC

Contents

Illustrations

Tables

Contributors

Campbell Fraser is Senior Lecturer in the Department of International Business and Asian Studies, Griffith Business School, Griffith University, Australia.

Yuko Hamada is Regional Migration Officer at IOM, Washington D.C., United States, and former regional migration officer for Asia and the Pacific, Bangkok, Thailand.

Samsul Hoque is Executive Officer of the Meghna Sub-district, Comilla Government of Bangladesh.

Moazzem Hossain is Adjunct Associate Professor in the Department of International Business and Asian Studies, Griffith Business School, Griffith University, Australia.

Munshi Israil Hossain is Assistant Professor at the Rajshahi University, Bangladesh, and a PhD candidate in the School of Social Science, University of Queensland, Australia.

Paul Howard is Lecturer in the Department of International Business and Asian Studies, Griffith Business School, Griffith University, Australia.

M. Adil Khan is Adjunct Professor in the field of Development Practice at the School of Social Science, University of Queensland, Australia.

Habibul Haque Khondker is Professor in the Department of Humanities and Social Sciences at Zayed University, Abu Dhabi, UAE.

Amina Maharjan is Livelihood Specialist (Migration) at ICIMOD (an International NGO) based in Kathmandu, and Consultant, Swiss Aid, Switzerland.

Patricia Short is Honorary Associate Professor of Sociology in the School of Social Science, University of Queensland, Australia.

Yenny Tjoe is a PhD candidate in the Department of International Business and Asian Studies, Griffith Business School, Griffith University, Australia.

Acknowledgements

We would like to take the opportunity to thank the School of Social Science at the University of Queensland and Griffith Asia Institute at Griffith University for their generous support for two international workshops in Brisbane, which facilitated seminar and workshop sessions among contributors to this collaborative project. Amy McMahon of the School of Social Science and Natasha Vary of Griffith Asia Institute made the workshops a great success at short notice, despite the challenges of international travel permits for contributors travelling from three to four different overseas destinations on each occasion. We also acknowledge the time and skill Roy Short has provided in shaping a chaotic manuscript into a presentable one. Without this support, it would have been almost impossible to meet the publisher's deadline.

Our sincere appreciations go to all the contributors for committing their time and efforts to the project and for so enthusiastically sharing their research and knowledge in this way.

The Editors
Brisbane, October 2016

Acknowledgments

1 An overview of South-South migration

Opportunities, risks and policies

Moazzem Hossain, M. Adil Khan
and Patricia Short

1. Introduction

In the contemporary world, South-South (developing country to developing country) migration constitutes the bulk of international migration. South-South migration, predominantly labour migration, contributes significantly to the development of the emerging economies of migration receiving countries and, at the same time, generates a major share of income flowing into migrant-sending countries. Over many years, international agencies such as the UN International Fund for Agricultural Development (IFAD), the World Bank (WB), and the International Organization for Migration (IOM) have documented key trends in international migration on a global scale, and in doing so have focused attention upon significant shifts in migration flows, forms and outcomes. Recent studies highlight the growth and significance of South-South migration, particularly in Asia – especially the increasing number of temporary labour migrants travelling from slower developing nations to growth economies in the Asian region, the associated increase in the flow of remittances within the region, and the emerging opportunities and costs for both sending and receiving nations, and migrant workers and their families. By capturing field experience and observations from a number of research studies, this volume provides a robust catalogue of data, practical experience, and observations focused on the significant issues, risks, and challenges that are associated with this evolving phenomenon in international migration. It focuses upon Asia as a significant and rapidly changing global hub of South-South migration, and attends to the interactions of macro- and micro-level processes and outcomes of migration and remittance, from the variable structural transformations in the economies and polities of the region to the experiences and impacts of migration and remittances at the local level. It does so in terms of livelihoods, poverty reduction, access to education and health care, gender empowerment and migrants' rights. The collection critically explores new perspectives and highlights new policy directions relevant to making South-South migration more efficient, attractive and mutually beneficial to sending and receiving countries, migrants, their households, communities and nations.

2.   Background

There has been increasing interest in migration and development issues in the era of economic globalization. Economic globalization contributes not only to advancing commodity trade; it also has brought a major shift in the flow of workers from labour abundant to labour scarce nations. According to the United Nations, there were 244 million international migrants (persons residing outside their country of birth) in 2015 from all over the world. Nearly 58 percent of these migrants lived in the developed regions (the global North) but some 61 percent originated from a developing country. Forty-two percent of the world's total migrant stock in 2015 resided in developing regions with the vast majority of these migrants (87 percent) originating from other parts of the developing world (the global South; United Nations 2016, p. 1). Approximately 40 percent of the world's migrants in 2015 originated from the Asian region, and nearly one-third were residing in Asia, almost equivalent to the number residing in all countries of Europe, and exceeding the number in North America. What distinguishes the patterns of migration in the Asian region is the very high proportion of migrants who originate from countries within the region. Of all of those migrating to Asian countries in the period 1990–2015, 90 percent came from other countries in Asia and, by 2015, Asia-to-Asia regional corridors constituted the largest in the world (United Nations 2016, pp. 2–3). This regional concentration contrasts with the patterns for Europe and North America, which are much more diversified, and reflects, in large part, the movement of semi-skilled and low-skilled migrant workers within the region (United Nations 2016, p. 12).

The destinations of the overwhelming majority of Asian migrants are the Gulf Cooperation Council (GCC) countries of the Middle East (or Western Asia), Southeast Asia and East Asia. Within the Asian region, three main migration flows have emerged over the past three decades: from South Asia and Southeast Asia to GCC countries; flows within the ASEAN region; and from Southeast Asia to East Asia. The largest of these is the flow towards the GCC countries. In 2015, almost 15.4 million migrants from South Asia and 3.5 million from Southeast Asian nations were residing in GCC countries (United Nations 2015). Five nations (Bangladesh, India, Indonesia, Pakistan and the Philippines) were the countries of origin for more than 17 million migrants residing in GCC countries (UN 2015).

Remittances, one of the most significant outcomes of international migration, are now estimated at more than USD600 billion globally (World Bank 2016a, p. xii). Remittances sent home by international migrants from developing countries in 2015 stood at around USD432 billion in 2015, a figure that exceeded that of International Development Assistance (Ratha et al. 2016, pp. 4–5). Although the growth of remittances (the personal transfers of employees working outside their country of permanent residence), worldwide, has slowed somewhat since 2014, largely due to weaker economic performance in remittance-source countries, remittances contribute very high proportions of foreign income to the economies of slower-developing nations of the South and, on a

Table 1.1 Remittance inflows to top seven Asian countries, 2012–2015 (USD billion)

Country	2012	2013	2014	2015	2016*
India**	68.82	69.97	70.39	68.91	65.45
China**	57.99	59.49	62.33	63.94	65.17
Philippines**	23.35	25.37	27.27	28.48	29.1
Pakistan**	14.01	14.63	17.24	19.31	20.3
Bangladesh**	14.12	13.87	14.99	15.39	14.85
Vietnam	10.00	11.00	12.00	13.00	13.35
Indonesia	7.21	7.61	8.55	9.63	9.84

* 2016 data are estimates.
** Among the top ten remittance-receiving countries, globally.

Source: World Bank (2016b)

global scale, are larger than official development assistance and demonstrably more stable than private capital flows (private debt and portable equity; Ratha et al. 2016, p. 5). Among the top ten remittance-receiving countries in the world in 2015, five were in Asia, a pattern that is likely to be sustained into the future. Table 1.1 presents a clear picture of the volume of remittance inflows to the top seven Asian receiving countries.

In addition to the flow of economic resources, migration involves the flow of noneconomic resources from migrant receiving countries to migrant-sending countries (and vice versa). Such flows include transfer of knowledge, technology and ideas that have made significant contributions to the sending economies in a macroeconomic sense and to migrant households, communities and local economies from a micro point of view. Experiences and outcomes of labour migration are not, however, all positive. Migration entails significant costs and inequities (among nations and individuals) in inputs, processes and outcomes. Migrant workers, their households and communities bear considerable costs, both financial and non-financial, sometimes outweighing the benefits, and as the scale and complexity of migratory flows has increased, related issues of governance in both sending and receiving nations have become matters of much concern and debate. It is these issues, as much as the evidence of rapid economic growth in some developing nations alongside the evidence of significant structural transformations in slower-growth, remittance-induced economies of the South, that have prompted production of this volume.

3. Overview

Rapid economic growth in some countries of the global South has triggered rising demand for foreign labour and, at the same time, rising population and slow economic growth in others have led to oversupply of unemployed and underemployed labour, creating opportunities for migration from the latter to the former countries (United Nations 2004). Contemporary patterns of migration, triggered by such uneven economic growth coupled with the technological potential for a highly mobile, international labour force, constitute a sharp break with the past. In the present day and age, the number and types of migration, as well as the configuration of the sending and receiving countries, have become truly global in the scope and direction of movement. In recent years, while the volume of migrants has increased exponentially, destinations of migration have also diversified and undergone significant change, shifting from predominantly South-North to South-South (Castles and Miller 2003; Massey 2003; IOM 2013a; United Nations 2014).

South-South labour migration and remittances have become major resources for development, construction and service industries in receiving countries and of development financing and poverty alleviation in sending countries. At the macroeconomic level, labour migrants' financial remittances make significant contributions to the gross domestic product of the migrant-sending countries. South-South labour migration and financial remittances also contribute to increasing human capital through education, health and training of migrants' household members, increasing household income and material resources and developing community capacity. However, international migration in general and South-South migration in particular pose several challenges that often either decrease net financial benefit or entail significant social costs, especially at the migrant household levels.

Evident inequities in the distribution of benefits and costs of migration, not only at the country level but also at the individual and household level among migrants and others engaged in the business of labour migration and remittance, have prompted our attention to macro-micro linkages in migration systems. Much of the research presented in this volume demonstrates the significant and positive impacts of labour migration and remittances at the national level for receiving and sending countries, respectively. It also reveals the local dimensions of labour migration and remittance; and how migrants themselves, in their households, families and local communities, and through their networks of association, make decisions about migration for employment, as a livelihood or income enhancement strategy. What becomes very clear is that, under the conditions of contemporary South-South migration, migrant workers embark upon their quest in a variety of circumstances that facilitate, but all too often constrain, their capacities to benefit from the opportunities that labour migration affords, and the costs, both economic and social, are unevenly distributed.

Taken together, the chapters in this volume highlight the importance of understanding the workings of migration systems at all levels, and the value of research that addresses not only macro- or micro-level structures, processes and impacts but also their interactions. There is a logic to the order of chapters. Chapter 2 offers an analysis of South-South migration as a contemporary phenomenon and thus provides a reference point for consideration of the range of case studies presented in the chapters that follow. Case studies (Chapters 3, 4, 5, 6 and 7) are arranged, broadly, in terms of the breadth of their focus; from macro-level or systemic to household level though the interactions of macro and micro structures and processes are salient in all. The last two chapters in the volume (Chapters 8 and 9) focus attention, again, at a broader level, upon policy and governance.

In Chapter 2, Khan and Hossain explore the phenomenon of South-South migration in the era of globalization. The chapter provides an analysis of the historical, political and regional underpinnings of South-South migration, and an overview of the patterns and forms of international migration that define contemporary South-South migration or 'Globalized South-South (GSS) migration'. By drawing in large part upon the case studies and other works in this volume, Khan and Hossain posit a theoretical framework highlighting the characteristics of GSS migration that distinguish it from other, earlier forms of international migration. They highlight, in particular, the temporary or cyclical nature of migration and the increasing engagement of semi- and low-skilled workers; the complementary macroeconomic dimensions of sending and receiving countries that work in a push-pull dynamic that solves both the problem of labour demand in receiving countries and the problem of surplus labour in sending countries; the rapidity of growth in demand for labour and the voluntary and accessible nature of labour migration that together have spawned the growth of massive, transformative but weakly governed markets in labour and remittance (cf. IFAD and World Bank 2013; Suttie and Vagas-Lundius 2016). How these features influence both the processes and the outcomes of South-South migration is a key consideration. Ultimately, Khan and Hossain point to the significance of effective policy and good governance for achieving more transparent and accountable systems of migration and remittance, and more equitable outcomes.

The study reported by Howard in Chapter 3 focuses on the political economy of labour migration within the Greater Mekong Sub-region (GMSR) of Southeast Asia and investigates cross-border migration from Cambodia and Laos into Thailand, and a related pattern of internal migration in Yunnan Province in China. These sites present differing political and economic contexts but there are underlying commonalities among them in terms of their emergence from economic disadvantage, and labour migration impacts on agricultural development in the sending communities. One such impact is the engagement with technology that is essential to the process of remitting income from the host country to the sending community, and the potential for investment of such knowledge in sending communities. Increased understandings of technology and production, coupled with the use of remittances for education and health care, provide impetus to socioeconomic development in the sending communities. However, the potential application of new knowledge returned to sending communities through remittance by migrant workers exposed to new technologies and work practices is curtailed by the limited capacity for investment of remittances (financial and technological) in agriculture.

Howard points to the exploitation of migrant workers, weak regulation, limited transparency and poor access to information as key factors that exacerbate migrant vulnerabilities and limit the benefits of migration. The chapter highlights the importance of enabling a freer flow of 'registered' labour in the GMSR through improved migration governance across the region, and the need for monitoring of border crossings and improved access to information among the most vulnerable groups (unskilled migrant workers, those with low educational levels, women and children and the unregistered). Howard argues that such improvements are essential to achieve a fair and equitable labour migration process in the GMSR, and that this is key to harnessing the full potential that intra-regional migration offers for sending communities and the region as a whole.

Continuing the focus on the Mekong sub-region, in Chapter 4 Fraser and Howard present a comparative study of Cambodian migrant workers returning from Thailand. Their analysis focuses attention on the effects of different drivers and conditions of migration by comparing the experiences and outcomes of migration in relation to the socioeconomic 'urgency' of migration. Some 247 migrants, repatriated from Thailand, were involved in the study. They were classified and analysed as two distinct groups: those migrating under an urgent socioeconomic imperative (classified as 'Involuntary Livelihood Pushed' migrants) and those migrating voluntarily in order to accumulate wealth (classified as Voluntary Income Enhancement migrants). The findings of the research, presented in Chapter 4, indicate that participants who were 'pushed' to migrate as a result of their dire economic circumstances not only endured worse conditions of both employment and living standards in Thailand, but they also were more willing to accept such poor conditions when compared to the group of migrants who had the opportunity to make more considered decisions in regard to their migration options. Through their comparative analysis of the experiences of 'livelihood pushed' and 'income enhancement' motivated migrants, Fraser and Howard explore, in some depth, the nature of employment brokerage and illustrate the wider role that brokers play in facilitating migration within the context of the political economy of the Mekong Sub-region, and South-South migration more generally.

Chapter 5 turns the focus to labour migration from Bangladesh, and an examination of the socioeconomic impact of remittance income, at the household level. Hossain, Tjoe and Hoque report findings from a household survey conducted in the Meghna Sub-district of Bangladesh in 2014–2015. Since independence in 1971, Bangladesh has sent more than eight million workers all over the world, the majority to the Gulf Cooperation Council countries and Malaysia. A recent study estimates that from remittances sent by these migrant workers up to 2014, the country had received some USD15 billion (Bangladesh Bureau of Statistics 2016); in 2015, the nation was the world's tenth-largest remittance recipient (World Bank 2016a, p. 12). The World Bank estimates that the average remittances to receiving households is equivalent to 80 percent of the receiving household's income and is twice the national per capita income (World Bank 2014). With this as the backdrop, Hossain, Tjoe and Hoque investigated household demographics and the distribution of income in migrant workers' households. They also compared the households of migrant workers with that of the non-migrant households in the survey area to estimate the impacts of remittance income on poverty and income inequality in the study area. They conclude that migration and remittances make a significant contribution to poverty reduction and equity among migrant households in the Meghna Sub-district.

The impacts of migration and remittances for migrants and their households are explored from a different perspective in Chapter 6. Taking a more ethnographic approach, Hossain and Short offer a descriptive account of the changing dynamics of migrant households at the village level, based upon a case study undertaken in a rural village of Bangladesh where labour migration to Malaysia, over some ten to fifteen years, has increasingly become a regular pattern of income earning among a substantial and increasing proportion of households. Hossain and Short focus on two key aspects of the experiences and circumstances of migrants and their households: first, how remittance incomes are used in the households of migrant workers, and how remittance income contributes to changing livelihood patterns and capital formation in migrants' households; second, the social dimensions of migration and changing livelihoods in migrants' households. The chapter also presents an overview of the economic context in which international labour migration has emerged as a significant livelihood strategy in the village and explores how a particular, localized pattern of middlemen-driven, limited-repeat cyclical migration and remittance to and from Malaysia has become established.

In Chapter 7, in the context of Nepal, Maharjan investigates the social as well as economic impacts of cross-border and international migration and remittance at migrant household level. Nepal has very high rates of internal, cross-border and international migration and is one of the most highly remittance dependent countries, with remittance inflows making up approximately 29 percent of GDP in 2014 (World Bank 2016a, p. xii). Overall, migration and income remittance has a positive impact on the livelihood outcomes of sending households in Nepal. Typically, households invest first in improving or purchasing physical assets – house, land and other assets. With more liquid cash remitted to households, their financial situation also improves both in terms of available cash as well as credit worthiness. Migration also helps to improve the skills (both technical and life skills) of the migrant himself/herself, as well as the remaining household members, particularly in relation to children's educational outcomes. Remittance income is also spent on accessing health services for members of the family who may be unwell, although at the same time working conditions for migrant workers at certain destinations put migrants at greater health risk. As the whole process of migration is influenced by social networks, migration in turn also enhances the social capital of households left behind and this, along with the inflow of remittances, has moderated the social hierarchy based on economic class and the caste structure. The impact of migration on gender equality is also significant; migration and the resulting opportunities for women clearly have significant potential for women's empowerment in Nepal.

Maharjan's study demonstrates clear benefits of migration and remittance at the household level but reveals differential outcomes for overseas migrants and cross-border migrants (those who travel across the national border to neighbouring India). It also reveals gaps in knowledge and understanding of sustainable impacts of migration and remittance. Maharjan concludes by highlighting the importance of systematic, longitudinal research to inform policy development, and ultimately, to increase the benefits of migration for migrant households and protect the rights of migrant workers.

Chapters 8 and 9 return to a broader view of South-South migration and consider the implications of benefits and risks for both sending and receiving countries with regard to improvements in policy and governance into the future. In Chapter 8, Hamada focuses attention upon the interests and rights of migrant workers, the perspective of South 'receiving countries' and the relevance and implication of the Sustainable Development Goals agenda for migration and migrants' welfare. The chapter presents broad-based evidence and documented examples illustrating that, despite the volume of labour migration and remittance in the contemporary, globalized world, migrant workers from the global South, overall, still have very limited access to safe and secure working and living environments in countries of destination.

In the fast-growing economies of the Asian region, the Newly Industrial Countries (NICs)[1] and countries of the Gulf Cooperation Council (GCC),[2] migrants are engaged in low-skilled work in construction, heavy industry, plantations, agriculture, fishing, food processing, timber and domestic services – that is, in so-called 3D jobs (dirty, dangerous and/or difficult), or a combination of the three (Koser 2010, p. 306). Such jobs pay relatively low wages, and employment conditions are often physically challenging and do not meet safety requirement standards. Migrant workers typically have little access to social security such as health and other public services, or education for their family members. In many instances, exploitation of migrant workers remains invisible due to the irregular status of many migrants and unethical practices of recruiting agencies. Hamada argues that in order to maximize gain from migration, attention to the wellbeing of migrant workers in receiving countries is essential. Migrants and mobile populations benefit from an improved standard of physical, mental and social wellbeing, which enables them to contribute substantially towards the social and economic development of their home communities and host societies alike (IOM 2013b). She argues for greater cooperation between countries of origin and countries of destination to improve migrant experiences and outcomes of migration, and points to the UN Sustainable Development Goals (SDG) agenda as a framework for improving policy and cooperation, especially among migrant-sending countries which, she argues, must move toward collective bargaining in their efforts to secure better and more sustainable conditions for their migrant workers abroad.

In Chapter 9, Khondker examines various existing institutions and processes at the global and/or international level that oversee migration processes in the Asian region, including the Colombo Process, launched in 2003. The chapter reviews the current status of global migration governance, and explores the dynamics of international migration governance by tracing the recent history of labour migration to the Arab Gulf states, a major receiving hub within the Asian region. Temporary labour migration or labour mobility has played a large part in the infrastructural development of the Arabian Gulf countries, and remittances from the Arab Gulf states (most particularly the member states of the GCC) have played an important role in the socioeconomic development of the labour-sending countries of South and Southeast Asia. Despite the enormity of the migration process and its growing economic importance, there is no single global institution in charge of administering this large trans-border process. Migration is still within the jurisdiction of national governance. Khondker argues that to improve the effectiveness of labour migration governance in ensuring safe migration, protecting the dignity and wellbeing of labour migrants, and ensuring their safe-return to their source countries, relations and processes at all the three tiers of governance (global, national and local) need to be improved and coordinated.

Taken together, the chapters in this book provide considerable insight on the potential for enhancing the links between migration, remittances and the broad-scale development agenda reflected in the UN SDGs. They also point to the importance of taking into account both the broader scale, macro-level economic and political relations that motivate the mass movements of people across the globe, and the local, micro-level social conditions and relationships that animate individual responses and experiences, and shape the outcomes of migration and remittances, at the individual, household and community level. Collectively, the contributions to this volume provide greater insight on the dynamics of what Khan and Hossain have called Globalized South-South migration. Though focusing upon the Asian region, the chapters in this collection encompass a multiplicity of forms, processes and experiences of migration and remittance, and hence reflect the complexity of drivers and outcomes of Globalized South-South migration.

This book, thus, provides a useful account of the state of present knowledge of South-South migration as a guide to students, academics and policy makers on the subject of migration and development of emerging nations. The book will generate further debate on the issues and challenges of migration and development in the nations of the global South, across the world. It points to the importance of sound research and policy development, and ultimately to good governance that guarantees transparency and accountability in migration processes, including protection of migrant rights, and their safety and security in receiving countries. These are the keys to improving the migration experience for migrants and their families and households, and to enhancing and sustaining development outcomes for both sending and receiving communities and nations.

Notes

1 China, Indonesia, India, Philippines, Malaysia, and Thailand
2 Kingdom of Bahrain, Kuwait, Sultanate of Oman, Qatar, Kingdom of Saudi Arabia (KSA), and United Arab Emirates

10   *Moazzem Hossain et al.*

References

Bangladesh Bureau of Statistics 2016, *Report of the Survey on Investment from Remittance (SIR) 2016*, Bangladesh Bureau of Statistics (BBS), Ministry of Planning, Dhaka.
Castles, S and Miller, MJ 2003, *The Age of Migration*, 3rd edn, Guilford Press, New York.
IFAD and World Bank 2013, *Sending Money Home to Asia: Trends, Opportunities in the World's Largest Remittance Marketplace*, International Fund for Agricultural Development (IFAD), Rome, viewed 15 October 2016, <https://www.ifad.org/documents/10180/352c6b0f-dc74-4637-81aa-8fda3677d054>.
IOM (International Organization for Migration) 2013a, *World Migration Report 2013: Migrant Well-being and Development*, IOM, Geneva.
IOM (International Organization for Migration) 2013b, *Migration Health: Healthy Migrants in Healthy Communities*, viewed 19 January 2015, <http://health.iom.int/>.
Koser, K 2010, 'Introduction: International Migration and Global Governance', *Global Governance*, vol. 16, pp. 301–15, viewed 23 August 2014, <http://www.thefreelibrary.com/Introduction:internationalmigrationandglobalGovernance.-a0237050213>.
Massey, DS 2003, 'Patterns and Processes of International Migration in the 21st Century', Paper Presented to the *Conference on African Migration in Comparative Perspective*, Johannesburg, South Africa, Johannesburg, South Africa, 4–7 June, viewed 6 June 2012, <http://worldroom.tamu.edu/Workshops/Migration06/GlobalMigration/Globa%20Migratio%20articles/Pattern%20an%20Processe%20o%20Internationa%20Migratio%20i%20th%2021S%20Centur%202003.pdf>.
Ratha, D, De, S, Plaza, S, Schuettler, S, Shaw, W, Wyss, H, and Yi, S 2016, *Migration and Remittances – Recent Developments and Outlook*, Migration and Development Brief 26, April 2016, World Bank, Washington, DC.
Suttie, D and Vagas-Lundius, R 2016, *Migration and Transformative Pathways: A Rural Perspective*, IFAD Research Series 02, International Fund for Agricultural Development, Rome.
United Nations 2004, *World Economic and Social Survey 2004: International Migration*, Department of Economic and Social Affairs, New York, viewed 11 June 2012, <http://www.un.org/en/development/desa/policy/wess/wess_archive/2004wess_part2_eng.pdf>.
United Nations 2014, *Population Facts*, Department of Economic and Social Affairs, Population Division, New York, viewed 1 April 2015, <http://www.un.org/en/development/desa/population/publications/factsheets>.
United Nations 2015, *Trends in International Migrant Stock: Migrants by Destination and Origin (United Nations Database, POP/DB/MIG/Stock/Rev.2015)*, UN Department of Economic and Social Affairs (DESA), Population Division, New York.
United Nations 2016, *International Migration Report 2015 (ST/ESA/SER.A/384)*, UN Department of Economic and Social Affairs (DESA), Population Division, New York.
World Bank 2014, *Migration and Development Brief 22*, The World Bank, Washington, DC.
World Bank 2016a, *Migration and Remittances Factbook, 2016*, 3rd edn, World Bank, Washington, DC.
World Bank 2016b, *Migration and Remittances Data: Inflows*, viewed 19 October, 2016, <http://www.worldbank.org/en/topic/migrationremittancesdiasporaissues/brief/migration-remittances-data>.

2 The emerging phenomenon of post-globalized, South-South migration

In search of a theoretical framework

M. Adil Khan and Munshi Israil Hossain

1. Introduction

International migration, meaning people moving from one country and/or from one region to another for economic and/or other reasons, is as old as human existence (Wickramasekara 2002). However, this study focuses on the new phenomenon of South-South migration, a post-colonial/post-globalization phenomenon that involves labour migration from mostly slower-growing developing to faster-growing developing countries. At the present time, this form of South-South migration constitutes a significant proportion of all international migration.

By drawing upon the case studies and other chapters included in this book, this chapter attempts to construct a theoretical framework that describes institutions, processes, patterns and outcomes that contribute to and are particular to South-South migration. To situate South-South migration in its current context, the chapter first defines contemporary patterns of international migration and, secondly, articulates at a theoretical level the differences between South-South and other forms of international migration. The chapter provides historical perspectives as well as an overview of the institutional contexts of different migration patterns: spatial (North-North, North-South, South-North, South-South) and historical patterns of pre-colonial, post-industrial revolution, colonial and post-colonial and post-globalization.

1.1 International migration and its North and South denominations

Defining 'North' and 'South' is difficult. According to IOM (2014) different methods have been used by different organizations. For analytical purposes this chapter adopts the definition used by the World Bank, which categorizes 'North' and 'South' on the basis of GDP per capita. In this definition, 'North' includes high-income countries such as the United States, Canada, Western Europe, developed countries of Asia, Australia and New Zealand; the Global South is made up of low to middle income countries of Africa, Latin America, the developing countries of Asia and the Middle East.

Defining migration can be equally complex because international migration, meaning the cross-border movement of people, is taking place under a range of historical and institutional contexts. In this chapter an attempt has been made to explain patterns of international migration that include cross-border voluntary, involuntary, legal and/or illegal movements of people that have been and/or are induced by factors such as (1) famine, drought, war, persecution; (2) exploration/trade and commerce; (3) treatment of people as tradable commodities – slaves and/or indentured labour – sent from one colony to another, during the colonial period or to the metropolis of the colonizing country; (4) colonial settlement by the colonial occupiers during the colonial period; and (5) conditions of contemporary globalization, including the movement of (a) skilled workers/professionals from 'North' to 'North' countries; (b) semi-skilled/skilled workers/professionals from 'South' (less developed) to 'North' countries mostly on permanent basis; and (c) skilled and mostly semi-skilled labour from less developing 'South' to faster-growing developing 'South' countries for short or medium term stays or on a rotational/cyclic residency basis. It is the latter type of migration that, typically, has come to be known as South-South migration (SSM), and is the focus of this volume.

International migration across different political, economic and historical contexts has encompassed all of these forms in the following main patterns: (1) North-North during the industrial revolution period; (2) South-South during periods of famine and internal strife; (3) North-South during the colonial trade and colonial occupation and settlement period; (4) South-North during the colonial period; (5) Colonial South/Colonial South during the colonial slave trade/indentured labour transfer period; and (6) North-North and South-North and South-South during the post-colonial/post-globalization period.

2. South-South migration: history and trends

The United Nations (2014) estimates that total global migrant stock stood at 76 million in 1960 and increased somewhat slowly till 1980, increased dramatically especially after the 1980's oil boom in some Gulf countries and rapid economic growth of several developing country economies that altered their respective labour markets to 82.3 million in 2013. This demonstrates that the volume of South-South movements (82.3 million migrants worldwide) is approximately the same as South-North flows (81.9 million). The 2013 World Migration Report also confirms this trend and observes that worldwide more than half of the top twenty migration corridors are along South-South corridors (IOM 2013).

Although the Asian Financial Crisis (AFC) of 1997–1998 and the Global Financial Crisis (GFC) of 2008 slowed rates of migration to some extent, especially in South-South migration corridors, the absolute number of migrants has nevertheless continued to rise. Furthermore, between 1990 and 2013, the number of international migrants worldwide rose by over 77 million or by 50 percent, and much of this growth occurred from 2000–2010. During this period, some 4.6 million migrants were added annually (compared to an average of 2 million per annum during the period 1990–2000), and there were 3.6 million per annum during the period 2010–2013 (United Nations 2014). Indeed, with the rise in migration globally, the directions of migration have changed. For example, in 2013, 41 percent of the world's total migrants were hosted by economically rapidly growing developing countries of the South. In addition, of the 136 million international migrants living in the North, 82 million, or 60 percent, originated from developing countries (United Nations 2014).

Figure 2.1 presents a comparative picture of total migration patterns between and within regions of the global South and North. Figure 2.1 illustrates that in 2013 South-South migration (36 percent of total migration) had become as important a feature of international migration as South-North migration (35 percent of the total). On the other hand, in 2013 North-North migration constituted only 13.7 percent of the total and North-South only 6 percent. South-South migration is now a global phenomenon that encompasses all continents, most significantly Asia, with South-South migration increasing at a time when there has been a worldwide increase in international migration.

Table 2.1 shows that the number of international migrants worldwide rose by over 77 million or by 50 percent between 1990 and 2013. In terms of region, the average annual growth rate of migration in developed regions was higher during 1990–2000 compared to developing regions, but the trend changed after 2000, when the rate was higher in developing regions from 2000–2010 and also from 2010–2013. In terms of continents, Table 2.1 illustrates that from 1990–2000 the annual growth rate of migration to North

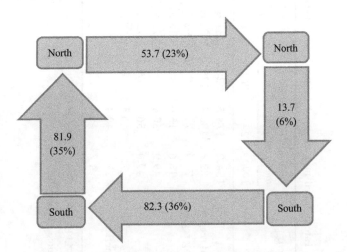

Figure 2.1 International migration stock by origin and destination, 2013 (million and percent)

Source: UN (2014)

Table 2.1 International migrant stock by development level and major area, 1990–2013

Destinations	International migrant stock (millions)				Average annual change in migrant stock (millions)			Average annual growth rate in migrant stock (%)		
	1990	2000	2010	2013	1990–2000	2000–2010	2010–2013	1990–2000	2000–2010	2010–2013
World	**154.2**	**174.5**	**220.7**	**231.5**	**2.0**	**4.6**	**3.6**	**1.2**	**2.3**	**1.6**
Developed regions	82.3	103.4	129.7	135.6	2.1	2.6	1.9	2.3	2.3	1.5
Developing regions	71.9	71.1	91.0	95.9	-0.1	2.0	1.6	-0.1	2.5	1.8
Africa	15.6	15.6	17.1	18.6	0.0	0.2	0.5	0.0	0.9	2.8
Asia	49.9	50.4	67.8	70.8	0.1	1.7	1.0	0.1	3.0	2.5
Europe	49.0	56.2	69.2	72.4	0.7	1.3	1.1	1.4	2.1	1.5
LAC*	7.1	6.5	8.1	8.5	-0.1	0.2	0.2	-0.9	2.2	1.8
North America	27.8	40.4	51.2	53.1	1.3	1.1	0.6	3.7	2.4	1.2
Oceania	4.7	5.4	7.3	7.9	0.1	0.2	0.2	1.5	3.1	2.6

* LAC refers to Latin America and the Caribbean

Source: United Nations (2013).

America was higher compared to all other continents, but from 2000–2010, migration to Oceania and Asia also increased from 4.7 million to 7.9 million and from 49.9 million to 70.8 million for the period 1990–2013. For 2010–2013 the rate was highest for Africa, followed by Oceania and then Latin America (LAC).

These trends confirm that South-South migration is a rising and important phenomenon in international migration and that as these migrations take place under particular conditions, the subject warrants special attention.

2.1　Past and present South-South migration

In this regard, it is important to mention that South-South migration is not as new a phenomenon as is often argued. Significant South-South migration did occur in the past. As in the present, South-South migration in the past involved large numbers of migrants, but migration occurred under conditions that contrast markedly with those of the present. Figure 2.2 presents overall migration patterns and characteristics in historical contexts. It portrays varied patterns and characteristics of international migration over time and demonstrates that South-South Migration has a long history, albeit under differing economic and political

Pre-colonial period **(premercantile-mercantile period, 1500–1800)** *Patterns* North-North; South-South; South-North; North-South	• Trade and commerce (North-North): Voluntary/mutually economically beneficial • Trade and commerce/exploration (North-South): Voluntary, some mutually economically beneficial, some exploitative • Slave trade (South-North; South-South): Involuntary/ Exploitative
Colonial **(1800-mid 1900s)** *Patterns* North-Colonized South; South-North; South-South	• Colonial expansion and occupation/' produced colonialism/ colonized settlement (North-South): Voluntary/ Exploitative • Indentured labour movements (Colonized South-Colonial North; Colonized South-Colonized South): Involuntary/ Exploitative
Post colonial/globalized period **(Mid-1900s to present)** *Patterns* South-North; South-South	• Growth and economic expansion in North (South-North): Voluntary, mutually beneficial • Growth and expansion under globalized conditions (South-North; less developing South-faster developing South): Voluntary/Mutually beneficial

Figure 2.2 Patterns and characteristics of international migration in historical contexts

Source: Hossain and Khan (2015)

Table 2.2 Features of colonial South-South (CSS) and globalized South-South (GSS) migration

---

Colonial South-South Migration

- From colonized South to colonizing North; to colonized South, to meet colonial economic and production arrangements, mostly as indentured labour in plantation/mining sectors
- Intra- and inter-regional
- Largely involuntary and enforced with no provision for return and/or 'backward linkage' (remittances both financial and 'social') to the country/place of origin
- Exploitation based and no migrant rights
- Socially excluded in receiving countries
- With decolonization most migrant workers got absorbed in their receiving countries where they continue to face several social, political and economic barriers

Globalized South-South Migration

- Complementary 'push' and 'pull' factors of migration between the sending and the receiving countries create opportunities for migration as a voluntary option
- Mostly intra-regional
- Temporary and rotational ('cyclic') in nature and includes mainly low to semi-skilled workers
- Predominantly male but number of female migrants also on the rise
- Modalities of migration include but not limited to kinship network, official formal means and most predominantly, through unofficial middlemen
- War and repressions in some sending South countries contribute to involuntary/ illegal migration including 'people smuggling' etc.
- A major source of foreign exchange earnings for the developing sending countries that accrue through remittances and for receiving countries a major and also a cheap source of labour for infrastructure development and services sector
- Governance deficits in both sending and receiving countries increase migrant vulnerabilities re safety, security and welfare at both ends, and reduce net benefits
- Low income and relatively high transaction costs prompt repeat or cyclic migration contributing to prolonged migrant absence that increase social costs at the migrant household level
- Most national and international level research and policy discussions on migration prioritize issues concerning remittance and development financing not so much on economic and social changes/costs incurred at the migrant individual and household levels

---

conditions, stretching through both pre-colonial, colonial periods into the present day post-colonial globalized period.

Table 2.2 illustrates more explicitly the distinguishing features of colonial South-South (CSS) and post-colonial/post-globalization South-South migration (GSS). The most important feature is that while CSS involved involuntary and exploitation-based migrations that were enforced by the colonial North, GSS migration is voluntary and accrues, albeit unequally, mutual benefits to both sending as well as the receiving countries.

The other striking contrasts between CSS and GSS migrations are that the former entailed both intra- and inter-regional migration (from colonial Asia to colonial Asia and Africa, for example), with no or limited provision of remittances of income earned by the migrants to the countries of origin. CSS also involved no or limited options of return to home countries and migrants also had no or limited options of communication with their home countries. Whereas in contrast to CSS, GSS is temporary and rotational ('cyclic'), where remittances are sent more or less regularly by the migrants back to their countries of origin with the provision, if not the obligation, to return to their home country.

Again, in terms of modalities of migration, while the colonial period involved enforced recruitment through colonial agents, present day recruitments are conducted by a plethora of organizations, both formal and informal, and in most cases through unofficial middlemen. Most importantly, unlike the colonial South-South migration that was mainly involuntary, exploitative, extractive and accumulative in character, contemporary South-South migration is voluntary and less exploitative, and helps meet the economic needs, albeit unequally, of both the sending and receiving countries.

2.2   Patterns and trends of globalized South-South migration

The globalization processes that have induced growing differences in economic growth between South countries (where one set of countries are experiencing much faster economic growth and thus are creating labour demand and the other set where the economies are growing more sluggishly and are producing surplus labour), have created the conditions for South-South migration, especially intra-regional South-South migration. Common history, cultural affinity, distance proximity, and skills compatibility are also playing important roles in promoting current trends in South-South migration (Ratha and Shaw 2007; Constant and Zimmermann 2009; IOM 2014).

One of the most significant reasons that South-South migration is predominantly intra-regional is that, within the same region, South countries have experienced different growth trajectories, creating relevant networks of labour demand and supply. For example, in Asia where the bulk of South-South migration occurs, two sets of countries provided the demand nodes of migration in the region – namely, the slow-growing Bangladesh, India, Pakistan, Sri Lanka and Nepal on the one hand, and faster-growing countries such as the oil-producing Middle East, fast-growing Malaysia, the Republic of Korea, Singapore and Thailand on the other (Egbula and Zheng 2011; IOM 2014).

Table 2.3 illustrates clearly such intra-regional patterns of migration. It presents the number of persons residing in a destination (major area), in 2013, who were also born in the same major area. The majority of international migrants born in Europe, Asia and Oceania were living in a country within their region of birth. Of the fifty-eight million international migrants born in Europe, thirty-eight million were residing in Europe (65 percent); fifty-four million of the ninety-two million international migrants from Asia were living in Asia (58 percent; United Nations 2014).

Table 2.3 Major migration movements by regions including South-South, 2013 (in millions)

2013		Origin							
		Africa	Asia	Europe	LAC	NA	Oceania	Various	Total
Destination	Africa	15.3	1.1	0.8	0.0	0.1	0.0	1.4	18.6
	Asia	4.6	53.8	7.6	0.7	0.6	0.1	3.4	70.8
	Europe	8.9	18.6	37.8	4.5	0.9	0.3	1.3	72.4
	LAC*	0.0	0.3	1.2	5.4	1.3	0.0	0.2	8.5
	NA*	2.0	15.7	7.9	25.9	1.2	0.3	0.0	53.1
	Oceania	0.5	2.9	3.1	0.1	0.2	1.1	0.1	7.9
	Total	31.3	92.5	58.4	36.7	4.3	1.9	6.4	231.5

* 'LAC' stands for Latin America and the Caribbean; 'NA' stands for North America.

Source: United Nations (2014, p. 1).

Table 2.4 Estimates of South-South and other international migration by different definitions, 2013

Definition by different sources/perspectives	Direction of migration			
	South-South	North-South	North-North	South-North
World Bank Income definition	42 percent	4 percent	16 percent	35 percent
UNDP HDI* Level	45 percent	4 percent	14 percent	37 percent

* The UNDP HDI is a measure of development that combines economic with social development indicators

Source: Campillo-Carrete (2013).

Table 2.4 presents patterns of migration according to different definitions of 'North' and 'South' adopted by different organizations, producing slightly varied, albeit consistent, estimates of South-South migration. By the World Bank's income definition of countries (low, middle and high), the estimate of the proportion of international migration that is South-South migration is 42 percent; by the United Nations Development Programme (UNDP) Human Development Index (HDI) measure, the estimate is 45 percent. Notwithstanding these differences in definitions of South and their corresponding estimates of South-South migration, what emerges as a key message is that South-South migration is a significant phenomenon in the post-colonial, post-globalized world.

2.3   Dominance of Asia in South-South migration

In South-South migration, Asia-to-Asia migration, especially that related to migration from slower-growing developing Asia to faster-growing developing

Asia, is most significant. It is estimated that 87 percent of the 21 million migrants who entered the Asian region between 1990 and 2013 originated from Asia. Asia gained from Asia itself an average of 1.7 million international migrants per annum during the period 2000–2010 and an additional 1 million per annum during the period 2010–2013. In 2013, some 54 million international migrants born in Asia were residing in another country in Asia, thus constituting the most substantial proportion of international or cross-border migration in the world (United Nations 2014).

Historically, the increasing trend of Asia-to-Asia migration has been triggered by three major successive waves of rapid economic growth experienced in certain parts of the continent. These three waves are very different from one another. Japan led the first wave in the 1950s and 1960s during the post-WWII period, with massive growth of its industries sector which also created significant demand for labour (Ohkawa and Rosovsky 1973; Koshiro 1991). The second wave came with the oil boom in Persian Gulf countries that continue to be major recipients of migrant labour from Asia (Birks and Sinclair 1980; Wickramasekara 2002; Massey 2003). The third and more recent wave started in the 1980s with (1) the emergence of Hong Kong, South Korea, Singapore, Malaysia and Thailand as a new receiving group (Hugo 1995; Kaur 2010); (2) the emergence of former communist countries such as Vietnam, Cambodia and Laos PDR as a new set of sending countries; and (3) continuation of the Philippines, Indonesia, Bangladesh, Sri Lanka and Nepal as major migrant-sending countries in Asia (Abella 1995).

While South-South migration generally takes place due to varied economic performance among the South or developing countries, the intra-regional character of Asia-to-Asia migration includes factors such as varied economic performance within regions as well as those that relate to geographic proximity and migrant networks, ease of access, cheap transportation, ethnic, linguistic, religious, historical and political affinities (UN 2004; Hugo 2005). Table 2.5 shows the major sending and receiving countries in Asia.

Table 2.5 Major sending and receiving countries in Asia

Sending country	Main receiving country
Bangladesh	Singapore, Malaysia, Jordan, India, Saudi Arabia, Kuwait, UAE, Oman, UK, United States, Italy
India	Nepal, Bangladesh, Sri Lanka, Saudi Arabia, Kuwait, UAE, Oman, UK, United States, Canada
Nepal	Thailand, India, Japan, Qatar, Saudi Arabia, UK, United States, Canada, Australia
Pakistan	India, Saudi Arabia, Kuwait, UEA, Qatar, Oman, UK, United States, Italy, Canada
Sri Lanka	India, Jordan, Saudi Arabia, Kuwait, UAE, Qatar, Oman, UK, Canada, Italy

Source: Compiled from World Bank (2016).

In recent years, migrations from Bangladesh, India, Pakistan and Sri Lanka to Singapore, Malaysia and Thailand have emerged as important migration corridors, although the Middle East has continued to remain the preferred destination of South Asian sending countries, especially for low- to semi-skilled workers. Only a small proportion who are skilled and professionals opt for another South country for migration, many preferring Europe and North America as destinations for higher incomes and, most importantly, for the opportunities of permanent residency in these countries (Chanda 2012; IOM 2014).

Although in earlier periods Asia-to-Asia migration included highly skilled workers from information technology, financial services, and engineering and other professional service sectors (Chanda 2012), at the present time, Asia-to-Asia migrations are predominantly on a temporary or short-term basis, where most migrants are engaged in low to semi-skilled labour-intensive activities such as agriculture, plantations, fisheries, construction, domestic service and factories that are regarded by the locals as '3D' work (dirty, dangerous and difficult; ILO 2016). Furthermore, as Table 2.4 reveals, some countries in the South, especially in Asia, such as India and Bangladesh, play alternate roles as both sending and receiving countries.

In summary, Asia-to-Asia migration, the largest component of contemporary Globalized South-South migration, has developed through different periods in two major phases: first, during the 1950s and 1960s, through importation of highly skilled workers by those that were resource rich but lacked highly skilled manpower, and more recently, through importation of low to semi-skilled workers in large numbers to contribute to infrastructure development activities and the services sector in faster-growing economies of the South. In the main receiving countries of the region, increases in per capita GDP have altered the structure of their labour markets, creating demand for semi- to low-skilled labour.

3.   Remittances in South-South migration

With the rise in South-South migration, remittances from South receiving countries have become an important source of foreign exchange in the South Sending Countries. Table 2.6 depicts that in 2016, South-South migration constituted 38 percent of all international migrations and generated 34 percent of all migration remittances.

In reading these data, it must be pointed out that complexities with formal remittances in both South receiving and sending migrant countries often prompt migrants to choose informal methods of transfer that involve higher per unit cost in remittances, which thus reduces the net amount sent as remittance. Conversion to US dollars from local currencies, sometimes a legal necessity, also reduces the net amounts received as remittances in sending countries (Ratha and Shaw 2007). Despite these complexities, particular countries, especially in South Asia, are emerging as the main source/s of labour in the faster-growing economies of Asia, as 'land[s] of migrant workers', and their economies are

Table 2.6 Migration and remittances (2016), by 'North' and 'South' dimensions

Migrants from/ Remittances to	Migrants residing in		Share of total migrants (South)	Share of total migrants (North)
	South	North		
South	93.1 million $206.7 billion*	84.3 million $27.9 billion*	38% of total migrants 34% of total remittances	34% of total migrants 5% of total remittances
North	14.2 million $223.8 billion*	55.7million $143.0 billion*	6% of total migrants 37% of total remittances	23% of total migrants 24% of total remittances
Total	107.3 million $430.5 billion*	140.0 million $170.8 billion*	43% of total migrants 72% of total remittances	53% of total migrants 28% of total remittances

* USD

Source: World Bank (2016).

Table 2.7 Remittances, foreign direct investment, and official development assistance in South Asia, in USD billion, 2009

Country	Remittances*	Foreign direct investment (FDI)**	Official development assistance (ODA)***
Bangladesh	10.5	0.7	1.2
India	49.5	19.0	2.5
Nepal	3.0	0.3	0.9
Sri Lanka	3.3	0.3	0.7
TOTAL	66.3	20.3	5.3

* Current
** Balance of payments, current
*** Net, current

Source: Ozaki (2012, p. 10)

transforming into 'remittance economies' (Ozaki 2012; Pettinger 2013). Table 2.7 shows the growing importance of remittances in South Asian sending economies.

It is evident from Table 2.7 how most South Asian migrant-sending countries are heavily reliant on remittances as one of their major sources of revenue to the extent that, in all of the countries listed, remittances inflows are much higher than those of foreign direct investment or official development assistance.

In addition to financial remittances, a less tangible but no less significant feature of international migration is 'social remittance', which is 'a local level form of cultural diffusion' where 'ideas, behaviours and identities and social capital' flow from receiving countries to sending countries and over a period of time get 'remodelled in sending countries' (Levitt 1998, p. 926). Some also argue that migrants equally influence the economic, political and social changes in the receiving countries as well (Levitt and Lamba-Nieves 2013).

Exactly how social remittances work in South-South migration is unclear, but given that migration cycles are rather short and also that most migrants work in low-skilled activities, 'social remittances' in terms of transfer of values, culture and technology are likely to be limited, though in some cases important behavioural changes in terms of attitudes towards children's education, punctuality, entrepreneurship have been noticed, especially among multi-cycle returned migrants (Constant and Zimmermann 2011; Campillo-Carrete 2013), and in some cases gender relationships have been 'reshaped' in limited ways (King, Mata-Codesal and Vullnetari 2013).

The issue of social remittances is complex, especially in South-South migration. Therefore, some suggest that there may be need

> to explore the embeddedness of economic remittances within a broader range of socio-cultural remittances (rather than vice versa); the interfaces between the categories of social remittances and social capital; the complex ways in which physical and social distance between senders and recipients affect the circulation of social remittances, as well as their impact on migrants' communities of origin.
>
> (Boccagni and Decimo 2013, p. 1)

Another important aspect of South-South migration is the social cost, but in comparison with other outcomes of South-South migration this is not well documented, though there is growing evidence that it is substantial. For example, temporary residency conditionality in migrating countries, a unique feature of South-South migration that also entails high transaction costs, low salary and regular payment of 'protection' money to law enforcement agencies for safety and security, results in low disposable income from workers' wages for remittance. The consequence of this is that one-time migration that typically runs between three and five years does not generate enough income to recover migration investment costs, prompting 'cyclic' or 'repeat' migration that may span from eight to ten years and entail significant social costs in migrants' households in the form of children's increased risk of school dropout, juvenile delinquency and, sometimes, marginalization of wives left behind. (See, for example, the collection of papers edited by Hujo and Piper 2010.)

4.   Governance characteristics of South-South sending and receiving countries and their implications

Governance in general and migration governance in particular are key factors affecting migration decisions, the processes employed in recruitment to journey and arrival at the destination country, the transaction costs, and migrant security, safety and welfare in receiving countries. Aspects that are more directly influential are transparency and accountability in organization of migration especially regarding information sharing and access at the sending county level and the aspects of rule of law, human rights, labour rights and migrant rights at the receiving country level. Deficits in any of these aspects of governance have the potential to directly affect both the processes as well as the outcomes of migration. For example, deficits in transparency and accountability and weaknesses and/or bias in dissemination of information concerning migration may contribute to uninformed or ill-informed decisions that ultimately would lead to a range of adverse outcomes, including loss of money and lives. Also, a sending country government's failure to reach out to the grass-roots and provide people with correct information may create space for middlemen who are often exploitative. Similarly, governance deficits in receiving countries relating to such matters as human rights, labour rights, the rule of law and the integrity of law enforcement agencies may jeopardize migrant safety, security and welfare, and increase transaction costs, ultimately reducing net income earned by migrants and thus their remittances. Prompted by governance deficits in terms of lax border control and/or corruption, migrants who employ unofficial means – illegal or undocumented migration – to migrate to another South country, especially within the same region, are often vulnerable to such injustices as extortion by the middlemen, broken promises, and slavery (see also Chapter 8).

In contrast to South receiving countries, North receiving countries tend to be more democratic, less corrupt, more transparent and accountable, practice better rule of law and are more committed to labour rights, and these attributes of the North influence both the processes as well as the outcomes of migration. In these countries migration happens in a selective, regulative and transparent manner (except in cases of illegal migration). Furthermore, all citizens, including those who are legal migrants and enjoy permanent residency status and/or hold a stay on work visa, are subjected to the same rules and regulations as citizens, such as those relating to human rights, labour rights and minority rights. By way of summary, Table 2.8 presents key governance characteristics of selected South-South sending and receiving countries.

Almost all countries listed in Table 2.8 score poorly on key aspects of good governance such as rule of law, human and trade union rights (as measured by the International Trade Union Confederation Global Rights Index; ITUC 2015), and corruption, revealing the prevalence of major governance deficits in both sending and receiving countries. This has implications for migration decision-making, transparency and accountability in recruitment, security and safety, net income earned and remittances. On the World Justice Project Rule of Law Index (World Justice Project 2015), Bangladesh, Nigeria and Guatemala, with respective scores of 0.42, 0.41 and 0.44, appear as the worst among the listed sending countries on this particular aspect of governance and their scores on labour rights ('no guarantee of rights') and corruption (25, 26 and 28, respectively) are similarly poor. Such governance deficits do seem to correlate strongly

Table 2.8 Key governance indicators of selected South-South migration receiving and sending countries

Selected sending countries	Key governance indicators			Selected receiving countries	Key governance indicators		
	Rule of Law Rank/Score*	ITUC Global Rights Index**	Corruption Perception Index Rank/Score***		Rule of Law Rank/Score	ITUC Global Rights Index	Corruption Perception Index Rank/Score
Bangladesh	92/0.42	No guarantee of rights	129/25	India	59/0.51	No guarantee of rights	76/38
Philippines	51/0.58	No guarantee of rights	95/35	Malaysia	39/0.57	Systematic violation of rights	54/50
Indonesia	52/0.52	No guarantee of rights	36/34	Korean Republic	11/0.79	No guarantee of rights	37/56
India	59/0.51	No guarantee of rights	76/38	Gulf states	NA	No guarantee of rights	48/52
Nigeria	96/0.41	Systematic violation of rights	136/26	South Africa	36/0.58	Repeated violations of rights	61/44
Guatemala	85/0.44	No guarantee of rights	123/28				

* Source: World Justice Project (2015). Ranking: 1 best, 102 worst; Score: 1.0 best, 0.00 worst
** Source: International Trade Union Confederation (ITUC) (2015)
*** Source: Transparency International (2015). Ranking: 1 least corrupt; 167 most corrupt. Score: 100 very clean; 0 highly corrupt.

with rent-seeking and opaqueness in processes involving selection and recruitment of migrants (De Lombaerde, Guo and Neto 2014).

What is also revealing from Table 2.8 is that the scores/ranks of the listed South receiving countries also indicate significant deficits. For example, on the Rule of Law Index, Malaysia, a major South receiving country, scores 0.57. This indicates a comparatively weak rule of law. On the Corruption Perception Index (CPI), its score of 50 means a relatively moderate level of corruption. Malaysia's record on the ITUC Global Rights Index is 'systematic violation of rights'. These deficits imply that migrant rights, a fair wage, safety, security and welfare are likely to be under threat in this particular receiving country. However, Malaysia is not unique in governance deficits. Most South receiving countries in the Asian region demonstrate similar governance challenges. For example, the Gulf States, a major South migrant receiving region, suffer several major governance deficits. Data for the Gulf States on Rule of Law is not available, but data on 'ITUC Global Rights Index' and CPI reveal 'no guarantee of rights' and a score of 52 (moderately corrupt), which implies that in these countries occurrences of incidents of migrant abuse and exploitation are more than likely.

Furthermore, as South-South migrations are mostly intra-regional where destination/receiving countries can be reached easily via land or sea routes, where border control is lax and corrupt and where conflicts and persecution against a particular group of people force them to migrate to neighbouring countries, opportunities are rife for illegal and undocumented migration, including 'people smuggling' (ABC 2015).

Lastly, a governance issue that has important ramifications in South-South migration in general and, with regard to migrant rights and welfare in particular, relates to the issues of bilateral relations between the South sending and South receiving countries that are essentially unequal. The sending countries are relatively poor and depend on the receiving country as an important source of foreign exchange and in such situations of dependency, the bargaining space for sending countries in securing desirable and satisfactory employment conditions and outcomes of migration for their migrating citizens is rather limited.

In summary, to understand the range of issues and outcomes relating to contemporary South-South migration, governance attributes that characterize both the sending and receiving countries and significantly affect both the processes and outcomes of migration need to be well articulated and understood. Characteristic patterns of South-South migration reveal a number of governance deficits in sending countries that render the processes of migration less transparent and less accountable and thus vulnerable to many tiers of manipulation and exploitation. These characteristics have significant bearing on migration decisions, transaction costs, and modes of journey and entry into the receiving countries. The presence of similar deficits at receiving country level, especially those that relate to migrant rights, rule of law, and corruption affect migration and migrants in a number of ways. Migrant rights are rarely protected, and their safety, security and welfare are almost never guaranteed. Such conditions of weak governance in both sending and receiving countries almost invariably result in rent-seeking, and threaten migrant safety and welfare at multiple levels.

Despite these challenges, South-South migration continues to grow as an important component of modern day international migration and an important contributor to development in both receiving and sending countries. The South receiving countries gain from the contributions migrants make in their infrastructure development and services sectors and the sending countries benefit from the remittances sent by the migrants that help provide valuable foreign exchange resources required in import financing for development and, importantly, to help reduce poverty at the migrant household level. Notwithstanding these benefits, there are a number of social costs associated with present day South-South migration, some of which have been highlighted in section three of this chapter. These are caused by particular features or conditions of South-South migration, such as migrant absenteeism from families and households, in repeating cycles of migration, an outcome of migrants' temporary residency status. Impacts upon families and households, especially children and left-behind wives, are increasingly the focus of research and policy (Hujo and Piper 2010) and include issues such as school dropout, juvenile delinquency, increased vulnerability and disempowerment of migrants' wives, and in cases where migrants fail to earn enough to offset migration-related debts, diminished status of migrants in their home communities, and risks of destitution.

5.   Summarizing key features of globalized South-South migration

In summary, the features unique to contemporary GSS migration are as follows:

- *Economic backdrop to South-South migration*. Differences in economic growth between the relatively slow growth and the faster-growing South developing countries create the basic 'push' and 'pull' factors of migration between these two sets of economies. In those sending countries where economic growth cannot match the demographic growth and produce surplus labour conditions and motivations (the 'push' factors), conditions are created for migration to those South developing countries that experience faster economic growth, and provide opportunities for employment in sectors that match the surplus manpower produced in the slow developing sending South countries. In addition, political instability, internal racial and/or other forms of discrimination also create conditions for migration where aspiring migrants from politically unstable countries target those South countries that are economically better off, culturally congenial and, most importantly, have easy accessibility. However, as a proportion of all South-South migration, the proportion of migrants who migrate due to political conflict in South countries is small.
- *Migration processes in South-South migration*. South-North migration is determined by clearly defined and rigidly implemented entry criteria in

receiving countries. In contrast, South-South migration is often a product of a myriad of arrangements such as government-to-government agreements between the sending/receiving countries and marketing (some false) of migration opportunities by networks of friends, relatives and middlemen. Also, due to lax border control and corruption in border control processes, migration processes between developing sending and developing receiving South countries are pursued by various means, some legal, some illegal, some documented, some undocumented and some opportunistic, meaning that some migrants enter some of the South receiving countries illegally and, after obtaining jobs, are able to register as legal.

- *Migration decisions and migration patterns in Globalized South-South migration*. Colonial South-South migrations which were mostly enforced and involuntary and involved both inter- and intra-regional destinations to various colonies of the North. However, contemporary South-South migrations are voluntary, predominantly intra-regional, temporary, and due to relatively high transactional costs and low net return, often are repeat or cyclical in nature.
- *Governance deficits and their influences on migration processes and outcomes*. In South-North migration, significant differences in governance arrangements exist between the South sending and North receiving countries. While most South sending and receiving countries have significant governance deficits that influence both the processes and outcomes of migration, North receiving countries that practice democratic governance, observe rule of law and uphold to a large measure the tenets of labour rights, produce vastly different outcomes, mostly positive, for migrants. In South-South migration, deficits of democracy and absence of transparency and accountability, weak information sharing and limited access to information in both South sending and receiving countries provide opportunities for misinformation and exploitation of migrants by multiple parties. These compromise the safety, security and welfare of migrants and, in the process, increase the transaction costs and minimize income earned. Such deficits contribute to 'cyclic' migration and prolonged migrant absenteeism (because migrant workers typically are not allowed to bring their families to the receiving countries), resulting in myriad changes in social and economic behaviour at the migrant household level, some positive and some not so positive.
- *Outcomes*. Unlike South-North migration, where economic back-flow to sending countries is rather limited, in contemporary or globalized South-South migration, benefits are mutual. Receiving countries experience forward linkage in terms of contributions that migrant labour makes to their infrastructure and services sector development and backward linkages to sending countries are created through remittances and in overall macroeconomic development, including poverty alleviation (IOM 2014).

This demonstrates, starting from the economic backdrop, that globalized South-South migration displays features that are unique and warrant a more insightful and analytical discussion, especially if the current arrangement is to be made more transparent, accountable and equitable; most importantly, this raises the debate at the theoretical level.

6. Understanding globalized South-South migration

In some ways, current GSS migration exhibits characteristics that are both structural and dialectical (Goss and Lindquist 1995; de Haas 2008), in the sense that globalization and liberalization have promoted, among other things, unequal growth both nationally and internationally. This has produced significant economic growth in some South countries that has altered labour markets and created significant demand for low-skilled foreign labour in other South countries. At the same time in some slow growing South countries, urban-centric unequal growth trajectories and rising population numbers have diminished livelihood options in rural areas, and this has produced surplus labour, creating impetus for migration first to the urban areas within these countries then internationally, especially to other developing nations in the same region where there is demand for labour. However, given the voluntary nature of GSS migration, under the agency of both migrants themselves and brokers at various levels, migration takes place under both legal and illegal, formal and informal institutional arrangements which reflect to some extent the features of 'push-pull' models of migration propagated by classical theorists (Ravenstein 1885; Macisco and Pryor 1963; Lee 1966; Bogue 1969; Brown and Moore 1970; Stark and Bloom 1985; Bell 1996). GSS migration is thus stimulated by contradictory tendencies: on the one hand, it is a product of a globalized capitalist system which is exploitative, and on the other, it is also functional and mutually beneficial for economic growth and development, though not equally.

Figure 2.3 portrays key features and thus a working, albeit evolving, analytical framework of globalized South-South migration. It demonstrates that, in comparison with present-day South-North and colonial South-South migration, present day, post-globalization South-South migration is characterized by features that are unique and are strongly associated with neoliberal economic modes of production. The governance arrangements that guide GSS migration (from recruitment to remittances) create opportunities for multiple levels of exploitation but also enable mutual benefits, albeit grossly unequally. The inequities of contemporary South-South migration (see Chapters 3, 4, 8 and 9 of this book) have generated debate and dialogue both at national and international levels, with demands that GSS migrations are made more transparent, accountable and equitable at all levels.

The growing evidence of social costs of migration in sending communities (Hujo and Piper 2010; also see Chapter 7 of this book), an aspect of GSS migration which so far has not been researched to the extent desirable, warrants more in-depth study to enable better understanding and minimization if not amelioration of risks, and points to the importance of examining the impacts of migration governance at all levels.

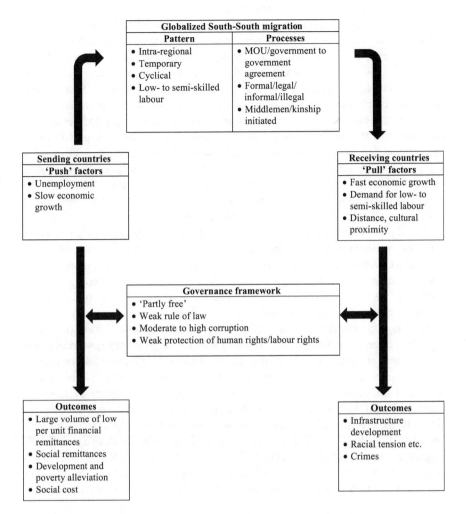

Figure 2.3 Globalized South-South migration: an analytical framework

Given the complexities of GSS migration, the aim of this chapter has been to examine and highlight key features from existing empirical works and propose an analytical framework (Figure 2.3), mainly to assist better understanding as well as theorizing of globalized South-South migration, an evolving phenomenon in present-day international migration. In this regard, it is important to mention that historical-structuralist theorists of migration have viewed migration as an inevitable consequence of the exploitative capitalist mode of production that results in inequities at multiple levels (Goss and Lindquist 1995; de Haas 2008). Whereas integrative and/or agency-inclined approaches (Bogue 1969; Brown and Moore 1970; Bell 1996) have examined migration more optimistically in terms of the unique relationships that exist between different social, economic and political entities from migrant household to community, to national and global level both within and across nations, and the ways these forces interact with each other and create impetus for migration from one set of South to another set of South countries. This latter school also argues that in comparison to colonial South-South migration, the institutional arrangements within which globalized South-South migration takes place are unique and vary significantly, and even though GSS migration arrangements are not completely abuse free, they produce outcomes that are mutually beneficial (see Table 2.2 and Figure 2.3). Post-globalization inequities in development, both within and across nations, have created the impetus for international migration, especially South-South migration. However, unlike colonial South-South migration (where another colonized migration receiving South country exclusively served the cause of the colonists), GSS migration is voluntary and accrues mutual benefits, albeit unequally.

At this point in time, construction of a general theory of South-South migration is perhaps neither possible nor desirable, though significant progress may be made, as Castles (2008) suggests, 'by re-embedding migration research in a more general understanding of contemporary society, and linking it to broader theories of social change across a range of social scientific disciplines' (Castles 2008, p. 1). In due course, a theory of migration studies in general, and South-South migration in particular, may consider more explicitly the political economic dimensions of all aspects of international migration. These include sending country governance and development strategies and their influence on livelihood opportunities; the import of governance for migration decision-making; recruitment; transit; remittances; and most importantly, issues of migrant rights, safety and security in receiving countries that influence the processes, the transaction costs and outcomes of migration. As an evolving phenomenon, more cross-continental and more focused issue-based research is needed to construct a theoretical framework of South-South migration that is spatially extensive and analytically more complete. The chapters that follow, as well as other relevant research works that highlight the evolving characteristics GSS migration, may help with this task in some way.

References

ABC 2015, *South-East Asian Migrant Crisis: The Boats and the Numbers*, viewed 20 May 2015, <http://www.abc.net.au/news/2015–05–17/migrant-refugee-crisis-south-east-asia-in-numbers/6476160>.

Abella, MI 1995, 'Asian Labour Migration: Past, Present, and Future', *ASEAN Economic Bulletin*, vol. 12, no. 2, pp. 125–35.

Bell, MJ 1996, *Understanding Internal Migration*, Australian Government Publishing Service, Australia.

Birks, JS and Sinclair, CA 1980, *International Migration and Development in the Arab Region*, International Labour Office, Geneva, Switzerland, viewed 10 April 2012, <http://www.popline.org/node/459542>.

Boccagni, P and Decimo, F 2013, 'Mapping Social Remittances', *Migration Letters*, vol. 10, no. 1, pp. 1–10.

Bogue, DJ 1969, *Principles of Demography*, John Wiley and Sons, New York.

Brown, LA and Moore, EG 1970, 'The Intra-urban Migration Process: A Perspective', *Human Geography*, vol. 52, no. 1, pp. 1–13.

Campillo-Carrete, B 2013, *South-South Migration: A Review of the Literature*, Working Paper No. 570, Migration Literature Review, No. 2, IDRC, CRDI and ISS, Netherlands.

Castles, S 2008, 'Understanding Global Migration: A Social Transformation Perspective', Paper Presented to the *Conference on Theories of Migration and Social Change*, St Anne's College, Woodstock Road, Oxford, England; Wednesday 2 July 9.30–11.00 Session 1: Theories of Global Mobility.

Chanda, R 2012, *Migration between South and Southeast Asia: Overview of Trends and Issues*, South Asian Diaspora, Institute of South Asian Studies, National University of Singapore, viewed 19 February 2014, <https://www.isas.nus.edu.sg/ISAS%20Reports/ISAS%20Working%20Paper%20140%20-Migration%20between%20South%20and%20Southeast%20Asia%20-%20Part%201.pdf>.

Constant, AF and Zimmermann, KF 2009, *Migration, Ethnicity and Economic Integration*, Discussion Paper Series, IZA DP No. 4620, Forschungsinstitut zur Zukunft der Arbeit (Institute for the Study of Labor), Bonn, Germany.

Constant, AF and Zimmermann, KF August 2011, 'Circular and Repeat Migration: Counts of Exits and Years Away from the Host Country', *Population Research and Policy Review*, vol. 30, no. 4, pp. 495–515.

de Haas, H 2008, *Migration and Development: A Theoretical Perspective*, University of Oxford, UK, International Migration Institute, viewed 16 March 2012, https://www.imi.ox.ac.uk/publications/wp-09-08.

De Lombaerde, P, Guo, F, and Neto, HP 2014, 'South-South Migration: What Is (Still) on the Research Agenda,' *International Migration Review*, vol. 48, no. 1, pp. 103–12.

Egbula, M and Zheng, Q 2011, 'China and Nigeria: A Powerful South-South Alliance', *West African Challenges*, vol. 5, pp. 1–20.

Goss, J and Lindquist, B 1995, 'Conceptualizing International Labour Migration: A Structuration Perspective', *International Migration Review*, vol. 29, no. 2, pp. 317–51.

Hossain, MI and Khan, MA 2015, 'International Migration History, Trends and the Emerging Phenomenon of South-South Migration: In Search of a Theoretical Framework', Paper presented to the *International Symposium on South-South Migration: Opportunities, Risks and Policy Imperatives*, School of Social Science, University of Queensland, Brisbane, Australia, 22 April.

Hugo, G 1995, 'International Labour Migration and the Family: Some Observations from Indonesia', *Asian and Pacific Migration Journal*, vol. 4, no. 2–3, pp. 273–301.

Hugo, G 2005, 'The New International Migration in Asia: Challenges for Population Research', *Asian Population Studies*, vol. 1, no. 1, pp. 93–120.

Hujo, K and Piper, N (eds) 2010, *South-South Migration: Implications for Social Policy and Development*, Palgrave Macmillan and United Nations Research Institute for Social Development (URISD), Geneva, Switzerland.

International Labour Organization (ILO) 2016, *Hazardous Work*, viewed 14 October 2016, <http://www.ilo.org/safework/areasofwork/hazardous-work/lang–en/index.htm>.

International Trade Union Confederation (ITUC) 2015, *ITUC Global Rights Index, 2015*, viewed 14 October 2016, <http://survey.ituc-csi.org/>.

IOM (International Organization for Migration) 2013, *World Migration Report 2013: Migrant Well-being and Development*, IOM, Geneva.

IOM (International Organization for Migration) 2014, South-South Migration: Partnering Strategically for Development', IOM, Geneva, viewed 20 June 2014, <https://publications.iom.int/system/files/pdf/rb23_eng_2oct.pdf>.

Kaur, A 2010, 'Labour Migration in Southeast Asia: Migration Policies, Labour Exploitation and Regulation', *Journal of the Asia Pacific Economy*, vol. 15, no. 1, pp. 6–19.

King, R, Mata-Codesal, D, and Vullnetari, J 2013, 'Migration, Development, Gender and the "Black Box" of Remittances: Comparative Findings from Albania and Ecuador', *Comparative Migration Studies*, vol. 1, no. 1, pp. 69–96.

Koshiro, K 1991, 'Labor Shortage and Employment Policies in Japan', in *Proceedings of Second Japan-ASIAN Forum on International Labour Migration in East Asia*, the UN University, Tokyo, 2 September.

Lee, ES 1966, 'A Theory of Migration', *Demography*, vol. 3, no. 1, pp. 47–57.

Levitt, P 1998, 'Social Remittances: Migration Driven Local-level forms of Cultural Diffusion', *International Migration Review*, vol. 32, no. 4, pp. 926–48.

Levitt, P and Lamba-Nieves, D 2013, 'Rethinking Social Remittances and the Migration-Development Nexus from the Perspective of Time', *Migration Letters*, vol. 10, no. 1, pp. 11–12.

Macisco Jr, JJ and Pryor Jr, ET 1963, 'A Reappraisal of Ravenstein's "Laws" of Migration: A Review of Selected Studies of Internal Migration in the United States', *The American Catholic Sociological Review*, vol. 24, no. 3, pp. 211–21.

Massey, DS 2003, 'Patterns and Processes of International Migration in the 21st Century', Paper Presented to the *Conference on African Migration in Comparative Perspective*, Johannesburg, South Africa, 4–7 June, viewed 6 June 2012, <http://worldroom.tamu.edu/Workshops/Migration06/GlobalMigration/Globa%20Migratio%20articles/Pattern%20an%20Processe%20o%20Internationa%20Migratio%20i%20th%2021S%20Centur%202003.pdf>.

Ohkawa, K and Rosovsky, H 1973, *Japanese Economic Growth: Trend Acceleration in the Twentieth Century*, Stanford University Press, Stanford, CA.

Ozaki, M 2012, *Worker Migration and Remittances in South Asia*, South Asia Working Paper Series, Asian Development Bank, No. 12, May 2012, Manila, Philippines.

Pettinger, T 2013, *Economic Impact of Migrants and Remittances*, viewed 12 September 2016, <http://www.economicshelp.org/blog/6784/economics/economic-impact-of-migrants/>.

Ratha, D and Shaw, W 2007, *South-South Migration and Remittances*, World Bank Publications, Washington, DC, viewed 4 March 2011, <http://siteresources.worldbank.org/INTPROSPECTS/Resources/SouthSouthMigrationandRemittances.pdf, 0821370731>.

Ravenstein, EG 1885, 'The Laws of Migration', *Journal of the Statistical Society of London*, vol. 48, no. 2, pp. 167–235.

Stark, O and Bloom, DE 1985, 'The New Economics of Labour Migration', *The American Economic Review*, vol. 75, no. 2, pp. 173–8.

Transparency International 2015, *Corruption Perceptions Index,* viewed 14 October, 2016, <http://www.transparency.org/cpi2015>.

UN 2004, *World Economic and Social Survey 2004: International Migration,* Department of Economic and Social Affairs, New York, viewed 11 June 2012, <http://www.un.org/en/development/desa/policy/wess/wess_archive/2004wess_part2_eng.pdf>.

UN 2013, *Trends in International Migrant Stock: The 2013 Revision,* United Nations Department of Economic and Social Affairs, (United Nations Database POP/DB/MIG/Stock/Rev.2013), viewed 10 August 2016, <https://esa.un.org/unmigration/TIMSA2013/Data/>.

UN 2014, Population Facts, Department of Economic and Social Affairs, Population Division, New York, USA, viewed 1 April 2015, <http://www.un.org/en/development/desa/population/publications/factsheets>.

Wickramasekara, P 2002, *Asian Labour Migration: Issues and Challenges in an Era of Globalization,* International Migration Programme, International Labour Office, viewed 11 December 2011, <http://www.ilo.org/asia/whatwedo/publications/WCMS_160632/lang – en/index.htm>.

World Bank 2016, *Migration and Remittances Factbook,* 3rd edn (Advance Edition), World Bank, Washington, DC.

World Justice Project (WJP) 2015, *World Justice Project Rule of Law Index 2015,* viewed 14 October 2016, <http://worldjusticeproject.org/rule-of-law-index>.

3 The political economy of labour migration within the Greater Mekong Sub-region

Paul Howard

1. Introduction

The states of the Greater Mekong Sub-region (GMSR) are diverse politically and economically. While this chapter concerns the GMSR generally, the more specific focus is on Cambodia, Laos, Myanmar and Yunnan Province in the People's Republic of China (PRC). In the case of Cambodia and Laos, the emphasis here is on migration into Thailand. By contrast, for Yunnan Province, the focus is on internal migration within the PRC. China's relative diversity in terms of both geography and development, coupled with the complex political economy of internal worker migration, provides the justification for this focus. While these places have differing political and economic contexts, there are underlying commonalities among them in terms of their emergence from economic isolation and/or disadvantage.

In the 1980s, Cambodia had emerged from the tragic period of the genocidal Pol Pot regime as an economically dysfunctional state. While Cambodia still remains a low income nation, the country has seen substantial economic growth in recent times and foreign investment, particularly from China, has resulted in spectacular growth which is evident in the pace of construction and changing skyline in Phnom Penh. Neighbouring Laos is also among the poorest and most disadvantaged countries in the world but is experiencing high economic growth and foreign investment in recent years. As a major source of investment capital in both Laos and Cambodia, China has itself risen from economic isolation to forge decades of sustained economic growth following the 'opening up' and modernising of the economy under the post-Mao regime of Deng Xiaoping. Similarly, Vietnam embraced the economic reforms of *Doi Moi* in the mid-late 1980s and, although progress was somewhat slower initially than in China, Vietnam also has opened to the world and has been developing rapidly in recent decades.

Myanmar has only in the last few years emerged from direct control by a military junta. While multiparty national elections were held in 2015, the military still hold great implicit and explicit power. The governmental focus is firmly on developing the economy and building social capital. In a sense, rapid development from political and economic isolation or dysfunction ties all these places together. In addition, Cambodia, Laos and Myanmar have borders with

Thailand, and there is significant worker migration, both legal and illegal, across those borders. The impetus for this worker migration is largely the incentive to earn more money than is possible in their home communities and the ability to remit money home. Additionally, migrant agricultural workers may bring back new knowledge on agricultural production from the host communities in the form of technology transfer or innovative methods. Moreover, remittances may enable capital investment to facilitate implementation of the acquired knowledge and policies.

While the economic impact of labour migration in the sending communities is potentially positive, that potential is not fully realized. The allocation of remittances for capital investment is often limited, as income from remittance is largely used for more routine daily expenditures. However, remittances may also be used for the education of migrants' children, something that has potentially positive effects for the sending communities' socioeconomic development. Another role that labour migration may play in these polities is in the engagement with technology essential to the process of remitting income from the host community to the sending community. In addition, entrepreneurialism may be spawned as enterprising 'agents' act as remittance facilitators. The negative aspect of unregulated entrepreneurialism is that some 'agents' may charge inflated fees and act contrary to the interests of the migrants.

It is clear that despite the potential benefits remittance income may offer, there are often problems with both remittance transfer and the limited use of remittances for capital investment. Newly acquired agricultural knowledge may not be fully leveraged without the capital investment needed. There are, though, other significant potential benefits for the sending communities. Increased understanding of technology and production, coupled with the use of remittances for education and health care, may provide the impetus for socioeconomic development in the sending communities. At a broader political level, the role of remittance income in socioeconomic development within sending communities is inextricably tied to the evolving political and economic narratives of both the respective states that constitute the region and that of the Greater Mekong Sub-Region as a whole. This linkage between the regional, national and local contexts provides the rationale for undertaking this analysis of migration and remittances within the GMSR.

In undertaking this analysis, this chapter first considers some of the limitations to the analysis of the issues before providing some background to migration and remittances in specific GMSR countries. Following this, the drivers of migration and related issues within the GMSR are discussed. This creates the basis for the subsequent analysis of the role of remittances in the development of the region and the constituent countries.

1.1 Limitations

Before discussing the core issues, it is worth noting some of the limitations to the study of labour migration and remittances in these places, particularly those related to the availability and reliability of data. In peripheral regions of the respective states, factors such as unregistered migrants, porous borders and reluctance among many interviewees to divulge earnings and/or movements are some of these limiting factors. For example, the International Organisation for Migration (IOM 2010) has noted the limitations of reliable remittance data for Cambodians working in Thailand, asserting that 'the volume of remittance flows, transfer costs, households' investment patterns, gender composition of the flows, and their impact on recipients and communities' are unclear. The IOM (2010) points to the lack of properly documented Cambodian migrants in Thailand with official data reflecting only appropriately registered Cambodian workers, as opposed to the actual numbers of Cambodians working in Thailand.

More specifically, Chan (2009) noted some of the challenges to obtaining accurate remittance data in surveys engaging Cambodian labour migrants. The first issue Chan (2009, p. 32) notes is that respondents were not generally declaring accurate remittance income, as they 'tend to hide their income'. Another problem is that migrants' recollection of amounts and periodization etc. may not be accurate in retrospect if the remittance income relates to periods of months or even years prior to the survey (Chan 2009, p. 32). Also, periods that migrants stayed before returning to Cambodia varied greatly (some returning daily and others staying for periods of up to a year), which was not always clearly communicated. In addition, survey respondents were not always sure when money would be sent by the remitter (Chan 2009, p. 32). Data on remittances is based only on officially declared remittances. The Asian Development Bank (ADB; Revenga, Yves-Fallavier, Larrison and de Paz Nieves 2006) has pointed to understated remittances due to factors including those previously listed, but has highlighted the overarching informal trade in remittance money. It is with these limitations in mind that the focus turns to the temporal development of migration and personal remittances in some of the countries of the GMSR.

2. Background analysis

The GMSR is formally comprised of Cambodia, Lao PDR (Laos), Myanmar, Thailand, and Vietnam in addition to Yunnan and Guizhou Provinces in the PRC. For the purpose of this chapter though, it is useful to provide some background on Cambodia, Laos, Myanmar and Vietnam as migrant 'sending' countries and, therefore, as remittance recipients. Some attention is also given to Yunnan Province in China, as it is considered in terms of migration and remittances within the PRC.

2.1 *Cambodia*

It is Cambodia's transition from a traumatized and underdeveloped society and economy that elevates the importance of labour migration and remittance income

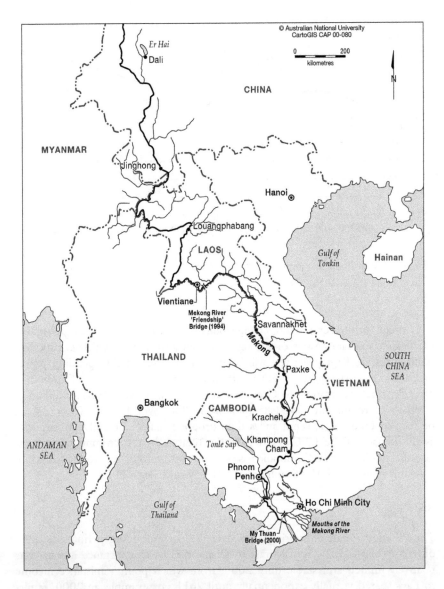

Map 3.1 Map of the GMSR showing major transport corridors

Source: CartoGIS, College of Asia and the Pacific, ANU (2016)

for the country. During the period 2000–2013, total remittances to Cambodia in USD varied significantly year to year. This could, perhaps, be largely explained by the impact of currency movements. For example, the Thai Baht's flexible exchange rate to the USD would be influential as a major source of Cambodian remittances.

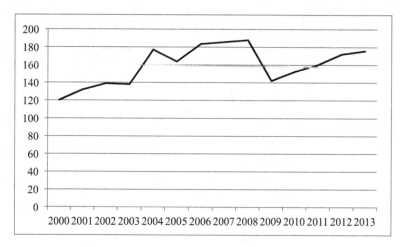

Figure 3.1 Cambodia personal remittances received (current USD million)
Source: World Bank (2015)

Consequently, given the interchangeability of the Riel with USD in Cambodia, the flexible exchange rates of the respective countries from which Cambodian remittances are largely derived will have a direct effect of the spending power in Cambodia, making the USD remittance data pertinent in the Cambodian case. Personal remittances to Cambodia rose from just over USD1.2 million in 2000 to approximately USD1.88 million in 2008 (World Bank 2015). As can be seen in Figure 3.1, remittances then dropped sharply in 2009, presumably as the impact of the GFC was felt in the region. In the ensuing years, total personal remittances to Cambodia rose steadily, with remittances to the Kingdom reaching around USD1.76 million in 2013 (World Bank 2015).

2.2 Laos

The situation for neighbouring Laos over the corresponding period was quite different (Figure 3.2). By contrast to Cambodia, Laos remittance income was relatively limited and stable until 2005, from which point remittance income to Laos soared virtually exponentially until 2011 For example, in 2000, remittances to Laos were only USD660,000, rising to around USD830,000 in 2005 (World Bank 2015). In 2006, remittance income to Laos had soared fivefold to more than USD4.23 million. In the ensuing years, remittance income rose significantly to more than USD110 million in 2011 (World Bank 2015).

It is worth noting that although remittance income to Laos rose only slightly in 2009 and 2010, it did not suffer the dramatic relative decline of Cambodian remittances in the corresponding period. In 2012 and 2013, though, Laos remittances were only USD58.5 million and USD59.62 million, respectively,

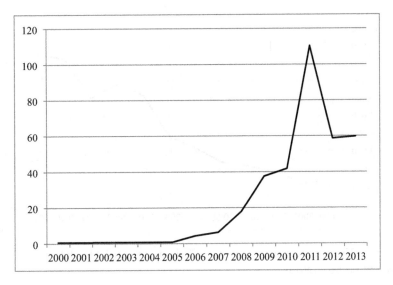

Figure 3.2 Lao PDR personal remittances received (current USD million)
Source: World Bank (2015)

having dropped well below the 2011 figure, whereas Cambodia experienced a modest rebound in remittance growth in the period from 2011 to 2013.

2.3 Vietnam

In the case of Vietnam, remittances have had a relatively linear trajectory from 2001, although there was a slight dip in 2009, most likely due to the GFC and/or currency movements associated with it (Figure 3.3). However, this dip in remittance income proved temporary, with remittance income received returning to its prior linear trend in 2010 and 2011 (data for Vietnam only available to 2011 at the time of writing). Overall growth for the ten-year period (2001–2011) was substantial, with remittance income rising from USD1.1 billion to USD8.6 billion in the period, almost an eightfold increase (World Bank 2015).

2.4 Myanmar

Emerging from decades under a strong authoritarian junta, Myanmar (Burma) is slowly thawing its release of data to the outside world. Indeed, data on labour migration have been scant and often unreliable. More recently though, data have begun to be collated more effectively by external observers, and there are useful clues in some of the data and the analyses conducted in recent years. The IOM, as of 2009, found that up to 10 percent of Myanmar's population was working outside the country (Hall 2012, p. 2). Based on March 2012 data

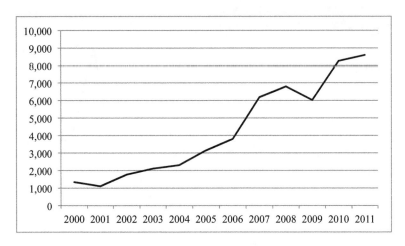

Figure 3.3 Vietnam personal remittances received (current USD million)
Source: World Bank (2015)

for officially registered migrant workers, Hall (2012, p. 3) provides the following breakdown of the major Asian countries for Burmese migrant workers (in descending order, Table 3.1):

Table 3.1 Burmese migrant workers in specific Asian countries

Thailand (est. 2–4 million)
Malaysia (est. 100,000–500,000)
Singapore (est. 100,000–200,000)
Bangladesh (est. 20,000–100,000)
Japan (est. 7,000–15,000)
Korea (est. 4,000–10,000)
China, India and Indonesia (no reliable estimates available)

Source: Hall (2012)

2.5   PRC-Yunnan Province

Despite the PRC's highly restrictive human migration policies, borders are often porous. The ugly side of this is human trafficking in the GMSR, something that has been a specific focus of the UN. In terms of non-illicit labour migration, it is impossible to know the extent of movements in these border areas. The situation is complex primarily because of communities, specifically ethnic minority communities, that straddle the borders in the area. Arbitrary borders determined politically often have borne no relationship to ethnic geography. For the

PRC though, internal labour migration is relevant to this discussion. China's geographic diversity is accompanied by great economic diversity and disparities. In the case of the PRC, the rural-urban shift is on a scale unprecedented in the planet's history of human movement. While the focus is on movements between specific countries, it is worthwhile to consider, first, the more general aspects of migration within the region.

3. Temporary migration within the GMSR

On January 13, 2007, Association of Southeast Asian Nations (ASEAN) leaders formally signed the 'ASEAN Declaration on the Protection and Promotion of the Rights of Migrant Workers', a document that specified objectives to protect the rights and interests of migrant workers (ASEAN 2007). While the specific objectives outlined are generally relevant to low or unskilled workers, there is explicit reference to both skilled and unskilled workers in regard to the need for education about regulations, requirements and processes both before and during migrant worker overseas employment. A decade earlier, at the second ASEAN informal summit, the broad 'ASEAN vision 2020' was adopted. It was a wide ranging document that subsequently led to more specific aims being identified in other declarations such as the Hanoi Plan of Action (HPA) (1999–2004), which was promulgated at the sixth ASEAN Summit in December 1998. The HPA had specific aims and objectives relating to diverse regional socioeconomic issues. Item (h) of Section 2.2 referred specifically to the need to 'Promote freer flow of capital, skilled labour, professionals and technology among ASEAN Member States' (ASEAN 1998).

While these aims may have been well intended, it is not clear that reality has matched those ambitions. A joint IOM-MPI (International Organisation for Migration-Migration Policy Institute) report considered the 'aspiration versus reality' of ASEAN's objective of freer skilled migration. The report asserted that progress toward that the free flow of skilled migrants within ASEAN had been limited. Rather, intra-ASEAN migration was largely characterized by low-skilled or unskilled workers constituting 87 percent of the migrants between ASEAN states (Sugiyarto and Agunias 2014, p. 4). Sugiyarto and Agunias (2014, p. 1) argue that the relatively low rate of skilled labour migration between member states has been due to several factors, which include

- Difficulty of adapting domestic policies and regulations
- Lack of political and public support
- Mutual recognition of qualifications not sufficient to 'facilitate mobility'
- Market demand for labour and supply gaps controlled by private sector

Addressing the factors identified as impediments to skilled migration within ASEAN may help promote skilled migration within the GMSR. That itself though will not negate the attraction of relative economic opportunity offered by mature economies. For example, the bulk of skilled migration within ASEAN is to Singapore, and a majority of those skilled migrants come from Malaysia and the Philippines (Migration News 2013). With its relatively high levels of GDP per capita and developed finance sector, Singapore has greater opportunities for many skilled workers to earn relatively high incomes. It is not surprising that this relative employment and earnings potential provides a strong pull factor for skilled migration. As the economies of the GMSR mature, it may be that opportunities will increase for intra-regional skilled migration.

3.1   Drivers of labour migration

The push factors for migration within the GMSR include demographic changes, poor agricultural yields and farming challenges, lack of land ownership, poverty and joblessness, credit obligations, a lack of market access, natural disasters and destruction of natural resources (Godfrey et al. 2001; Maltoni 2006; CDRI 2007; Chan 2009; Neth 2009; IOM 2010; Lamy 2013). Lamy (2013, p. 43) identifies the pull factors as 'rapid economic growth, lack of unskilled labour, major demands for low-skilled workers, large wage differences between origin and host countries or intensive creation of economic zones'.

Given the cross-border worker migration from Cambodia and Laos into Thailand, the GDP per capita (USD) reflects the 'pull factor' of Thailand's relative prosperity. For example, Thailand's GDP per capita in 2013 was USD6006, which was about four times that of Laos (USD1512) and nearly six times that of Cambodia (USD1043; ADB 2014a). While GDP per capita may not be a direct representation of relative purchasing power, it does graphically illustrate the clear link between macroeconomic performance and the economic incentive for worker migration.

In terms of the overall rates of poverty, the relative prosperity of Thailand is also highlighted and again correlates strongly with the flow of worker migration

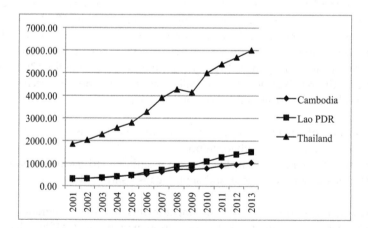

Figure 3.4 GDP per capita (USD per person), 2001–2013
Source: ADB (2014a)

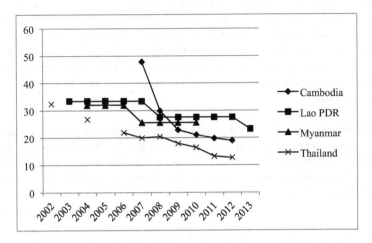

Figure 3.5 Poverty rate (percentage) in selected GMSR countries*
*Data not available for all years
Source: ADB (2014b)

within the Mekong Sub-region. As shown in Figure 3.5, Thailand's poverty rate in 2012 was 12.6 percent compared to Laos at 27.6 percent in the same year. The most recent yearly data for Myanmar was 2010, when the poverty rate was 25.6 percent of the population as against Thailand, which had a poverty rate of 16.4 percent in the same year.

3.2 Unregistered migrants

In June 2015, at the seventh Greater Mekong Sub-region (GMSR) Economic Corridors Forum in Kunming, participant countries committed to further 'promote the development of economic corridors, facilitate cross-border transport and trade, and enhance cooperation and private sector participation' (ADB 2015). The freer flow of goods and people was specifically mentioned as was the development of 'e-commerce' in the border areas. While the commitment to working toward this freer flow of people and goods is worthwhile, there currently exist problems, particularly with respect to the movement of unskilled or lowly skilled labour. The very people that are members of this cohort are among the most vulnerable to exploitation and abuse.

They may also find themselves paying hefty 'fees' just to ensure their continued ability to participate in the labour market of the receiving country. Workers from Myanmar crossing into Thailand must pay THB20 for a visa stamp in order to be registered to work. However, brokers reportedly may charge THB120–150 to organize the visa stamp in an unofficial process so that they can get work in Thailand without the wait (ThaiVisaNews 2015).

Burmese workers in Thailand often find it difficult to get the required documentation from their government, perhaps explaining in part the large numbers of unregistered Burmese working in Thailand, particularly in fisheries and farming where they may be treated poorly (Nyein 2015). Apart from potential abuse at the hands of employers, many Burmese workers, such as the following unnamed worker, also report being subject to overcharging by corrupt border officials or police.

> 'Despite the fact that I had a valid visa in my passport and a work permit, the police detained me and . . . said I must pay a 2,000 baht [about USD60] fine for staying in Tak Province for more than 24 hours,' he said. 'It happened not only to me, but also to other Burmese migrants travelling from Mae Sot to Bangkok or other areas.'
>
> (Nyein 2015)

On the Thai-Cambodia border, Thai authorities have struggled to control illegal logging by unregistered Cambodian migrants. For example, on April 25, 2015, after having been imprisoned for illegal logging in Thailand, 54 Cambodian loggers were deported by the Thai government (Sobratsavyouth 2015). In June 2014, the ruling junta in Thailand threatened a 'crackdown' on illegal Cambodian migrant workers, resulting in more than 200,000 unregistered Cambodians fleeing (Sumon 2015). The major incentive for Thai businesses to employ unregistered migrant labour is the substantially lower rates of pay they receive. For example, in agriculture, unregistered migrants may be payed literally half that of their registered counterparts (Caouette, Sciortino, Guest and Feinstein 2007, p. 39), and the situation is similar for factory and domestic workers. Unregistered workers in 'fish processing' and those engaged in 'general labour' may earn a fraction of that paid to registered workers (Caouette et al. 2007, p. 39).

Table 3.2 Registered versus unregistered migrant incomes in Thailand by industry

Sector	Registered migrant (THB)	Unregistered migrant (THB)
Agriculture	3,000–4,000	1,500–3,000
Domestic work	2,000–4,000	1,000–3,000
Construction	4,500–6,000	3,000–3,300
Fisheries	3,000–4,500	2,400–4,000
Fish processing	3,000	500–2,400
General labour	3,000	600–3,000
Factory	3,000–5,000	1,000–3,000
Entertainment	–	3,000–10,000

Source: Caouette et al. (2007)

3.3 Gender division

Women are proportionately more represented in some of those very areas that see abuse and underpayment of unregistered workers. In an ADB study of migration in the GMSR, despite the fact that hard data were not collected, it was found that women were represented strongly in seafood processing, domestic services, care-giving, shop-keeping, and to some extent, manufacturing (Caouette et al. 2007, p. 21). However, migrant women were also working in the 'entertainment' sector. This generic term may encompass numerous occupations that include restaurant work (waitresses) but also incorporates prostitution. Being unregistered and subject to dangerous working conditions leaves them at high risk of physical abuse and health problems. Trafficking victims, though, are completely vulnerable and without protection once under the control of traffickers.

> Thanh (name changed to protect identity) was 16 when she decided to leave home in her mountainous village in Vietnam's Yen Bai Province to help her poor family. A man who described himself as a labor broker offered her a good job in the provincial capital and she accepted. Instead of making good on his offer, the man spirited her over the border to China and sold her to a brothel. Thanh tried to get help to leave; she begged the brothel's owners to let her go, but they only beat her into submission. After a month in the brothel, a compassionate individual helped Thanh escape and flee home to Vietnam. Life back in her home town was far worse than before. The teenager suffered from severe psychological trauma and numerous health problems. Eventually, she required hospitalization for gynaecological and liver ailments caused by forced sex work.
>
> (Van 2013)

The case of Thanh illustrates the nature and implications for victims of abuse at the hands of traffickers who treat them as nothing more than a commodity. The cost, though, to the defenceless individuals caught up in the 'trade' can be life altering.

4. Role of remittances in development

4.1 Agricultural development

Having considered some of the drivers of worker migration and associated issues, it is pertinent to consider the role that remittances may play in development. Barney (2012) has noted that labour migration on the Laos-Thai border has precipitated change in agricultural practices. The importing of ideas is only part of the picture, as this mobility of agricultural labour occurs as a 'youth out' migratory process and does so in concert with shifts in government policies to land use.

Migration and agrarian transformation are explained as recursive processes in that the remittances from village youth – particularly from young women – are shown as contributing to the adoption of new practices of production in the sending community. Alongside excisions of communal land from a large agribusiness concession, smallholder rubber plots have become a factor in villager-directed privatization of communal property (Barney 2012, p. 60).

It is worth noting that Barney (2012) considers two main forms of migration among youth in Laos. One is the cross-border migration from Laos to Thailand. The other is internal rural-urban migration. Despite the clear differentiation between these two forms, both can invoke similar transference of ideas and technological knowledge. The cross-border migration may lead to new understandings of cultivation; technology or business practices from Laos' relatively developed neighbour. The internal rural-urban shift may lead to new understandings of technology and business practices in the busy urbanized major cities which can then be transferred to the rural host community.

The other side to this is that the incentive of gaining income in higher paying industries in major urban centres draws many away from agricultural production. This paradox was the subject of a study by Manivong, Cramb and Newby (2014), who considered 'crop intensification versus labour migration in Southern Laos'. The study focused on the Southern Laos Province of Champasak adjacent to the Laos-Thai border. Interestingly, the researchers did not draw absolute conclusions in terms of a hollowing out of agricultural production. Rather, they found that farm households seem to view farming as functioning at subsistence or slight surplus level. The attainment of this is seen as a 'platform on which to construct a diversified livelihood strategy in which the use of family labour within and beyond the farm is the key element' (Manivong, Cramb and Newby 2014, p. 373).

4.1.1   PRC-Yunnan

The process of rural youth moving to urban areas for work and returning to their host communities has precedent in the PRC. The relevance of the PRC's experience is made more so by the fact that Laos shares a land border with Xishuangbanna Prefecture in the south of China's Yunnan Province. As with Barney's Laos example, rice and rubber have served as cash crops in that pocket of China. This is not surprising given the common topography and climatic conditions between the respective border areas of the two countries. Interestingly, there may be lessons for Laos in the Xishuangbanna experience. In Xishaungbanna's burgeoning capital, Jinghong, the past decades have seen a 'sleepy' little hamlet transform into a bustling centre, a transformation exacerbated perhaps by the Prefecture's proximity and linkages to bordering Vietnam, Myanmar and Laos.

As capital of Xishuangbanna, Jinghong's economic growth over three decades has seen labour migration from other Provinces as tourism, construction and the related service sector market all boomed. It is in some senses a microcosm of the PRC's development since economic reform began in the post-Mao era from the late 1970s. Migrant remittance workers were on the move to areas of opportunity as the economy transformed. The potential indirect impact of remittance workers on local socioeconomic structures was highlighted in the case of the transformation of the ethnic Dai (Thai) village of Manjinglan, which lay at the Southeastern periphery of Jinghong. Manjinglan had been a rice and rubber growing village, but during the tourism-led development boom of the 1990s, officials moved to purchase the villagers' land to make way for general development (Evans 2000).

The villagers received a one off 'share profit' for the sale of the land and many used that windfall to 'brick-in' the underneath of their traditional Thai stilted homes, which had generally been used to house chickens and pigs. They divided this newly enclosed area into rooms which they rented out to migrant workers who had poured into Jinghong to work in a variety of lowly skilled occupations as labourers, cyclo-drivers and 'bar-girls'. The villagers enjoyed their newfound wealth, but Evans (2000, p. 172) presciently observed:

> While some may joke about the fact that they now house Chinese where they used to house pigs, the Dai grip on this extra income is vulnerable to a sudden change of heart by the city government, which could quickly crack down on this informal arrangement, which has evolved out of necessity.

The combination of the government purchase of land and the influx of remittance workers had created the impetus for a complete transformation in the villagers' socioeconomic structure. No longer farmers of rice and rubber, the formerly agrarian villagers had become landlords harvesting rental income from the remittance workers living under their dwellings.

The author of this chapter made subsequent field trips to the area in both 2004 and 2012. By 2012, it was not possible to locate many of the traditional structures. The area had given way to sprawling urban development characterized by low, medium and high-rise apartment blocks. I was not able to ascertain whether most of the villagers had simply sold their dwellings to the government and/or developers. However, the transition of Manjinglan was complete.

In regard to temporary worker migration from Yunnan, the International Fund for Agricultural Development (IFAD) conducted research involving 1,500 rural households from three townships in Eshan County, Yunnan Province. As part of this larger study, in 2008, interviews were conducted with 884 rural migrant households living in Beijing on the way their remittance income is spent (IFAD 2015). According to the data collected from the interviews, migrant households reported that their largest expenses related to their daily requirements (food and other consumption), looking after their parents and fees for their children's education. By contrast, 'savings' accounted for 5.6 percent, and 6.4 percent was allocated for agricultural production (IFAD 2015). With this aspect as the core focus of the study, IFAD noted the need for a significant proportion of remittance income to be directed to improving agricultural production in host communities. As with Cambodian and Laotian rural migrants, the process of transferring remittances to the host community remains difficult.

Remittance-receiving processes are the main problem, as they are related to poor financial services in rural China. A community approach is needed to help farmers gain better access to remittances and financial services, while building the capacity of villagers on financial and agriculture issues by providing training and knowledge (IFAD 2015).

4.2   *Thriving money transfer business: entrepreneurship*

The issue of the need for easier and cheaper channels for remitting money is important to both the migrant workers and their households. This was highlighted in survey data in a report for the International Organization for Migration (IOM 2010), concerned with labour migration from Cambodia to Thailand. The survey considered dual responses from both the workers and their home households. In response to the question of what services were most wanted, 91.7 percent of the migrant worker group and 91.1 percent of the household group responded that they wanted 'establishment of cheaper and safer money transfer channels' (IOM 2010, p. 61). Of the service categories nominated, this was the highest level of response in the affirmative for both groups. It was also the only category in which both groups expressed a similar level of affirmative response.

For example, in the area of microfinance, 68.9 percent of the household group responded that they wanted better access to microfinance (IOM 2010, p. 61). In stark contrast, only 5.9 percent of the migrant worker group saw microfinance access as a priority (IOM 2010, p. 61). Chan (2009, p. 37) provides a number of examples garnered from interviews conducted in September 2009 of informal remittance running businesses using the telephone, including the following case of an entrepreneur from Prah Netr District in Beanteay Meanchey:

> He charges 2.5 percent, and the broker in Svay Sisophon takes 0.5 percent for the service. In addition, a broker in Thailand charges 50 Baht from the workers each time they send remittances. He has to pay 50,000 Riels a month to the post office and 2000 Baht for the Thai telephone service, which can increase to 3000 Baht during Khmer New Year, Pchum Ben and other major ceremonies. . . . His capital of 100,000 Baht is not enough because sometimes the workers together transfer up to 200,000 Baht per month. As a result, he needs to borrow from a friend and pay interest of 3–4 percent per month. He has not had any problems because the broker is in the same village as him. In Phnom Lieb commune, there are seven agents providing this service. He can make a profit of about 1500 Baht per month.

There are points regarding the role of remittance transfer entrepreneurialism that are worth considering. Firstly, the engagement with technology that is necessitated by the remittance transfer process is educating participants in the use of the technologies involved. This may be true for some who become active in the remittance transfer process as a means of earning income but ultimately are drawn into the fabric of the cross-border economy. While this may be true for the 'middlemen/women', it may be the case that some of the remittance senders ultimately engage with technology and become educated in the relevant processes.

In addition, among the migration labour force, there will be information sharing on better and/or cheaper ways of remitting income. The agents will also likely learn quickly of the fluidity of business in terms of responses to demand or a drop in demand. Similarly, remittance workers themselves may become better educated in the power of choice and the power inherent in both the market demand for them as clients. While it is likely that, initially, many may be naïve to the remittance transfer processes, the economic imperative of remitting money for as little cost as possible will see them become savvy about the options available. This is also dependent on information sharing among migrant workers, something that may also implicitly strengthen the migrant worker community as a whole.

4.3 Information and Communications Technologies (ICTs)

While the use of ICTs in the process of remitting income may play an important role in engaging migrant labour with technology, the process of remitting income can leave many potentially exposed to unscrupulous operators or even merely just paying far too much for services rendered. Even in the case studies cited by Chan (2009), percentages charged by remittance agents for transferring remittances vary between operators. At a more extreme end of the fee spectrum, anecdotes of exorbitant fees being charged to remitters are common in the relevant literature. In recognition of this lack of understanding of the processes associated with remitting income, the ILO has developed a 'training kit', which includes modules that cover such aspects as how income can be remitted, how savings accounts/plans can be set up and how remitted money may be invested (Tunon and Rim 2013, p. 14).

4.4 Use of remittance money for growth

One of the central questions with regard to the impact of remittances on host countries is how remittance money is being spent by recipient households. In an ADB report, Caouette et al. (2007, p. 63) assert much of the remittance income sent to the developing GMSR countries is used for daily necessities, medical care and food staples. An ILO report on remittance income among Laotian and Cambodian labour migrants in Thailand found variance between the two countries in regard to how the remittance income was spent, based on surveys conducted with both groups. Among both Cambodian and Laotian migrants, the largest proportion of remittances was spent on 'daily needs', with 37 percent and 32 percent (expressed as a mean) of the remittance income spent on 'daily needs' respectively (Deleen and Vasuprasat 2010, pp. 25–26). Cambodian migrants reported spending of 14 percent on 'health' as the next biggest percentage of remittance expenditure, 'paying debt' at 10 percent, with the equal next biggest expenditure categories being 'savings', 'education' and the generic 'others' category each recorded as 8 percent of income on average (Deleen and Vasuprasat 2010, p. 26).

Laotian migrants spent 14 percent of remittances on 'health', substantially less than their Vietnamese counterparts and slightly less on education (6 percent) than Vietnamese respondents. In contrast, though, Laotian migrants spent 19 percent of remittance income on 'housing/home improvements' and 12 percent on 'Transport (cars, motorbikes, tricycles)' as the second and third largest expenditure items, respectively (Deleen and Vasuprasat 2010, p. 25). Vietnamese respondents reported spending only 1 percent and 2 percent on those items, respectively. Precisely why there is such variance is the percentage expenditure on those items is not clear. In particular, the use of remittances for education may provide the greatest long term benefits for the economic development of the remitting countries. Greater access to and level of education may provide a pathway for socioeconomic development within the sending countries, along with greater social capital for integration with both the regional and global economies.

5.   Conclusion

Migration within the countries of the GMSR is implicitly tied to the political narrative of the respective states that constitute the region. There is, among many of the states, a common thread of emergence from relative economic underperformance. This emergence has given way to rapid development throughout the region, and remittance income from worker migration has followed a similar trajectory. The impact of this remittance income on sending communities is mixed. It seems there is greater expenditure on education and health care, which in itself is a positive development.

Without appropriate capital investment in agricultural development though, knowledge gained by remittance workers is not being fully leveraged. In some respects, it is probably far more tangible to the observer to comprehend the immediacy of economic inputs to the developing economy than it is to fathom the myriad of social inputs that labour migration may bring. These inputs may range from positive developments such as increased knowledge and usage of ICTs to pernicious influences.

In addition to the purely economic considerations, unregistered remittance workers are particularly vulnerable to exploitation by employers. Registered workers and unregistered workers alike are also vulnerable to overcharging by unscrupulous remittance transfer agents. In contrast to this vulnerability, though, remittance workers may share information on remittance transfer, which could presumably expose them to technology. This engagement with technology may also help educate remittance transfer agents and provides a vehicle for entrepreneurialism.

In terms of development in sending communities, little remittance money is allocated to capital investment in agriculture. This limits the potential for application of new knowledge brought by remittance workers exposed to more efficient and productive technology and processes in the host communities.

The freer flow of 'registered' labour in the GMSR needs to be enabled, particularly in the border areas, and border crossing areas need to be monitored and audited by an independent agency to ensure a fair and equitable labour migration process. Access to information assistance for particular at-risk groups should be a priority (unskilled labour, migrant workers with low educational levels, women and children, unregistered migrant workers). Specific scrutiny should be applied to industries that employ large numbers of unregistered workers to ensure compliance with basic international standards of working and living conditions.

These issues all highlight the link between labour migration within the countries of the GMSR and the political narrative, both of the respective countries and the region as a whole. The emergence of many of the states of the GMSR from economic disadvantage is tied to the issues and challenges in harnessing the full potential that intra-regional migration offers.

References

ASEAN, 15–16 December 1998, 'Hanoi Plan of Action', *Sixth ASEAN Summit, Hanoi*, viewed 29 August 2015, <http://www.wright.edu/~tdung/hanoi_plan.htm>.

ASEAN 2007, 'ASEAN Declaration on the Protection and Promotion of the Rights of Migrant Workers (ACMW)', *12th ASEAN Summit Cebu, Philippines*, viewed July 2015, <http://www.asean.org/archive/23062.pdf>.

Asian Development Bank (ADB) 2014a, *Gross Domestic Product Per Capita (Current Prices) (US$/Person)*, viewed 30 June 2015, <http://www.gms-eoc.org/gms-statistics/overview/gross-domestic-product-per-capita-current-prices>.

Asian Development Bank (ADB) 2014b, *Poverty Rate*, viewed 30 June 2015, <http://www.gms-eoc.org/gms-statistics/overview/poverty-rate>.

Asian Development Bank (ADB) 2015, *Ministers Endorse Plans to Develop New Special Economic Zones in Mekong*, viewed 15 June 2015, <http://www.adb.org/news/ministers-endorse-plans-develop-new-special-economic-zones-mekong>.

Barney, K 2012, 'Land, Livelihoods and Remittances', *Critical Asian Studies*, vol. 44, no. 1, pp. 57–83.

Caouette, T, Sciortino, R, Guest, P, and Feinstein, A 2007, *Labor Migration in the Greater Mekong Sub-region*, Asian Development Bank, Bangkok.

CartoGIS, College of Asia and the Pacific, The Australian National University 2016, *Greater Mekong Subregion Map*, viewed 24 October 2016, <http://asiapacific.anu.edu.au/mapsonline/base-maps/greater-mekong-subregion>.

CDRI (Cambodia Development Research Institute) 2007, *Youth Migration and Urbanisation in Cambodia*, CDRI Working Paper Series No. 36.

Chan, S 2009, *Costs and Benefits of Cross-Country Labour Migration in the GMS: Cambodia Country Study*, Working Paper Series No. 44, CDRI, Phnom Penh.

Deleen, L and Vasuprasat, P 2010, *Migrant Workers' Remittances from Thailand to Cambodia, Lao PDR and Myanmar: Synthesis Report on Survey Findings in Three Countries and Good Practices*, ILO, Geneva.

Evans, G 2000, 'Transformation of Jing Hong, Xishuangbanna, PRC', in G Evans, C Hutton and Kuah Khun Eng (eds), *Where China Meets Southeast Asia: Social and Cultural Change in the Border Regions*, Institute of Southeast Asian Studies, Singapore, pp. 162–82.

Godfrey, M, Sovannarith, S, Saravy, T, Dorina, P, Katz, C, Acharya, S, Chanto, SD, and Thoraxy H 2001, *A Study of the Cambodian Labour Market: Reference to Poverty Reduction, Growth and Adjustment to Crisis CDRI*, Working Paper No. 18.

Hall, A 2012, *Myanmar and Migrant Workers: Briefing and Recommendations*, Mahidol Migration Center, Institute for Population and Social Research, Mahidol University.

IFAD 2015, *Yunnan Institute of Development YID: Expanding Financial Services to Rural China through Remittances*, viewed 27 March 2015, <http://www.ifad.org/remittances/projects/asia/china.htm>.

International Organization for Migration (IOM) 2010, *Analyzing the Impact of Remittances from Cambodian Migrant Workers in Thailand on Local Communities in Cambodia*, International Organization for Migration, Phnom Penh.

Lamy, M 2013, 'The Impact of Migration on Household Expenditure Patterns: Evidence from Cambodia', *Cambodian Economic Review*, issue 6, pp. 37–77.

Maltoni, B 2006, *Review of Labour Migration Dynamics in Cambodia*, International Organization for Migration (IOM), Phenom Penh.

Manivong, V, Cramb, R, and Newby, J 2014, 'Rice and Remittances: Crop Intensification Versus Labour Migration in Southern Laos', *Human Ecology*, vol. 42, pp. 367–79.

Migration News 2013, 'Southeast Asia: ASEAN 2015', vol. 20, no. 4, viewed 29 May 2015, <https://migration.ucdavis.edu/mn/more.php?id=3868>.

Neth, N 2009, *Human Trafficking in Cambodia: Reintegration of Cambodian Illegal Migrants from Vietnam and Thailand*, RSIS Working Paper No. 181.

Nyein, N 2015, 'Labor Official Warns Migrants to Complete Thai Work Registration', *The Irrawaddy*, 27 February, viewed 12 October 2015, <http://www.irrawaddy.org/burma/labor-official-warns-migrants-complete-thai-work-registration.html>.

Revenga, A, Yves-Fallavier, P, Larrison, J, and de Paz Nieves, C 2006, *Labour Migration in the Greater Mekong Sub-region: Synthesis Report Phase I*, viewed 18 March 2015, <http://siteresources.worldbank.org/INTTHAILAND/Resources/333200–1089943634036/475256–1151398858396/LM_in_GMSs_Nov06.pdf>.

Sobratsavyouth, H 2015, 'Thailand Deports Dozens of Cambodians Jailed for Illegal Logging', *Radio Free Asia*, 27 April, viewed 23 November 2015, <http://www.rfa.org/english/news/cambodia/deportation-04272015123646.html>.

Sugiyarto, G and Agunias, D 2014, 'A Freer Flow of Skilled Labour within ASEAN: Aspirations, Opportunities and Challenges in 2015 and Beyond', *Issue in Brief*, no. 11, December, pp. 1–11.

Sumon, N 2015, 'Cambodia Blames Thailand as 220,000 Migrant Labourers Cross Border', *The Guardian*, 18 June, viewed 23 June 2015, <http://www.theguardian.com/world/2014/jun/18/cambodia-thailand-migrant-labourers-border>.

Thaivisanews 2015, 'Lack of Jobs and High Cost of Living Drive Migrant Workers Back to Thailand', viewed 16 June 2015, <http://news.thaivisa.com/thaivisa-news/lack-of-jobs-and-high-cost-of-living-drive-migrant-workers-back-to-thailand/45333>.

Tunon, M and Rim, K 2013, *Cross-border Labour Migration in Cambodia: Considerations for the National Employment Policy*, ILO Regional Office for Asia and the Pacific, Bangkok.

Van, T 2013, 'Trafficking Study Urges Governments to Facilitate Safe Migration in Mekong Sub-Region', *Thanh Nien News*, December 23, viewed 16 April 2015, <http://www.thanhniennews.com/society/trafficking-study-urges-governments-to-facilitate-safe-migration-in-mekong-subregion-35552.html>.

World Bank, 2015, *World Development Indicators: Data Personal Remittances Received (Current US$)*, viewed 18 March 2015, <http://data.worldbank.org/indicator/BX.TRF.PWKR.CD.DT/countries/1W?display=default>.

4 Temporary migration of Cambodians into Thailand

A study of repatriated workers in Siem Reap

Campbell Fraser and Paul Howard

1. Introduction

This chapter reports on the findings of interviews with 247 Cambodian temporary labour migrants upon repatriation from Thailand. The chapter first discusses the socio-political context that has created the conditions that lend impetus to this temporary migration, before reporting the findings of a detailed analysis of the data collected from migrants in the peri-urban areas of Siem Reap.

Previous studies of temporary migrations have positioned their analyses in terms of push and pull factors; however, this study additionally considers the issue from the dimension of the *urgency* of the migration. From this added perspective, the migrants may be classified and analysed as two distinct groups: first, those migrating under an urgent socioeconomic imperative, and second, those migrating voluntarily in order to accumulate wealth. Following convention, these distinct groups are classified as Involuntary Livelihood Pushed (ILP) migrants and Voluntary Income Enhancement (VIE) migrants.

The overarching objective of this chapter is to critically analyse key environmental and social factors pertaining to the experience of Cambodian temporary worker migration in Thailand. The conceptual framework of this study is based on an explanatory approach to a specific South/South migration scenario. This particular scenario has been chosen due to the unique circumstances of Cambodian temporary migrants during the period 2014–2015. A sudden and unexpected change in Thai government policy in 2014 prompted an immediate and unplanned exodus of many of these temporary migrants from Thailand back to Cambodia. While in 2015 these migrants began to re-migrate back to Thailand, in the interim many of them were provided with social support through community centres in the major metropolitan centres throughout Cambodia. This research focuses on a group of returned Cambodian migrants accessing these community centres in the city of Siem Reap.

The findings of the research indicate that participants who migrated as ILP migrants not only endured worse conditions of both employment and living standards in Thailand, but they also demonstrated a higher willingness to accept these poor conditions when compared to the group of migrants who had the opportunity to make more considered decisions in regard to their migration options. These adverse conditions included deprivation of liberty and willingness to work in a different industry and perform different, more arduous tasks, from that initially agreed to with their broker.

The reasons for such ILP migration includes the need to service debt – pay for a family emergency or in some way fear for their immediate safety in their current location. The VIE migration group took the decision as a long term strategy to accumulate savings and, therefore, were in a stronger position to refuse migration contracts which they considered unfavourable. The marked difference in the treatment of the two groups of migrants can be explained by their respective levels of economic and social vulnerability.

The migrant groups studied in this research are considered here as being part of the broader picture of South-South migration more generally and of the political economy of the Mekong Sub-region. Consequently, the paper begins by exploring relevant issues in the Cambodian political economy to demonstrate the linkage between the national and regional contexts. Following this, the chapter provides an analysis of Cambodia's economic performance relative to Thailand's and the development of Cambodia's recent economic situation. Consideration of this regional political and economic context provides the background for the study.

2.   Regional context

2.1   The 2008 law

In 2008, the Cambodian Senate passed the 'Law on Suppression of Human Trafficking and Sexual Exploitation' (Royal Kram 2008). While the law is wide ranging, as the title suggests, Chapter 2 deals specifically with 'The Act of Selling/Buying or Exchanging a Person'. Within that chapter are specific articles relating to cross-border movements. Many of the articles deal with forced removal or labour but there is also provision for the greyer area of deceptive recruitment. For example, Article 12 concerns the 'Unlawful Recruitment for Exploitation' whereby 'the act of unlawful recruitment in this law shall mean to induce, hire or employ a person to engage in any form of exploitation with the use of deception, abuse of power, confinement, force, threat or any coercive means.'

Conviction under Article 12 may result in imprisonment from seven to fifteen years and longer terms (fifteen to twenty years) may be imposed if the victim is a minor, the offence is committed by a public official who abuses his/her authority over the victim or the offence is committed by an organized group. Consequently, the law is applicable to situations where migrants are lured under false pretences. The 2008 law does, therefore, have relevance to migrants who may have migrated of their own free will but have been given false hope by agents. The law, of course, also directly and explicitly applies to those forced to work under duress and to those trafficked against their will.

One of the explicitly stated objectives of the Cambodian law was to 'implement the UN Protocol to Prevent, Suppress, and Punish Trafficking in Persons, Especially Women and Children', supplementing the United Nations Convention against Transnational Organized Crime'. Therefore, this law, promulgated at national level, links directly to the international political sphere. In turn, there is a strong regional connection with other ASEAN states enacting similarly focused legislation (ATUC 2015) since 2004:

> Brunei – The Trafficking and Smuggling Persons Order (December 22, 2004)
> Myanmar – The Anti-Trafficking in Persons Law (September 13, 2005)
> Indonesia – The Eradication of the Criminal Act of Trafficking in Person (April 19, 2007)
> Malaysia – Anti-Trafficking in Persons Act (date of royal assent: July 18, 2007)
> Cambodia – The Law on Suppression of Human Trafficking and Sexual Exploitation (passed on January 18, 2008)
> Thailand – The Anti-Trafficking In Persons Act, B.E. 2551 (January 30, 2008)
> Vietnam – Anti Human Trafficking Law (effective January 1, 2012) with a National Plan of Action on Human Trafficking (2011–2015)
> Singapore – Prevention of Human Trafficking Act 2014

This enactment of similarly themed law across the ASEAN orbit is largely a result of the collective commitment of states within the regional body in the 2004 'ASEAN Declaration Against Trafficking in Persons Particularly Women and Children' (ASEAN 2004). The 2004 ASEAN Declaration and the various laws subsequently promulgated by member states demonstrates the positive influence a regional body may have in giving impetus to individual states taking action. Conversely, though, political developments within member states can have implications for migrant worker populations, as evidenced by the 2014 Thai coup.

2.2   *Thai coup (2014)*

The 2014 military coup in neighbouring Thailand saw Cambodian migrant workers 'fleeing' on mass out of fear of the incoming junta led by Prayuth Chan-ocha. By June 19th, a month after the coup, the IOM (International Organisation for Migration) had estimated that more than 200,000 migrant workers had returned to Cambodia (The Economist 2014). Such was the tide of humanity that the Cambodian Army collected the migrants in trucks from the border areas (The Economist 2014). The reason for the mass panic was largely due to the uneasy relations between the Thai junta and Hun Sen's Cambodian regime.

Thaksin Shinawatra, the former Thai Prime Minister and a media mogul, had lived in exile following a prior coup. Thaksin's sister, Yingluck Shinawatra, had been leader of the government in recent years prior to her government being ousted by the military in the lead up to the May 2014 coup. Thaksin is seen as being close to the Hun Sen government, leading to the Thai junta harbouring suspicions and a degree of paranoia due to the perceived influence of Thaksin, particularly in the rural areas, including those adjacent to the Thai border. The Thai junta had also accused the Cambodian government of harbouring the leader of the pro-Thaksin Red Shirt movement, Jakrapob Penkair (Leng 2014).

Subsequently, the focus of the Thai Junta was on deporting migrants who were unregistered or lacking appropriate documentation. In October 2015, a deal was struck between the Cambodian and Thai regimes under which Thailand agreed to 'relax enforcement' of deportation rules in the case of Cambodian migrant workers having expired documents, something that is triggered if the migrant changes employers in the absence of the prior employer's written consent (Sen 2015).

3. Political economy

While sudden political developments can prompt or even force migrants to leave, broader economic factors play a major part in migration choices. Movement into Thailand from its immediate neighbours largely relates to the 'pull factor' of the more prosperous economy and perceived opportunities. A direct comparison of Cambodia and Thai GDP per capita over time illustrates Thailand's relative prosperity (Figure 4.1). Cambodia's GDP per capita grew from USD315 in 2001 to USD1043 in 2013. During the same period, Thailand's GDP per capita grew from USD1853 to USD6006 (ADB 2014a). This represents a threefold increase in Cambodia's case and slightly more than threefold increase for Thailand in the period. A clear disparity remains, with Thailand's 2013 GDP per capita being 5.75 times that of Cambodia.

The 'poverty rate', as measured by the ADB, has fallen substantially in Cambodia from 48 percent of the population in 2007 to 19 percent in 2013. By comparison, the poverty rate in Thailand has fallen from 20 percent of the

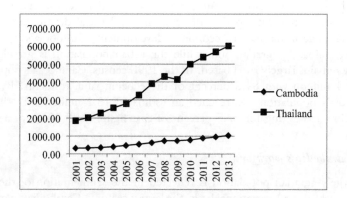

Figure 4.1 GDP per capita (USD per person), 2001–2013
Source: ADB (2014a)

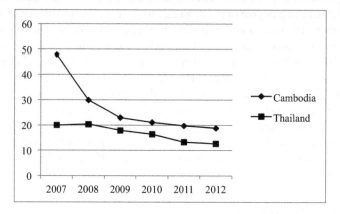

Figure 4.2 Poverty rate in Thailand and Cambodia (percentage)
Source: ADB (2014b)

population in 2007 to around 12 percent 2013 (Figure 4.2; ADB 2014b). It is worth noting that the steepest fall in Cambodia's poverty rate in the period was in 2007 and 2008. Subsequently, the poverty rate differential of the two countries was relatively steady. Despite the rapid reduction in the gap between poverty rates in the two countries, the relative prosperity of Thailand, with its high GDP per capita and correspondingly better perceived opportunities, remained the key attraction for Cambodia's temporary migrant workers.

3.1   Economic emergence

Cambodia's relatively low GDP per capita is largely symptomatic of past political developments. In the early 1990s, under the initial supervision of UNTAC (United Nations Transitional Authority in Cambodia), Cambodia began to emerge from a traumatic period of economic and social devastation. At that formative stage in its modern economic development, Cambodia's population was predominantly agrarian and, while the urban population is growing, the country remains largely rural based. In the 1998 census, Cambodia's population was 11.4 million with 84.3 percent of those being rural residents. By 2014, Cambodia's population had reached an estimated 15.2 million with the rural population accounting for 77.5 percent of that figure (NIS 2015. p. 3).

3.2   Cambodia's workforce

This largely agrarian population is reflected in the segmentation of the Cambodian workforce. On a national basis, the largest sector in Cambodia's workforce for both genders is that defined as 'skilled agricultural, forestry and fishery workers', with 41 percent of females and 38 percent of males identified as being

Table 4.1 Number of Cambodian workers by industry sector and gender (2014)

	Female	Male
Agriculture (Primary)	1,853,000	1,873,000
Industry (Secondary)	956,000	1,045,000
Services (Tertiary)	116,000	134,000

Source: NIS (2015, p. 73)

employed in that category of work. Significantly, approximately 40 percent of Cambodians are employed in the agricultural, forestry and fishery enterprises (NIS 2015, p. 72). Women working in that area comprise 41 percent, a slightly higher number than the percentage of males (38 percent) in that sector (NIS 2015, p. 72). In terms of the main sectors of the economy, agriculture is by far the largest area of employment with 1.85 million women and 1.87 million men working in that sector (Table 4.1; NIS 2015, p. 73).

This large number of people engaged in the agricultural sector provides a pool of potential workers for similar employment in neighbouring Thailand. Because a major source city of this labour pool is Siem Reap, the authors have chosen Siem Reap and its surrounds as the location of this study of temporary labour migration.

4.   Methodology

The authors have a long association with the city of Siem Reap through their longstanding work on human trafficking in the city. This was achieved through broad ethnographic study of the city by the authors over an extended period of time. While the authors' main interest in the city has been specifically its role in human organ trafficking, the NGO volunteers that the authors work with in this role are also involved in resettlement assistance of returned migrants. It was through these ongoing professional relationships that the planning and development of this current project evolved.

A total of 247 returned migrants were interviewed in the safety of their respective community centres. The interviews were highly structured, and adapted from an instrument used in the study of victims of human organ trafficking. The questions appear in the following list. Apart from the first question, which established the main reason why the temporary migration took place, each required an answer on a scale of 1–5, ranging from strongly disagree to strongly agree.

1   The main reason for seeking employment in Thailand.
2   It was my personal decision to migrate to Thailand.
3   I feel my family pressurized me into migrating to Thailand.

4 I volunteered to be the family member to migrate in order to prevent another family member from having to do so.
5 There was general agreement within the family that I should be the one to migrate.
6 I believe that there were other family members who could have migrated.
7 I believe the broker is a good person.
8 The broker provided me with options as to the where in Thailand I would be posted.
9 The broker provided me with options as to who my employer would be.
10 I was permitted to move around freely when not working.
11 Other migrants played a role in my decision to migrate.
12 Other migrants pressurized me into migrating.
13 The broker treated me respectfully.
14 I believe I was sometimes underpaid.
15 I believe that my employer is a good person.
16 I was detained against my will during the migration process.
17 My employer required me to perform tasks that I did not feel I should be doing.
18 The work I was asked to perform went against my morals.
19 I was treated differently because I was a foreigner.
20 I was subjected to violence at work.
21 There would have been negative consequences if I complained about the work I was asked to perform.
22 I felt safe while I was in Thailand.
23 I was overall better off after I migrated.
24 I remitted most of my income home.
25 Without my remittance my family would not have not have survived.
26 My status within the family increased after I migrated.
27 My status among my friends has increased since I migrated.
28 I have had difficulty integrating back into life in Cambodia.
29 I have a desire to return to Thailand.
30 I regret the decision to migrate.
31 I would migrate again if I could.
32 I would recommend others to migrate.

The participants were grouped according their responses to the main reason for seeking employment in Thailand, in addition to their gender and stated age.

A To pay general household expenses
B A family emergency
C To pay debt
D To accumulate savings
E On instruction of family without given reason
F To seek safety
G To establish business

The stated reasons for the migration were consolidated into two broad classifications – namely, Involuntary Livelihood Pushed migrants and Voluntary Income Enhancement migrants.

While the quantitative data obtained from the research participants provides the foundation of the analysis, rich qualitative data were additionally obtained during less formal social interaction with the Cambodian participants, their supporters and translators. Likewise, Thai employers' opinions were obtained through similar informal discussions, enabling a balanced analysis of both viewpoints. Issues discussed in these exchanges are discussed in this chapter and provide a useful context to the foundation quantitative data.

5. The case of Siem Reap temporary migrants

Siem Reap is not only the name of Cambodia's third largest city, but it also defines a Provincial area for statistical purposes. With the core attraction of Angkor Wat, Siem Reap has grown to be the premier focus for tourists in Cambodia. According to the Ministry of Tourism, international tourist numbers grew from 1.6 million in 2011 to 2.2 million in 2013, a 38 percent increase in the period (Morton 2014). As at 2013, tourism registered establishments in the Siem Reap city included 390 hotels and guesthouses, 178 restaurants, 49 massage parlours and 17 karaoke bars (Morton 2014).

Siem Reap ranks first among Cambodia's twenty-four Provinces for the percentage of business registered as 'street business',[1] accounting for 13.1 percent of the Province's businesses compared to a national average of 8.3 percent (NIS 2013, Sec 1, p. 4). This suggests a relatively large informal sector, something that may be connected to Siem Reap's status as a tourism-driven economy.

There is a long history of temporary labour migration from Cambodia to Thailand, including Siem Reap. The authors have spent time embedded in the region, meeting returned migrant workers in Siem Reap through the network of returned migrant social and support organizations. Using an ethnographic approach, the authors have gained an insight into the antecedent conditions that motivate temporary migration, the migration experience itself, and the reintegration of the migrant upon return to Siem Reap. This has given the authors a rich insight into the mechanics of the temporary migration, and the reported themes are presented and summarized. In total, the authors have interviewed 247 returned migrants across six support organizations. The 2014 Thai immigration enforcement drive, as described previously, resulted in a mass repatriation of migrants to Siem Reap, thereby providing the authors with a unique opportunity to interact with them.

The interviews conducted with Siem Reap migrants found that they universally used specialist migration employment brokers to secure both passage to and employment in Thailand. These brokers, who actively recruit migrants from Siem Reap to feed into their Thai employer networks, are often agents of larger brokerage organizations with a presence in both Cambodia and Thailand. The authors have met with fifteen brokers involved in this trade.

Migration brokers in Siem Reap have lucrative relationships with employers in a variety of business environments. These businesses share the common theme that to sustain profitability they require a continuous supply of inexpensive labour willing to perform highly repetitive, physically demanding tasks. The fish processing, garment manufacturing and entertainment industries are major employers.

While it is well known that temporary migration occurs for many reasons, the literature generally classifies these into 'push' and 'pull' factors. The 'push' factors are primarily concerned with the unfavourable conditions in the home country, such as unemployment, underemployment, low wage rates, family difficulties and political or social persecution. Conversely, the 'pull' factors of host countries include the prospect and expectation of more promising employment options with possibly improved working and living conditions. In most cases, however, the decision to become a migrant is based on a combination of push and pull factors, which combine to formulate the overall desirability of the move.

During discussions with this particular population of returned migrants in Siem Reap, a persistent theme of *urgency* of migration quickly became apparent. As a result, in this chapter we consider the migration, not only in terms of *push* or *pull* factors, but additionally from the perspective of the *urgency* of migration. By focussing on the *urgency*, we can examine the quality of the decision to migrate in terms of how well considered and rational the decision to migrate has been. This has also permitted the identification of two distinct groups within the population – the urgent Involuntary Livelihood Pushed migrants (ILP) and the non-urgent Voluntary Income Enhancement (VIE) migrants.

5.1   Decision to migrate temporarily with urgency – Involuntary Livelihood Pushed (ILP) migrants

ILP migration occurs in response to a specific, singular event. In the context of Cambodian migrants, the specific event that triggers an ILP migration is often a family emergency, where money is urgently needed to pay for medical treatment of a sick loved one. The decision to proceed with medical treatment may be based around several variables, including the gender of the sick family member, their status within the family hierarchy and the expected economic productivity of the family member both before and after medical treatment.

If the family does decide to treat the sick member, then a junior family member may be nominated to seek employment overseas in order to raise the necessary funds. The prospective migrant will very likely engage with a broker in the local neighbourhood to arrange transportation to, and employment in, Thailand, and will provide an advance to families to pay for the commencement of medical treatment once the migrating family member has left home to take up the work placement. This is such a common scenario in Cambodia that medical service providers known to the author work directly with brokers. The broker may directly refer patients to a specific medical service provider, with whom they have an established a profitable relationship.

While there are clear benefits to the family unit by being able to now procure medical treatment, this may come at great personal cost to the migrant themselves. The Siem Reap migrants report that brokers may garnishee wages directly, and that they may be forced to live in crowded and insanitary shared accommodation. Migrants report poorer working conditions than local workers, deprivation of liberty, and believe they would be subjected to violence if they complained. The migrant is, however, very unlikely to complain, as the employer is paying the brokers who in turn pay the doctor who is keeping alive the family member in Siem Reap.

The authors believe that both the costs and duration of treatment are inflated to sustain the motivation of the migrant in Thailand. The employer, the broker and doctor/hospital therefore all have incentives to retain the services of the migrant for as long as possible.

5.2 ILP migration due to the social environment

The social environment of temporary migrants can create the need for ILP temporary migration, both within and external to the migrants' families. A form of ILP migration frequently reported by participants in Siem Reap is where, within the family unit, an authority figure, usually the father, decides to contract a junior member of the family (usually a daughter) to a broker, and therefore the child unwittingly becomes a migrant in Thailand. While these young women may commence the migrant experience in fish processing or garment manufacturing, they will very likely, ultimately, be recruited into the entertainment industry.

The popular media frequently report this phenomenon as 'fathers selling their unwanted daughters'; however, this is a simplistic explanation. The situation arises principally where senior male members of the family have fallen into debt with the illicit gambling industry. Illegal gambling in Siem Reap is a major social problem, and with such large numbers of debtors, sophisticated logistic operations are in place, which permit gambling debts to be forgiven in exchange for the trafficking and employment of a family member, usually a daughter, into Thailand. The gambling debtor is classically given little choice in this and is, importantly, given very little time to consider alternative options. From interviews conducted, the time between receiving the initial migration proposal from the creditor and the actual trafficking of the family member can be less than one week.

Another social environmental factor, reported to the authors by the Siem Reap participants, that creates ILP temporary migration to Thailand is the situation where either an individual or family find themselves at risk of violence related to the thriving illicit drug industry. The illicit drug industry is controlled by a number of rival organizations that filter down into numerous gangs throughout neighbourhoods. Each competing organization controls elements of drug distribution and consumption, and has wider involvement in the entertainment industry. People who become involved with the drug and entertainment trade, either as employees or clients, frequently find themselves at risk of violence, especially if they are believed to have associated with a rival organization.

Our participants report that victims of violence from one cartel may be offered protection from another, but this refuge may ultimately involve the individual being trafficked into Thailand to work in either the entertainment or drug distribution industry. By becoming a migrant under such conditions of power imbalance, the cycle of misery continues unabated. The migrant may be subjected to further violence, have wages withheld and may not be permitted to autonomously make decisions regarding the type of work they are told to perform. Regardless of the drivers of ILP migration, two factors common throughout the Siem Reap group are that (a) the decision to migrate has been made very quickly and under both duress and coercion, and (b) there is a major power imbalance between the individual and the complex trafficking network of the broker and employer.

5.3   Non-urgent Voluntary Income Enhancement (VIE) temporary migration

VIE migration tends to occur where the decision to migrate is made over a considerable period of time and the individual has weighed up other available options before deciding on taking such action. The reasons for migration in such circumstances, as reported by the Siem Reap participants, include migration simply to be in a better position to pay for general household expenses or to accumulate savings. The authors have additionally interviewed a group of women who temporarily migrated in order to pursue ambitions to operate their own small businesses as brokers themselves.

The mechanics of temporary migration to Thailand, when not faced with an immediate financial or social environment crisis, is very different from that of more desperate migrants. Migrants in the VIE category may have considered migration over an extended period of time, perhaps over a period of months or even years. While they still use brokers to arrange employment and accommodation in Thailand, the fact that their initial contact with the broker is not made under coercion or duress increases the likelihood that the migrant can negotiate a better deal for themselves, and indeed they may well negotiate with a number of brokers before deciding on one.

The prospective VIE migrant in Siem Reap, in this more favourable situation, will also very likely seek recommendations from current and returned migrants, as to the quality of their experience with both individual brokers and employers. In 2016, the widespread use of social media among migrants has resulted in real time feedback being made available to prospective migrants, and constitutes a major factor in the decision to select one broker rather than another.

Brokers are acutely aware of the online feedback system that is now in place regarding their services, with investigations suggesting that this has resulted in improvements in migrant employment conditions. Notwithstanding the benefits of these developments, the contractual terms that VIE migrants agree to still cannot, by any objective measure, be considered to be fair, equitable or just. The brokers still hold great power over the migrant and they are still at risk of violence, of being forced into occupations other than those they agreed to, and of being discriminated against because of their nationality. In addition, some brokers have ceased doing business with new clients unless they present requiring urgent transportation to Thailand. VIE migrants pose a greater risk of exposing the brokers' abusive practices and, overall, are less profitable.

An interesting group within the classification of VIE migrants are those individuals who make a strategic decision to temporarily migrate to Thailand with the specific goal of earning and accumulating savings. Within our group of Siem Reap participants, these are often young people, 18–30 years old, who take the decision in the knowledge that they will have to endure a specified period of time doing unpleasant work in poor conditions. These prospective migrants are well connected by social media to current migrants in Thailand, and enter into arrangements with brokers fully informed of their dubious business practices. These migrants may, when compared to urgent migrants, have received a comparatively good education and be both numerate and literate. They may be determined individuals who are migrating to Thailand, against the wishes of their family, for their own economic benefit.

A defining characteristic of this sub-group of VIE migrants is that while they do save the bulk of their wages, the remittance of the savings back to Cambodia is not intended for the benefit of the migrant's family, but is reserved for the migrant themselves upon return to Cambodia. The decision not to share the fruits of the sojourn to Thailand would perhaps be expected to be a source of friction within the family, but the investigations performed by the authors revealed that the reaction of the family can be unpredictable. Male members of the family do appear to feel that the migrant, particularly if they are a daughter, has shown disloyalty to the family, and may make attempts to punish them. However, conversations with mothers in Siem Reap reveal an interesting mix of reactions, with some being supportive of their children's attempts to escape the cycle of subsistence living.

However, as is perhaps expected, some migrants in our Siem Reap group who have attempted to 'break free' from the family do, in time, subsidize their family, especially when family financial emergencies occur. In addition, as it becomes known that a returned migrant has accumulated savings, they become a direct target of both physical and psychological coercion, from both family and friends. This situation becomes more acute when the family members are in urgent need of funds to support a gambling or drug habit.

5.4 Engaging brokers

The chapter has emphasized the major role that brokers play in the migration process. These brokers vary from specialists involved only in the Thai migration trade, to generalists, involved in other forms of human trafficking, often including human organ trafficking. Trafficking in people for both the selling of a kidney and labour migration provides a broad cash flow profile for the broker. Human organ trafficking is a low-volume, high margin brokerage activity, whereas labour migration is a high-volume, lower-margin activity.

In Siem Reap, brokers are often also the local moneylenders. Individuals may take out small short-term loans from these brokers, and the brokers are known to suddenly demand repayment in full without notice to the debtor. This can happen even when the debtor has serviced their debt within the previously agreed terms. In Cambodia, with great shame being attached to being seen to be unable to pay debt, debtors are very likely to remain compliant with demands of the broker for fear of being publicly revealed as a debtor in default.

There is, therefore, a great incentive for moneylenders to create an artificial default status on their debtors, as it can trigger an extremely profitable chain of events. The moneylender will either be a broker themselves or be in alliance with one and may, therefore, attempt to coerce a debtor or one of their family members into accepting a migrant position, in exchange for forgiveness of the debt. Moneylenders in Siem Reap known to the authors, actively solicit for new clients with the intention of converting short term micro-loans into long term lucrative temporary employment arrangements. The experience of Siem Reap migrants who have been coerced into accepting such debt agreements is similar to that of those migrating to pay for a family emergency. However, the employer in Thailand, as a business partner of the broker, will know that the migrant is a 'debtor'; they enter into the relationship with the employer in an even weaker position and are, therefore, potentially subject to even more severe working and living conditions.

Brokers can also be previous migrant workers themselves, and a sub-group of the Siem Reap participants interviewed consisted of individuals who migrated to Thailand in order to establish their own brokerage business. This group of new brokers tend to be older than typical migrant workers, in their late thirties and early forties. All the Siem Reap participants in this new broker group were women, but this was due to the fact that they were met by the authors in a social club specifically catering to Cambodian women entrepreneurs. In every case known to the authors, migrants who have become brokers have experienced at least one previous sojourn to Thailand as an employee. These migrants have learned the business of trafficking migrants intimately, and indeed are likely to have had first-hand experience of the brutality of the industry.

These new broker start-ups report that they were provided with funding from Thai employers in the fish processing, garment manufacturing and entertainment industries with the intention that they maintain a consistent and reliable flow of labour from Cambodia. Given the nature of the business, there is a constant need to replace brokers who have departed the industry, voluntarily or otherwise. The Thai employers need a representative in every region in Cambodia where labour can be sourced, and have ready trained replacements in place whenever a particular existing broker ceases to trade. The Siem Reap participants believe that this is why they have been established as brokers by these employer groups.

The brokers that the authors met in Siem Reap report that employers pay them both an upfront fee for each migrant and an ongoing commission to provide incentive to the broker to ensure migrant retention and compliance. The brokers place representatives in the locale of the employer, throughout the transit routes, and in the main recruiting centres in Cambodia. The new brokers established by the employers appear to remain loyal to that one employer for a lengthy period, but in time may take on other business activities related to trafficking of Cambodians into Thailand, including sourcing and managing migrants for other employers. Brokers who have previously worked as migrants in Thailand also appear to enjoy a major marketing advantage over brokers that have not, with several migrants interviewed by the authors specifically choosing to deal with brokers who had previously been a migrant. This is reported to be because they perceive they will be treated with more empathy, and will be more likely to understand the new migrants' specific needs, concerns and aspirations.

In the authors' experience, however, the contrary is more likely to be true. Brokers who have previously worked as migrants but now find themselves with money, and in business, appear to be the most brutal. Several of the Siem Reap participants suggested that the older established brokers, who have been relatively wealthy throughout their lives, treat migrants more uniformly, realising that those who systematically abuse migrants are less likely to have viable businesses in the long term.

6. Discussion

The authors have found that individual workers who have made an ILP migration not only accept comparatively inferior conditions; they additionally report that these poorer conditions create less of a feeling of dissatisfaction than found in migrant workers who have migrated under more favourable circumstances.

For example, many migrants interviewed by the authors claim they were underpaid. For VIE migrants, this affects overall satisfaction of the migration experience and is a deterrent to them ever seeking subsequent migration opportunities. However, ILP migrants who have migrated under urgent or emergent circumstances appear to be more accepting of underpayment.

Similar circumstances exist cross a range of variables. Both groups (ILP and VIE migrants) reported being held against their will; being asked to perform duties that they had not agreed to; being asked to perform tasks that went against their morals; being fearful of the consequences of complaining; and being fearful of threats of violence. Each of these variables were effectively 'deal-breakers' for many VIE migrants, but taken almost as a given by the ILP migrant groups.

Several ILP migrants provided explanations of this phenomenon to the authors. They know the conditions are bad, but are better than any alternative that they have. The ILP migrant has need for the security and shelter that employment brings. Higher order needs, while desirable, are not considered essential to their mission. VIE migrants, however, require higher order needs to be satisfied before they consider the mission to have been satisfactory.

The research has shown that Cambodians who have temporarily migrated to Thailand as an ILP in an urgent and emergent fashion will very likely experience very poor employment and living conditions in Thailand, but will be comparatively satisfied with the onerous demands placed on them by their employers. It is also possible that ILP migrants, therefore, may be preferable to unscrupulous employers and brokers, given their greater likelihood of compliance with their unreasonable and possibly illegal demands when compared with VIE migrants.

The authors discussed the findings with middle management and supervisory staff of a major fish processor in Thailand, which has been an employer of Cambodian migrant labour. Management of this organization does associate different employment brokers with whom they work with different classifications of migrant workers. There are brokers known to be specialist suppliers of ILP migrants; therefore employees from these brokers are immediately classified as such from the commencement of their employment. Specifically, this information appears to be openly shared with other Thai employees, at all levels, including entry level fish processers. Therefore, on the same production line, there is active discrimination, with Thai workers not only knowing that their Cambodian colleagues were trafficked through a broker, but also the personal circumstances of that trafficking.

This revelation is worsened by the fact that when it becomes common knowledge that the Cambodian worker has been forced to take up the position for reasons of being unable to service debt, then they potentially become stigmatized by their co-workers. The resultant loss of face and dignity adds to the probability that the Cambodian employee will have to endure a particularly arduous, and possibly humiliating, employment experience.

It is therefore incumbent upon researchers and policy makers in the field to address factors regarding not only the urgency of the migration, but also in-country employment conditions. Temporary migrant workers are extremely vulnerable, particularly when they find themselves far from home, where they do not speak the language and are at the mercy of unprincipled and shameless employers and brokers. Specifically, there is great need to reconcile the micro-level issues explored with individual migrants with developments in the wider macro socio-political environment.

6.1   Macro-micro linkage

Developments at national level can be directly correlated with migration and remittance at the local level. The period of political turmoil in Cambodia, from the late 1960s until the UN intervention in 1992, saw the country's economy devastated. Such was the political and economic isolation of Cambodia during that period that accurate GDP data are not available. In 1993, Cambodia's GDP per capita was USD253 (World Bank 2015a). However, as the economy developed, GDP per capita rose steadily to reach USD1090 by 2014 (Figure 4.3; World Bank 2015a).

While per capita GDP rose rapidly from the year 2000, the continued relative prosperity of other countries, particularly neighbouring Thailand, saw significant economic incentive for Cambodians to migrate and remit money home. In 2000, Cambodian personal remittances were approximately USD120 million. Following the Global Financial Crisis, remittances first declined but then increased to approximately USD175 million by 2013 (Figure 4.4; World Bank 2015b). In 2014, however, remittances soared to USD363 million, a figure

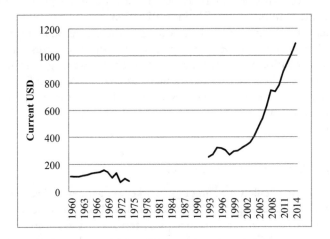

Figure 4.3 Cambodia GDP per capita, 1960–2014 (current USD)
Source: World Bank (2015a)

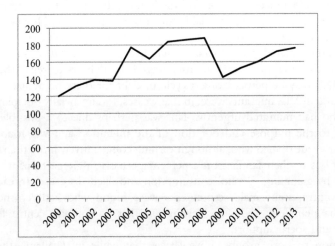

Figure 4.4 Cambodia personal remittances, received (current USD million)
Source: World Bank (2015b)

that would be an underestimation given the high rate of unregistered immigration and remittances via unofficial means (Sor 2015).

Remittances to Cambodia from migrant workers have risen substantially in recent years, with Chanleas Dai commune, at a local level, providing an example of some of the drivers of that shift. Chanleas Dai's location on the western edge of Siem Reap, approximately 100 km from the Thai border, has resulted in the development of a large community of migrant workers (Bylander 2014). According to Bylander (2014), the early 1990s saw the beginning of migration from Chanleas Dai into Thailand. This period is directly associated with major national political developments, as discussed earlier – a tumultuous period resulting in the direct intervention of the UN in 1992–1993.

Bylander (2014) argues more specifically that the expansion in migration from Chanleas Dai over two decades has coincided with lower costs and risks. By 2007, the vast majority of Chanleas Dai households were 'using migration as their primary livelihood strategy' (Bylander 2014). While Chanleas Dai is not one of the peri-urban areas of Siem Reap central to the case study, it provides a useful example of the local drivers of migration in terms of the larger state political narrative.

6.2   Expenditure at the household level

This chapter has detailed how migrant workers engage with brokers either on an urgent ILP or non-urgent VIE basis, but it is also important to understand the differences between the two groups in terms of expenditure. Across both groups, there is a difference between actual and intended expenditure.

The ILP migrants interviewed, without exception, intended to use remittances to pay for urgent medical treatment or debt repayment. In most cases the actual expenditure did indeed pay for the medical treatment, with no respondents reporting having any surplus available for further expenditure. However, several of those respondents who migrated to pay debt did partially repay the debt, and spent the remainder on general household expenditure and consumer goods. It appears that the moneylenders discouraged the debtors to repay their loans in full. This may be perpetuating a cycle of debt for these migrants.

Non-urgent VIE migrants were, in many cases, less financially disciplined than those who had migrated urgently. This was perhaps due to a possible lack of focus as to the purpose and duration of the migration and was found to be particularly true of men who, although earning comparatively more than women, remitted less to their families on a percentage basis. Male participants became tempted by gambling, alcohol consumption and illicit drug use. In each community centre, some male respondents were found who had returned from Cambodia penniless, and were relying on that community centre for both financial and social support.

Common to both groups, however, is that while in Thailand, they were earning significantly more than they would have at home and many appeared to lack financial literacy. In many cases they had never had a bank account, and their first dealings with financial institutions took place when remitting funds overseas. Female respondents, overall, appeared to have a more comprehensive understanding of financial management than men, and did not succumb to temptations the way men did.

Women who remitted high proportions of their income back to Cambodia reported possible financial abuse by their families. They reported that a proportion of remittances were used to fund male family members' indulgences in gambling, alcohol or illicit drug use. Most serious of all was the small number of cases where remittances, intended to fund family medical emergencies, were squandered for other less worthwhile purposes.

7. Conclusions

This chapter has provided a broad-based analysis of the experiences of Cambodian temporary migrants upon repatriation from Thailand to Siem Reap. It has provided, through the study of Siem Reap migrants, an overview of the socio-political environment of regional temporary migration in the form of a macro-analysis, and provided examples of how this translates at the micro household level.

The chapter has made a distinction between those who migrate on an urgent or non-urgent basis, classifying them as either Involuntary Livelihood Pushed (ILP) migrants or Voluntary Income Enhancement (VIE) migrants. It has explored how these classifications form the basis of a power imbalance between themselves, their employers and the brokers they work through. The nature of employment brokerage has been explored in depth, illustrating the wider role that brokers play in this environment.

While ILP migrant workers who have had to urgently migrate do report poorer contact conditions than those of non-urgent migrants, these poorer conditions do not appear to lower their overall satisfaction with the migration. There appears to be an acceptance the part of the urgent migrants that, as they present in a position of low-power, they have no reason to expect better conditions.

The conditions that urgent ILP migrants face is, by any objective measure, exceptionally poor. They may be threatened or subjected to acts of violence and be coerced into undertaking work which, prior to migrating, they had not agreed to. They may be held against their will in crowded and unsanitary accommodation. Despite this, migration still occurs, and new migrants continue to seek employment opportunities in Thailand.

As a recommendation for further study, the analysis of groups in other major centres of migration would provide a useful comparison, as well as considering the experience of migrants in other host countries. Further study of the gender differences in migration could be based on the factors introduced in this study, across a wider range of age groups. This study focussed primarily on relatively young migrants, most of whom were under 30 years old. The impact of migration among older migrants would provide comparison which would create a broader data set which may help develop a more universal model for analysis.

Note

1 'Street Business' is defined in the Economic Census of Cambodia 2011 as 'An establishment such as a stall, a booth etc. that runs at a fixed location on the sidewalk or the roadside, or around but outside a market'.

References

ASEAN 2004, *ASEAN Declaration against Trafficking in Persons Particularly Women and Children*, adopted by the Heads of State/Government of ASEAN Member Countries on 29 November 2004 in Vientiane, Lao People's Democratic Republic, viewed 16 November 2015, <http://www.asean.org/index.php/communities/asean-political-security-community/item/asean-declaration-against-trafficking-in-persons-particularly-women-and-children-3>.

Asian Development Bank (ADB) 2014a, *Gross Domestic Product Per Capita (Current Prices) (US$/Person)*, viewed 30 June 2015, <http://www.gms-eoc.org/gms-statistics/overview/gross-domestic-product-per-capita-current-prices>.

Asian Development Bank (ADB) 2014b, *Poverty Rate*, viewed 30 June 2015, <http://www.gms-eoc.org/gms-statistics/overview/poverty-rate>.

ATUC (ASEAN Trade Union Council) 2015, *Looking Back: First Anti-trafficking Law in Southeast Asia*, viewed 16 November 2015, <http://aseantuc.org/2015/05/2652015-looking-back-first-anti-trafficking-law-in-southeast-asia/>.

Bylander, M 2014, 'Are Migration and Microcredit Mutually Enabling? Evidence from Rural Cambodia', *Development Viewpoint*, No. 74, SOAS, Centre for Development Policy and Research, viewed 8 February 2016, <https://www.soas.ac.uk/cdpr/publications/dv/file93549.pdf >

Leng, T 2014, 'The Cambodian Fallout from Thailand's Coup', *East Asia Forum*, 27 June 2014, viewed 10 November 2015, <http://www.eastasiaforum.org/2014/06/27/the-cambodian-fallout-of-thailands-coup/>.

Morton, E 2014, 'Business Flocks to Tourist Town', *Phnom Penh Post*, 9 September 2014.

National Institute of Statistics 2013, *Economic Census of Cambodia 2011 Provincial Report 17 Siem Reap Province*, Ministry of Planning Phnom Penh, Cambodia, Supported by: Government of Japan and Japan International Cooperation Agency (JICA).

National Institute of Statistics 2015, *Cambodia Socio-Economic Survey 2014*, Ministry of Planning, Phnom Penh, Cambodia, Supported by: Swedish International Development Cooperation Agency (SIDA).

Royal Kram 2008, *Law on Suppression of Human Trafficking and Sexual Exploitation*, English Translation, viewed 11 November 2015, <http://www.unodc.org/res/cld/document/khm/2008/law_on_suppression_of_human_trafficking_and_sexual_exploitation_html/Cambodia_03_-_Law-on-Suppression-of-Human-Trafficking-and-Sexual-Exploitation-15022008-Eng.pdf >.

Sen, D 2015, 'Deal Struck for Migrant Workers', *Phnom Penh Post*, 8 February 2015, <http://www.phnompenhpost.com/national/deal-struck-migrant-workers>.

Sor, C 2015, 'Bank Data Show Remittance Flows Rising', *Phnom Penh Post*, 8 February 2015, <http://www.phnompenhpost.com/business/bank-data-show-remittance-flows-rising>.

The Economist 2014, 'Migrant Workers in Thailand: The Exodus', 21 June 2014, p. 40.

World Bank 2015a, *GDP Per Capita Data Tables*, viewed 9 December 2015, <http://data.worldbank.org/indicator/NY.GDP.PCAP.CD/countries?display=default>.

World Bank 2015b, *World Development Indicators: Data Personal Remittances, Received (Current US$)*, viewed 18 March 2015, <http://data.worldbank.org/indicator/BX.TRF.PWKR.CD.DT/countries/1W?display=default>.

5 Socioeconomic impact of remittance

An analysis of household level data from Bangladesh

Moazzem Hossain, Yenny Tjoe and Samsul Hoque

1. Introduction

Economic globalization contributes not only to advancing commodity trade but it has also brought a major shift in the flow of workers from labour abundant to labour scarce nations. According to the UN, transnational migrants (persons working outside their country of birth) constituted approximately 232 million in 2013 from all over the world (Baruah 2014). Almost one-third of these migrants originate from Asian developing nations. The destinations of the overwhelming majority of Asian migrants are Middle Eastern countries (Gulf Cooperation Council or GCC countries), Southeast Asia (Malaysia, Singapore and Thailand) and East Asia (South Korea). Over the past three decades, three major migration flows have developed within Asia: from South Asia and Southeast Asia to GCC countries; flows within the ASEAN region; and from Southeast Asia to East Asia. The World Bank estimates that there were six Asian countries among the top ten remittance-receiving countries of the world in 2013 (World Bank 2014). The GCC countries received almost 3.5 million workers from South Asia and Southeast Asian nations in 2012. Among them, five nations (Bangladesh, India, Nepal, Pakistan and the Philippines) sent more than half a million each. Nepal alone sent approximately 1.5 million. Almost half a million workers migrated overseas from Bangladesh in 2012.

In recent years, Bangladesh has become the major source of unskilled workers for the GCC countries and Southeast and East Asian nations (Malaysia, Singapore, Hong Kong and Korea). This nation, since independence in 1971, has sent more than eight million workers all over the world. The majority have gone to the GCC countries and Malaysia. A recent study estimates that more than USD15 billion was sent by more than eight million migrant workers as remittances in 2014 (BBS 2016). The current level of remittances makes this nation the world's eighth-largest remittance holder. The World Bank argues that the average value of remittances to receiving households is equivalent to 80 percent of the receiving household's income and is twice the national per capita income (World Bank 2014).

With a focus on Bangladesh as a major migrant-sending nation in the global South, the major aim of this chapter is to investigate the distribution of household income among the households of migrant workers. The investigation also compares the income of migrant households with that of the non-migrant households in the same area. Further comparison of patterns of distribution of household income of migrant workers is made in relation to different migrant destinations and among non-migrant households in relation to (in-country) occupation or profession. The data presented here are derived from a field survey, conducted in 2014 and 2015, of 205 households. The Griffith Asia Institute, Griffith University and the Meghna Sub-district of Bangladesh provided support for the fieldwork in cash and in kind, respectively.

2. Background

The family remittance industry of migrants of the world now exceeds USD420 billion per annum and is predicted to grow further in the years to come. Asian countries are making a major contribution towards this industry in terms of both inflows and outflows. Seven of the world's top ten remittance-receiving countries are in Asia, namely, India, China, the Philippines, Bangladesh, Pakistan, Vietnam and Indonesia. More than 10 percent of the GDP of these nations is derived from the family remittance sector. Among these nations, India alone has 11 million unskilled labourers working abroad. In recent years, the outflow of remittances from Asia has been mainly from three countries: Singapore, Malaysia and Thailand (World Bank 2011).

The opportunities for expanding the industry in the future were recognized by the world's leading economies as early as 2006, with the International Fund for Agricultural Development (IFAD) taking a major initiative through the formation of a consortium to investigate the long term development of the remittance industry (IFAD 2013). In 2009, the G8 put the issues of remittances firmly on the global agenda in the L'Aquila summit in Italy, and the G20 summit in Cannes in 2011 with the leaders endorsing a 5 percent reduction target for average costs of sending remittances from the then 10 percent. If achieved this would return some USD5 billion annually to migrants' households globally.

Migration involves the flow of both economic and noneconomic resources from the migrant receiving countries to migrant-sending countries. Such flows that include transfer of money, knowledge, technology and ideas have made significant contributions to the sending economies from a macroeconomic perspective and to migrant households from a micro point of view.

Historically, the eastern part of South Asia has sent unskilled workers to different parts of the world. In the British period in the late nineteenth century, the workers from East Bengal were moved to different tea plantations in Assam and Sri Lanka. The workers from Southeast Bengal (coastal districts) were a major source of shipping industry workers and sailors' hands all over the world during the nineteenth century. Thus the subject of remittances or 'cash payment or in kind gifts sent home by relatives living and working abroad with permanent and temporary status' is not new (Hobbs and Jameson 2012).

However, since WWII the newly found independent nations of Asia, Africa and South America have experienced a period of mass emigration, despite the constraint of restrictive policies in destination countries (e.g. the United States, UK, Canada and Australia). There were four waves of migration from the 1950s to the 2000s:

> 1950s – European migration to the United States, Canada and Australia
> 1960s – Latin American migration to the United States
> 1970s – Asian migration to the Global North
> 1990s to present – South to South migration
> (Stark, Taylor and Yitzhaki 1986; Mughal and Makhlouf 2013)

As a nation of the Global South, Bangladesh, has experienced strong growth in remittances which are contributing not only to the improvement of household incomes in migrants' households but more broadly to the macroeconomic balances of the nation. It is in this context that the authors undertook the household survey reported here, to compare the household incomes of migrants and non-migrants in Meghna Sub-district of Bangladesh.

3.   Literature review

Since there are both costs and benefits of all types of migration, skilled or unskilled, a study by Hobbs and Jameson (2012) conducted on Nicaraguan migration to both the United States and Costa Rica investigated the impact of remittances on poverty and income distribution and compared the outcomes for Nicaraguan emigrants to the United States (Global North) and to Costa Rica (Global South). The emigrants were fairly evenly distributed between these two nations. However, the study shows poor migrants overwhelmingly migrate to Costa Rica, richer migrants favoured the United States. The outcomes of the study were presented in relation to three indicators. It was found, first, that migration to Costa Rica increased the per capita consumption of the poor households compared to similar households where 'no-migration' had occurred, while migration to the United States led to an increase in the number of middle class households. Second, in both cases the rate, depth and severity of poverty decreased only slightly. Third, inequality appeared to increase because the US migrants were more likely to come from the middle class with relatively high income to begin with, while those going to Cost Rica were more likely to be poor. Thus, while both groups were likely to improve their household incomes, there were greater advantages for the better off households of the middle class and inequality widened.

Taking a different perspective and the case of Nepal, the vast and impoverished Himalayan mountain region, a study by Maharjan, Bauer and Knerr (2012) investigated the position of women who were left behind by migrant male household heads, and their roles and responsibilities in caring for the family unit. There were three main aspects analysed: first, the change in women's workload; second, expansion of their roles, their ownership and access to productive resources; and third, the part they played in household decision-making. The results suggest that

> women have broadened and deepened their involvement in rural society as a result of male out-migration, which could lead to either the empowerment or disempowerment of women. The nature and the extent of this impact has been conditional on the migration pattern and the remittances received by the households.
>
> (Maharjan, Bauer and Knerr 2012, p. 95)

The net effects of migration on income distribution have been analysed by several studies in developing countries over the last three and a half decades (Lipton 1980; Oberai and Sing 1980; Stark et al. 1986; Adams 1989; Bharam and Boucher 1998; Taylor and Wyatt 1996; Adams and Page 2005; Brown and Jimenez 2007; Adams 2010). At a regional level, in their study of two Pacific Island nations, Fiji and Tonga, Brown and Jimenez (2007) measured inequality and poverty based on a comparison of 'with-migration' income and remittances and a 'non-migration' income scenario. The study maintains that

> counterfactual household incomes are estimated, taking account of what the migrant members would have earned had they not migrated. The results are compared with alternative income estimates in which remittances are treated simplistically as exogenous transfers. The positive effects of migration and remittances on poverty alleviation and income distribution are found to be stronger when the more rigorous, counterfactual income estimates are used.
>
> (Brown and Jimenez 2007, p. ii)

Remittance, in the context of Bangladesh nationally, has been studied by many researchers, but recent work by Siddiqui and Mahmood (2015), based on a primary survey of five thousand households from seventeen of sixty-four districts, is significant. Siddiqui and Mahmood (2015) suggest that the migrant households suffered from poverty at half the rate of the national level in 2014, at 13 percent and 26 percent, respectively.

In the study conducted by the Bangladesh Bureau of Statistics cited previously (BBS 2016), the aim was to estimate the average amount invested from remittances sent by the expatriates overseas in 2015 for the purposes of policy planning and development. The analysis suggested that only one half of the households made investments from their remittances. The average investment per household was only USD1000 across various sectors in 2015, which is approximately 25.33 percent of total remittances to this country. This suggests that remittance income as a source of investment remains very low. The remittances flown to Bangladesh in recent decades are presented in Table 5.1.

Table 5.1 Flow of remittance to Bangladesh, 2005–2015 (in USD billion)

Year	Amount	Growth rate (%) from the previous year
2005–2006	4.80	24.70
2006–2007	6.00	25.00
2007–2008	7.91	31.80
2008–2009	9.69	22.50
2009–2010	10.99	13.42
2010–2011	11.65	6.01
2011–2012	12.84	10.21
2012–2013	14.46	12.62
2013–2014	14.23	−1.60
2014–2015	15.32	7.66

Source: BBS (2016)

4.   Bangladesh's ascendancy

Bangladesh became an independent state through armed struggle against Pakistan in 1971. Since then, the nation has been characterized by political and economic instability and natural disasters, resulting in adverse effects on the economy during the initial twenty years of its liberation. Table 5.2 compares the major economic indicators between 1983 and 2015. Bangladesh had more than 90 million people with a density of population over 590 per square kilometre in 1983. The annual rate of population growth was 2.7 percent. The GDP per capita was very low at USD590 at 1983 prices. The growth rate in 1982 was only 0.1 percent. The readymade garment (RMG) and shrimp exports had been nil or negligible. The remittances from abroad were only USD300 million in 1983. The population under the poverty line (headcount ratio) was 60 percent in the same year. The production of rice was only thirteen million tonnes, and inflation was running at 19 percent.

The picture has changed dramatically over the last three decades to 2015 (Table 5.2). Population increased by 80 percent as a result of a drop in growth rate by 60 percent. Population density per square kilometre increased by 70 percent. The GDP per capita increased almost ninefold, as a result of sustained growth in GDP, to between 5 percent and 6.5 percent in recent decades. The difference in population growth and GDP growth in 2015 indicates that GDP has grown more than fourfold. In 1983, the population growth rate was more than twenty-seven times that of the GDP growth rate. The value of garment exports reached more than USD25 billion and shrimp exports were worth USD650 million in 2015. Remittances rose to USD15 billion, and foreign reserves peaked at USD27 billion in 2015. In the production of rice, the nation had a surplus of two million tonnes in 2015, compared with a deficit of the

Table 5.2 Bangladesh's achievements, 1983–2015

Items	1983	2015	Increase
Population (millions)	90	160	1.80
Population growth rate (%)	2.7	1.7	–1.60
Population per sq. kilometre	590	1,030	1.70
GDP (USD billions)	NA*	205	–
GDP per capita (USD)	150	1,300	8.67
Growth rate (%)	0.1	6.5	65.00
Garments exports (USD billions)	Nil	26	–
Shrimp exports (USD billions)	Neg.**	0.64	–
Remittance (USD billions)	0.3	15.50	51.67
Foreign reserve (USD billions)	NA	27	–
Under poverty line % of total population)	60	23	–2.60
Rice production (million tonne)	13	33	2.54
Inflation rate (%)	19	6.5	–3.00

* NA = Not available
** Neg. = Negligible

Source: Hossain (1983) and Haider (2016)

same amount a few years earlier. Rice production at the time of writing has risen to thirty-three million tonnes. The inflation rate reduced to single digits (6.5 percent) in 2015 after running at double digit level since 1983.

4.1 Poverty reduction

In terms of reducing extreme poverty in Asia, certainly the East Asian nations have been ahead of South Asia. The Headcount Ratio (HCR) suggests that almost half of the population in Bangladesh and 41 percent in India lived below a Purchasing Power Parity (PPP) of USD1.25 per day. Recently, the Bangladesh Planning Commission (PC) published a report on the country's achievements and non-achievements in poverty reduction to 2014. The PC's assessment was based on data collected by the Bangladesh Bureau of Statistics (BBS). Table 5.3 presents a picture of poverty reduction between 2002 and 2014. Figures for 2014 are very encouraging. The national poverty level was reduced to one-fourth of the population compared to almost one half in early 2000. More interestingly, the 'hard-core poor' in 2014 comprised 10.6 percent of the 24.3 percent of the total population deemed to be living in poverty. This suggests that if the current momentum can be maintained, the nation may well be in a position to eliminate poverty for another 15 percent by 2021, and potentially eliminate hard-core poverty. In absolute terms, this would be less than twenty million under

Table 5.3 Poverty reduction in Bangladesh, 2002–2014 (percentage)

Year	People under poverty level	Hard-core poor	People above poverty level
2002	44.6	–	55.4
2006	38.4	–	61.6
2009	33.4	–	66.6
2013	26.2	–	73.8
2014	24.3	10.6	75.5

Note: The Bangladesh Planning Commission defines poverty in terms of calories a person requires per day. In Bangladesh this is about 2,122 Kcal. To purchase the required calories, the income of a person per month has been considered to determine who are poor or people under poverty and the hard-core poor. It has been estimated that BDT3,000 per capita per month is needed to buy 2,122 Kcal per day. The categories of 'people in poverty' and 'hard-core poor' used here are those based upon estimates provided by the Planning Commission for these groups (Shah 2015). 'People living under the poverty level' are those who have incomes below BDT3,000 per month per person; 'hard-core poor' are those who have incomes below BDT1,600 per month per person.

Source: Shah (2015), Alam (2016), Hossain and Hoque (2016) and Kabir (2016)

the poverty line as compared with the present total of forty million. Nonetheless, poverty will remain a major challenge for the nation in the years to come (Hossain and Hoque 2016).

With all these achievements on the economic front, according to the World Bank's definition of prosperity, Bangladesh has now advanced to lower-middle income status. The next step is to achieve middle income status. It appears that, based on current developments in economic activities, it is indeed likely to be achieved by 2025, providing the country maintains political stability. In politics, the cloud in the sky has not cleared at the time of preparing this chapter. There is a stalemate between the sitting government and the opposition. A general election is due in 2019, and it remains to be seen whether or not the present politics of confrontation improves over the next two years.

4.2 Sanitation access

While poverty reduction has been a priority in Bangladesh under the Millennium Development Goals (MDGs) program of the UN since 2000, sanitation access was also a major goal. In this regard, rural Bangladesh has been experiencing major improvements. For example, compared to its immediate neighbours, Bangladesh performed quite well overall in terms of improved and shared sanitation access. India, with 53 percent access (improved plus shared facilities) to sanitation performs almost equally to Pakistan (54 percent access), with Bangladesh (81 percent access) in 2010.

Comparing national performance in rural and urban areas, the differences at the urban level were Bangladesh, 83 percent; Pakistan, 78 percent; and

India, 77 percent (Hossain and Howard 2014). At the rural level, the differences have been phenomenal. For example, in Pakistan 40 percent of the rural population has access to an improved plus shared sanitation facility, which is significantly higher than the 27 percent of rural people in India. In stark contrast to both India and Pakistan, in Bangladesh 80 percent of rural people have access. The main reason for Bangladesh's improvement in this area has been the availability of microfinance to the poor in rural areas. Bangladesh is the home of large microfinance institutions (MFIs) of the world such as BRAC, Grameen Bank, ASA and others (Hossain 2015). In the present study, it has been observed that, in addition to sanitation improvements afforded through microfinance, migrant households are highly likely to have established sanitation access in their homesteads which was almost absent in the pre-migration period.

5.   Analysis of remittances

5.1   *Conceptual framework*

Economists view remittance in terms of potential income earning opportunity from employment off shore (as a result of migration) in relation to the wellbeing of a person, a community or even a nation. At household level, the sense of wellbeing depends not just on the amount of remittances from off-shore, but also its impacts on costs and benefits to the households (Rosewarne 2012; Beneria, Deere and Kabeer 2014).

The costs are generally less than the benefits. The major benefits are in terms of migrant households' (micro-level) contribution to the national economy (macro-level) in the following ways:

- Additional sources of earning foreign exchange
- Contribution to macroeconomic stability
- Enabling better management of external debt
- Providing additional sources of investment funds with multiplier effects
- Contribution to sustainable GDP growth
- A source of increased consumption in turn contributing to the growth in aggregate demand and hence employment
- A mechanism of poverty alleviation
- A means of reducing income inequality

While these are certainly welcome achievements from a macroeconomic point of view, at household and community levels there are some costs or negative impacts in both social and economic terms, as argued by Rosewarne (2012). The present chapter does not address the costs of remittances at micro-level but analyses remittance income in relation to the issues of poverty and income inequality among migrant and non-migrant households in villages within a bounded locality in Bangladesh.

5.2   *Household survey*

A large body of statistics on Bangladesh's village economy has been collected from central household surveys by the Bangladesh Bureau of Statistics (BBS), Bangladesh Institute of Development Studies (BIDS) and Bangladesh Academy for Rural Development (BARD). Unfortunately, they are too generalized; understanding the village economy requires household data collected simultaneously on agricultural production, consumption, investment and income. For our purpose, in the present study we have obtained data on all of these economic dimensions. The data have been collected from 205 households from 10 selected villages under Meghna Upazila (Figure 5.1) in Comilla (North) district (see Appendix 5.1). From each village, two types of households were interviewed by the local enumerators. The households surveyed included 139 with migrant workers and 66 with non-migrant workers only. They were selected under a purposive respondent-driven, referral sampling method in ten selected villages. The survey was initially directed at migrant households to gather remittance and related data. It was realized that for comparison with non-migrant households, comparable data from a sample of non-migrant households were also needed. A smaller sample of non-migrant households was included due to funding limitations.

This area is one of the deep-water rice zones of the nation, which include those areas which flooded in most years to more than one metre during the rainy season. The area is located between the southern and eastern banks of the mighty river Meghna, one of the three largest rivers of Bangladesh (see Figure 5.1). The survey questionnaire includes questions on the socioeconomic and demographic structure of the household, including some open-ended questions on improvements in livelihoods. There were thirty questions asked of migrant households. Only twenty-three questions were relevant to non-migrant households. The questions asked were the same for the migrant and non-migrant households, except that additional data relating specifically to migration and remittances were recorded for migrant households.

5.3   *Characteristics of migrant and non-migrant households*

The major characteristics of migrant and non-migrant households are presented in Table 5.4. Regarding demographics, 51 percent of migrant households had more than four members, whereas 74 percent of non-migrant households had more than four members. The remaining characteristics shown in Table 5.4 are aggregate numbers. For example, 30 percent of migrant households fall under the owner-operator farmer category, while 56 percent of non-migrant households are owner-operator farmers. The lower level of owner-operator farming activity among migrant households may reflect an investment in migration, instead of investment in farming, and reliance upon remittance income, but it is also apparent that migrants' families have been investing more in the education of minor members of the family, due to their relatively better economic

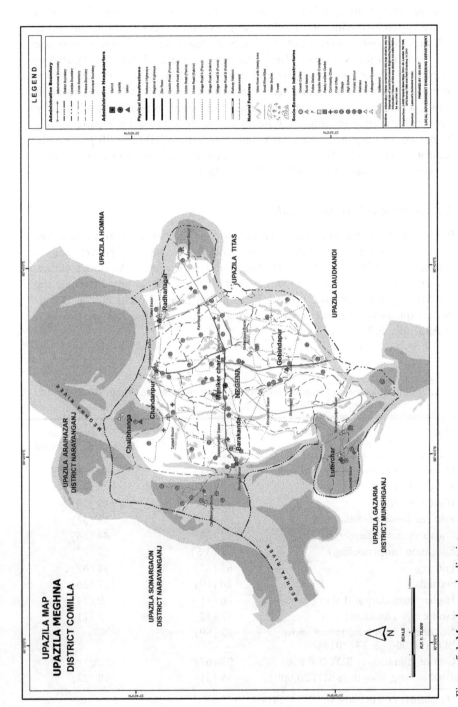

Figure 5.1 Meghna sub-district

Source: GIS Unit, Local Government Engineering Department, Bangladesh (n.d.)

circumstances resulting from the receipt of regular remittances. It might be expected that relativities between migrant and non-migrant households with regard to levels of education might change in the future. Currently, the survey indicates that only 4 percent of migrant households surveyed have at least one household member with secondary or higher secondary education compared to 14 percent of non-migrant households surveyed. Migrants also are semi-skilled or unskilled workers without a secondary school certificate, which is consistent with a general pattern for migrant workers from rural areas of Bangladesh. The income distribution for migrant households also reflects a general pattern, with 61 percent of migrant households earning more than BDT20,000 per month, compared with only 27 percent for non-migrants in the sample. (See more detailed data in Appendix Tables 5.4a to 5.4d.)

5.4   Micro-analysis: some results

In view of the previously listed characteristics of the two types of households, micro-analysis was undertaken to analyse comparative levels of poverty among migrant and non-migrant households in the survey area. As noted earlier, poverty has been measured in three different ways: the headcount ratio, the poverty gap index and the poverty gap squared index (Vecchi 2007). Definitions, explanation and methods of estimation of these measures are provided in Appendix 5.2.

Table 5.4 A comparison of migrant and non-migrant households, Meghna sub-district, Bangladesh, 2014–2015

Item	Migrant HH (%) N = 139	Non-migrant HH (%) N = 66
Household size (> 4 members)	71 (51)	49 (74)
Self-employed*	3 (2)	5 (7.5)
Wage labourer	3 (2)	15 (20)
Paid employment/Small bus.	85 (61)	21 (32)
Owner-operated farmer	42 (30)	34 (56)
Education (no schooling)	5 (3.5)	15 (23)
Primary	52 (37)	44 (67)
Secondary	26 (19)	17 (26)
Higher Secondary and above	6 (4)	9 (14)
House type (Building)	17 (12)	7 (11)
No. of HH with remittances above BDT150,000 (2013–2014)	82 (59)	Nil
Cost of migration (>BDT200,000)	93 (67)	NA
Total income/month (>BDT20,000)	85 (61)	18 (27)

*Employment status in the year 2014–2015

5.4.1   Poverty reduction of migrant and non-migrant households

Table 5.5 provides the estimates of poverty in migrant and non-migrant households using the three measures mentioned earlier. First, the headcount ratio (HCR) is the proportion of the population that is regarded as poor under a specific poverty line. In this study the food poverty line has been assumed as BDT500 per household of four persons per week (USD1.50 per person per day in purchasing power parity (PPP) terms in 2015. (See also the note in Table 5.5.)

The poverty gap index is defined as the average poverty gap (PG) in the population as a proportion of the poverty line, where the non-poor have zero gaps. The PG accounts for the intensity or depth of poverty – in other words, how poor the poor are. The estimates suggest that for the migrant household group, the poor have an average expenditure shortfall of 3.37 percent from the poverty line. This estimate suggests that the poor migrant household will have to earn only BDT17.00 per week (.0337 × 500) per capita extra to rise above the specified poverty line. The squared poverty gap index (SPGI), which estimates inequality among poor households, attributes more weight to the poorest among the poor. The SPGI estimates suggest that for 1.56 percent of poor migrant households, the poverty gap is greater than the estimated average (PG), and these households will need to increase their income by more than BDT17.00 per week to overcome poverty.

Based on the three measures above, for non-migrant households the HCR is 36.36 percent. In other words, 24 of 66 non-migrant households were found to be poor. The PG estimates suggest that the non-migrant poor households have an average expenditure shortfall from the poverty line of 8.63 percent. With these estimates the non-migrant poor household will have to earn BDT44.00 extra per week (.0863 × 500) per capita to overcome poverty. Finally, SPGI estimates suggest that among the non-migrant poor households,

Table 5.5 Poverty estimates of migrant and non-migrant households, 2014–2015

Item	Poverty estimates (%)	
	Migrants N = 139	Non-migrants N = 66
Headcount ratio	9.35	36.36
Poverty gap ratio	3.37	8.63
Poverty gap squared	1.56	3.30

Note: The 'food poverty line' is assumed at BDT500 per household. The Bangladesh Planning Commission defines poverty in terms of calories a person requires per day. In Bangladesh this is about 2,122 Kcal. To purchase the required calories, the income of a person per month has been considered to determine who are poor or people under poverty, and hard-core poor. It has been estimated that BDT3,000 per capita per month is needed to buy 2,122 Kcal equivalent food items per day. Based on this assumption, BDT1.40 is needed to consume 1 Kcal equivalent of food. In the present study it has been estimated that it takes approximately BDT1 to buy 1 Kcal per day (Hossain and Hoque 2016). See more on poverty reduction analysis in Kabir (2016).

3.3 percent have a larger poverty gap – in other words, a gap of more than BDT44.00 per week per capita.

The data presented in Table 5.5 indicate that, on average, the migrant households surveyed have been doing much better than the national poverty averages. The HCR for migrant households in Meghna Sub-district appears to be approximately 15 percent less than the national average HCR (compared with the HCR for non-migrant households surveyed, which is a little more than 10 percent above the national average HCR). Comparison of the data from Meghna Sub-district with national averages of HCR (see Hossain and Hoque 2016) suggests that remittances to migrant households have had substantial impact in reducing poverty in the study area, over time, based on national HCR averages (Hossain and Hoque 2016). While HCR is a crude method of estimating poverty, the PG and PG squared measures also reflect the HCR outcome.

6. Inequality analysis: Gini ratios at household level

There are debates in the literature surrounding the subject of income inequality in developing countries, the international migration of family members and their sending of remittances to their families (Barham and Boucher 1995). Empirical studies suggest that migration and remittances can either increase or decrease the inequality of household income distribution (Lipton 1980; Oberai and Sing 1980; Stark et al. 1986; Adams 1989). Barham and Boucher (1998) have developed a method for estimating the Gini coefficient of total income by following the Gini decomposition framework developed by Stark et al. (1986) and Stark (1988) to identify the contribution of income sources (remittance plus domestic) of households to the Gini coefficient. This is presented as follows in equation (1)

$$G_0 = \sum\nolimits_{k=1}^{k} R_k G_k S_k, \tag{1}$$

where, for a given population of households, the left-hand-side of the equation, G_0, is the Gini coefficient of total income. The three right-hand-side terms in the equation, namely, R_k, G_k and S_k are, respectively, the Gini correlation of income component 'k' (remittances) with total income; the Gini coefficient corresponding to the income component 'k' (the inequality of remittances) and the share of component 'k' in total household income. We applied this approach to our data for these four variables to determine the contribution of remittances to income inequality in the Meghna area.

6.1   *Data and estimation of Gini from Meghna sub-district*

A summary of households and migrant statistics are presented in Table 5.6. The majority of the migrant households consist of more than 4 persons. The average number of migrants per household was 1.3, and the remittance income received by the households was 94 percent of their total income. The yearly remittance

Table 5.6 Summary statistics, migrant households (N = 139)

Variable	Study sample statistic
Household level	
Average number of international migrants per migrant household (HH)	1.3
Share of migrant remittances in total household income received (HH)	94 percent
Migrants' households	
Formal schooling (no. of HH)	117
Yearly remittances per migrant (USD)	1,875
Major countries migrated (KSA, UAE, Malaysia)	KSA
Non-migrant households	
Major occupation	Farming and wage labour

Note: KSA = Kingdom of Saudi Arabia; UAE = United Arab Emirates

per migrant was USD1,875, with the majority of migrants working in Saudi Arabia, the United Arab Emirates and Malaysia. For the majority of non-migrant households, farming and wage labour are their main occupations.

The observed income distribution in the migrant households with remittance income plus home earnings (total income of households) generates a Gini coefficient of 0.29, while the overall domestic earnings of non-migrant households (no remittance involved) generate a Gini coefficient of 0.41. In other words, income inequality among the non-migrant households is greater than among the migrant households (see Lorenz curve presented in Appendix 5.3A).

Table 5.7 presents the Gini decomposition figures for the two sources of income for the migrant group only. The decomposition estimates suggest that, for migrant households only, the Gini coefficient of remittance income was lower (0.29) than that of home earnings (0.69). Kendall's (R) correlation suggests that the migrant households' inequality has a very high (0.94) correlation with remittance income and only a moderate correlation with home earnings (0.31).

These two factors combined indicate a strong inequality-reducing effect of remittances, since the share of remittances (S) in migrants' households is more than 90 percent of the overall income of migrant households. The last column in Table 5.7 presents the percentage change in the Gini coefficient for a 1 percent change in remittances or income from other sources. For migrant earnings, a 1 percent increase in remittances would further reduce the Gini coefficient by approximately 3 percent. The opposite is the case for home earnings for migrants' households, where a 1 percent increase in household income is predicted to increase the Gini coefficient by approximately 3 percent.

Considering the consumption data of the two household groups (migrant and non-migrant), the consumption Gini appears to be relatively low for both

Table 5.7 Gini decomposition

Income source	Share in total household income (S)	Gini coefficient for income origin (G)	Gini correlation: income origin with total income rank (Kendall's R)	% change in Gini of total income from 1% change in income source
Migrant households				
Remittance income migrant HHs	0.94	0.29	0.94	−3 percent
Home earnings of migrant HHs	0.06	0.69	0.31	3 percent
Total income of migrant HHs (combined)	1.00	0.29	–	–

Table 5.8 Income Gini and consumption Gini of two groups of households

Income source	Income Gini (G) from remittance	Income Gini (G) from home earnings	Consumption Gini
Migrant households	0.29	0.69	0.21
Non-migrant households	Not applicable	0.41	0.22

(see Table 5.8 and Appendix 5.3B). Table 5.8 indicates that the consumption Gini for migrant households is 0.21, compared with 0.22 for non-migrant households. Unlike the income Gini coefficient, the consumption Gini coefficient is almost equal for the two groups (see Table 5.8). This suggests that in rural areas, food intake or the quality and price of food items are found to be no different for relatively high and low income earners who buy consumables from the same local bazaars or markets weekly. It was found that the majority of the migrant households spent a large portion of their remittances on education for children left at home. The next largest expenses among migrant households are industrial goods and construction materials.

Table 5.8 also compares the income Gini coefficients for two groups. The G (0.69) for migrant households from home earnings indicates that marked inequality exists in home earnings compared to non-migrant households with G at 0.41. However, in the case of migrant households, the contribution of home earnings to total income is very limited at approximately 6 percent, whereas in the case of non-migrant households, they derive all of their income from home earnings. The major source of income for migrants' households is remittances and their combined income G is only 0.29, which is much lower than for non-migrant households (0.41).

7.   Conclusions

In this chapter we have addressed the socioeconomic impact of migration and remittances at household levels in the context of a localized (sub-district) study in Bangladesh. The analysis was conducted taking into consideration two groups of households, migrants and non-migrants, in estimating the impacts of remittances in terms of poverty reduction and distribution of income. Most importantly, the impact of remittances on poverty and income distribution was estimated for migrant households, with a view to assessing the significance of remittances for their livelihoods, compared with the incomes and livelihoods of a sample of non-migrant households. The FGT model was applied to the household data collected from both the groups in a primary survey of 205 households conducted in the period 2014–2015 (Foster, Greer and Thorbecke 1984). The seminal work by Stark et al. (1986) was employed to estimate the impact on income distribution of remittance and non-remittance income data in investigating the differences in terms of poverty and inequality between the two groups of households by comparing their respective Gini ratios.

Remittances would appear to contribute significantly to poverty reduction, in headcount terms, with 9 percent of migrant households compared with 36 percent of non-migrant households living below the poverty line. The current national average for poverty remains at approximately 25 percent. The number of non-migrant households in the study area living below the poverty line is almost 10 percent higher than the national average, whereas the number of migrant households living below the poverty line is almost 15 percent less. In the case of income distribution, migrant households were found to be much more homogeneous than non-migrant households, with greater inequality among non-migrant households reliant upon domestic income. However, with regard to the distribution of food consumption, the two groups of households were found to be very similar. Both groups had relatively low levels of consumption inequality, with Gini ratios of 0.21 and 0.22. This study can therefore draw a reasonable conclusion that migration and remittances are having a major positive impact, in economic terms, among the rural migrant population in the study area. However, the study also found that more than one-third of the non-migrant households remain poor in absolute terms when only domestic income is considered. Remittances have certainly limited poverty among migrants' households in the study area to below one-tenth.

Appendix 5.1
Comilla district map

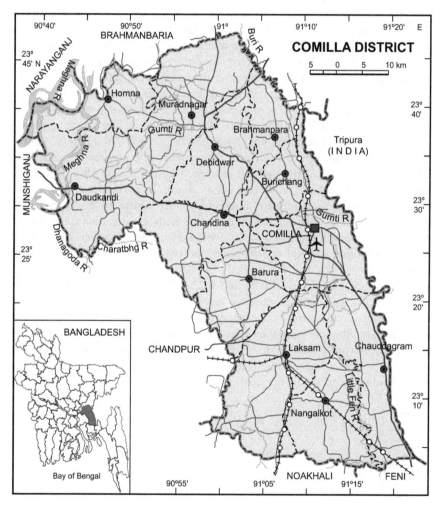

Map 5A.1 Comilla district map. Upazilas (sub-districts) in Comilla North and South
Adapted from: Maps of Bangladesh (2011).

Appendix 5.2

Poverty measures

The poverty measure is based on the Foster, Geer, Thorbecke (FGT) Index (Foster et al. 1984). This measure can be presented in the following equations:

$$FGT_\alpha = \frac{1}{N} \sum_{i=1}^{H} \left(\frac{z - y_i}{z} \right)^\alpha, \tag{1}$$

where z is the poverty line, N is the number of people in the economy, H is the number of poor, $\mathbf{y}_i$ is the individual consumption figure and $\propto$ designates the meaning of the indicator which can be put in terms of HCR, PG and SPG. These are presented in equations 2, 3 and 4 (Vecchi 2007).

The headcount ratio (HCR) is the proportion of the population that is classified as poor. Let q denote the number of poor households and N the total households:

$$HCR = \frac{q}{N} = \frac{1}{N} \sum_{h=1}^{n} I(x_h \leq z) \tag{2}$$

The PG index is defined as the average poverty gap in the population as a proportion of the poverty line (where the non-poor have zero gaps):

$$PG = \frac{1}{N} \sum_{i=1}^{n} \left(1 - \frac{x_i}{z} \right) I(x_i \leq z) = \frac{1}{N} \sum_{i=1}^{q} \left(1 - \frac{x_i}{z} \right) \tag{3}$$

The squared poverty gap (SPG) index attributes more weight to the poorest among the poor:

$$SPG = \frac{1}{N} \sum_{i=1}^{N} \left(1 - \frac{x_i}{z} \right)^2 I(x_i \leq z) = \frac{1}{N} \sum_{i=1}^{q} \left(1 - \frac{x_i}{z} \right)^2 \tag{4}$$

Appendix 5.3A

Lorenz curve: income – income
compared, 2014–2015

Gini ratio: migrant households (0.29)

Non-migrant household (0.41)
Perfect equality (0)
Perfect inequality (1)

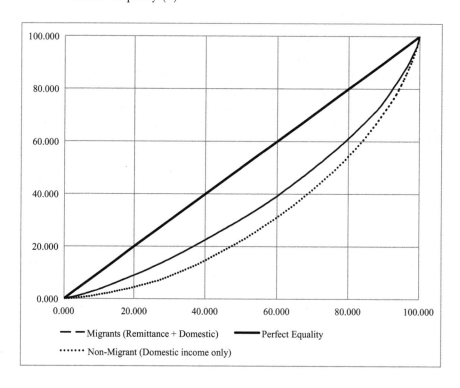

Appendix 5.3B

Lorenz curve: consumption-consumption compared, 2014–2015

Gini ratio: migrant households (0.21)

Non-migrant household (0.22)
Perfect equality (0)
Perfect inequality (1)

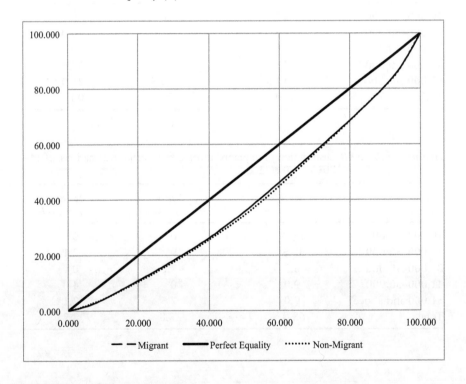

Appendix 5.4

Appendix Table 5.4A: Distribution of migrant households by destination, 2014–2015 (percentage)

Income/month (BDT)	Middle Eastern nations	Malaysia/ Singapore	South Africa/ Italy
10,000–19,000	19.0	0	0
20,000–30,000	46.0	38.5	25.0
31,000–40,000	8.0	31.0	0
41,000–50,000	13.5	0	50.0
51,000 and above	13.5	30.5	25.0
Total	100	100	100

Appendix Table 5.4B Distribution of migrants' income from major destinations, 2014–2015 (percentage)

Income/month (BDT)	Middle Eastern nations	Malaysia/ Singapore	South Africa/Italy
10,000–19,000	13.0	0	0
20,000–30,000	31.5	9	2.1
31,000–40,000	5.5	7.3	0
41,000–50,000	9.0	0	4.0
51,000 and above	9.0	7.5	2.1
Total	68.0	23.8	8.2

Appendix Table 5.4C Distribution of non-migrant households by occupation, 2014–2015 (percentage)

Income/month (BDT)	Farming	Job/business	Wage
Below 5,000	80.0	27.0	68
5,100–7,000	3.23	11.5	21.0
7,100–10,000	3.23	15.5	11.0
10,100–15,000	3.23	19.0	0
15,100 and above	10.31	27.0	0
Total	100	100	100

Appendix Table 5.4D Distribution of non-migrant income by occupation, 2014–2015 (percentage)

Income/month (BDT)	Farming	Job/business	Wage
Below 5,000	33.0	9.2	17.1
5,100–7,000	1.3	3.9	5.3
7,100–10,000	1.3	5.3	2.6
10,100–15,000	1.3	6.6	0
15,100 and above	3.9	9.2	0
Total	40.8	34.2	25.0

References

Adams, R 1989, 'Worker Remittances and Inequality in Rural Egypt', *Economic Development and Cultural Change*, vol. 38, no. 1, pp. 45–71.

Adams, R 2010, 'Evaluating the Economic Impact of International Remittances on Developing Countries Using Household Surveys: A Literature Review', *The Journal of Development Studies*, vol. 47, no. 6, pp. 809–29.

Adams, R and Page, J 2005, 'Do International Migration and Remittances Reduce Poverty in Developing Countries?', *World Development*, vol. 33, no. 10, pp. 1645–69.

Alam, S 2016, 'An Overview of SDGs and Bangladesh', Keynote Presentation of the Planning Commission, in the Seminar on *Implementing SDGs in Bangladesh: Challenges and Policy Options* Organised by the Bangladesh Institute of International and Strategic Studies (BIISS), 24 August, Dhaka.

Barham, B and Boucher, S 1998, 'Migration, Remittances and Inequality: Estimating the Net Effects of Migration on Income Distribution', *Journal of Development Economics*, vol. 55, pp. 307–31.

Baruah, N 2014, *Labour Migration Landscape in Asia*, ILO Regional Office for Asia and the Pacific, Bangkok.

BBS 2016, *Report of the Survey on Investment from Remittance (SIR) 2016*, Bangladesh Bureau of Statistics (BBS), Ministry of Planning, Dhaka.

Beneria, L, Deere, CD, and Kabeer, N 2014, 'Gender and International Migration: Globalization, Development, and Governance', *Feminist Economics*, vol. 18, no. 2, pp. 1–33.

Brown, R and Jiménez, E 2007, *Estimating the Net Effects of Migration and Remittances on Poverty and Inequality: Comparison of Fiji and Tonga*, Research Paper, UNU-WIDER, Japan.

Foster, J, Greer, J, and Thorbecke, E 1984, 'A Class of Decomposable Poverty Measures', *Econometrica*, vol. 52, pp. 761–6.

GIS Unit, Department of Local Government and Engineering, Bangladesh n.d. *Upazila Map, Upazila Meghna, District Comilla*, viewed 24 October 2016, <http://www.lged.gov.bd/UploadedDocument/Map/CHITTAGONG/comilla/meghna/meghna.jpg>.

Haider, A 2016, 'Bangladesh Out of the Basket', *The Daily Star*, 23 January, Dhaka.

Hobbs, A and Jameson, K 2012, 'Measuring the Effect of Bi-directional Migration Remittances on Poverty and Inequality in Nicaragua', *Applied Economics*, vol. 44, no. 19, pp. 2451–60.

Hossain, M 1983, *Quantitative Analysis of Policy Alternatives for Bangladesh's Future Agrarian Development*, Unpublished Doctoral Thesis, Department of Agricultural Economics, The University of Western Australia, Perth.

Hossain, M 2015, 'Microfinance Creating Micro Entrepreneurs: Is Climatic Hazard Spoiling the Party?', in G Nehme (ed), *Entrepreneuriat et PME: Enjeux et Perspectives*, a Université Antonine, Beirut, pp. 11–24.

Hossain, M and Hoque, S 2016, Rhetorical Bottomless Basket Case versus Bangladesh's Success with the MDGs, *Outlook 2016*, World Association of Sustainable Development, Emerald Press, London.

Hossain, M and Howard, P 2014, 'The Sanitation Access to Developing Asia: India's Performance Over 2001 and 2011', *World Journal of Science, Technology and Sustainable Development*, vol. 11, no. 2, pp. 93–101.

IFAD 2013, *Sending Money Home to Asia: Trends and Opportunities in the World's Largest Remittance Market Place*, International Fund for Agricultural Development, Rome, viewed 13 April 2015, <www.ifad.org/documernts/10180/>.

Kabir, M 2016, 'Poverty and Inequality', Presented in the Seminar on *Implementing SDGs in Bangladesh: Challenges and Policy Options* Organised by the Bangladesh Institute of International and Strategic Studies (BIISS), 24 August, Dhaka.

Lipton, M 1980, 'Migration from Rural Areas from Poor Countries: The Impact of Rural Productivity and Income Distribution', *World Development*, vol. 8, no. 1, pp. 1–24.

Maharjan, A, Bauer, S, and Knerr, B 2012, 'Do Rural Women Who Stay Behind Benefit from Male Out-migration: A Case Study in the Hills of Nepal', *Gender, Technology and Development*, vol. 16, no. 1, pp. 95–123.

Maps of Bangladesh 2011, *Comilla District*, viewed 24 October 2016, <https://mapofbangladesh.blogspot.sg/2011/09/comilla-district.html>.

Mughal, M and Makhlouf, F 2013, 'Labour Effects of Foreign and Domestic Remittances – Evidence from Pakistan', *International Review of Applied Economics*, vol. 27, no. 6, pp. 798–821.

Oberai, AS and Sing, HKM 1980, 'Migration, Remittances, and Rural Development: Findings of a Case Study in the Indian Punjab', *International Labour Review*, vol. 119, pp. 229–41.

Rosewarne, S 2012, 'Temporary International Labour Migration and Development in South and Southeast Asia', *Feminist Economics*, vol. 18, no. 2, pp. 63–90.

Shah, J 2015, 'Four Crore (40 Million Out of 160) People Are under Poverty', *Prothom Alo* (Bengali Daily), 12 February, Dhaka.

Siddiqui, T and Mahmood, R 2015, *Impact of Migration on Poverty and Local Development in Bangladesh*, SDC-RMMRU, Dhaka.

Stark, O 1988, 'Migration, Remittances and Inequality: A Sensitivity Analysis Using the Extended Gini Index', *Journal of Development Economics*, vol. 28, pp. 309–22.

Stark, O, Taylor, J, and Yitzhaki, S 1986, 'Remittances and Inequality', *Economic Journal*, vol. 96, no. 383, pp. 722–40.

Taylor, J and Wyatt, J 1996, 'The Shadow Value of Migrant Remittances, Income Inequality in a Household Farm Economy', *The Journal of Development Studies*, vol. 32, no. 6, pp. 899–912.

Vecchi, G 2007, 'Poverty Measurement', *Bosnia and Herzegovina Poverty Analysis Workshop*, 17–21 September, Universita' di Roma "Tor Vergata".

World Bank 2011, *Migration and Remittances Factbook 2011*, 2nd edn, The World Bank, Washington, DC.

World Bank 2014, *Migration and Development Brief 22*, The World Bank, Washington, DC.

6 Migration processes and impacts, and the emergence of a limited cyclical pattern of migration in rural Bangladesh

Munshi Israil Hossain and Patricia Short

1. Introduction

Since Bangladesh's independence in 1971, but particularly from the mid-1970s, Bangladeshi migration to the emerging economies of the global South has contributed considerably and increasingly to the national economy, especially by comparison with migration to the global North. The increasing trend of migration to the South began in a context of dire economic conditions imme-diately after independence – coinciding, historically, with the growth of the 'emergent tiger' economies of Southeast Asia and the Gulf nations.

Apart from the fragile economy, post-independence, Bangladesh experi-enced political instability, widespread corruption, and systematic governance failure (Mahmud, Ahmed and Mahajan 2008). A significant proportion of the economy of Bangladesh was decimated during the liberation war, and the country faced a trajectory of low economic growth (Rahman and Yusuf 2010). In the decade following independence, Bangladesh experienced too little investment, limited export gain, a stagnated financial sector and a low level of per capita income, due to the extensive state-controlled economic policies. By 1981, extreme poverty (70 percent of the total population lived under USD1 a day) caused by high unemployment, underemployment and landlessness, had resulted in widespread malnutrition (World Bank 2015). Further, more than 90 percent of the rural population lived below the sub-sistence level, and infant malnutrition caused extremely high child mortality (approximately 240 deaths for every 1,000 children). Through the 1980s, the agriculture sector was stronger than the industrial sector. The contribu-tion of agriculture to GDP, at that time, was approximately 32 percent, while the industrial sector contribution was approximately 20 percent. From the 1990s onward, increasing population in rural areas, decreasing availability of arable land, and slower growth in the agricultural sector has meant con-sequent unemployment and underemployment and pressures on rural workers to move elsewhere for employment. The industrial sector has absorbed labour but, because of a severe dearth of skilled labour and lack of managerial and entrepreneurial capabilities, growth in this sector also has been limited (World Bank 2015).

Despite these challenges, Bangladesh developed socially and economically, and by 2010 had emerged as one of the best performers in the UN Department of Economic and Social Affairs 'Least Developed Countries' list, having adopted many reform policies in the 1980s, particularly in trade and finance, moving towards a liberal economic regime (Rahman and Yusuf 2010). Identified as a 'rising star' in the 2013 UNDP Development Report (UNDP 2014), Bangladesh has done well to improve gender equity, literacy, life expectancy, education participation rates, gender parity in education, and food production and also to reduce fertility, child mortality, population growth, poverty and unemployment. Other factors, such as the availability of monetary capital and labour, and Total Factor Productivity (TFP), a measure related to improvements in technology and efficiency, also contributed to this development (Rahman and Yusuf 2010). A degree of economic liberalization and financial integration has further assisted the social and economic development of Bangladesh (Bashar and Khan 2007; Hossain 2013).

Such improvements in social and economic development indicators have led to Bangladesh appearing as the only nation in South Asia that has met Millennium Development Goals (MDGs), achieving a number of key social and economic goals. In 2011, this led Amartya Sen to comment that Bangladesh was no longer a 'bottomless basket', as it had been referred to by Henry Kissinger at the time of Independence in 1971, but rather 'a model for progress'.[1] The World Bank's (2015) estimates indicate that Bangladesh, along with some other low-income countries, continues to show improved economic and social performance, and has moved into the lower-middle income band of countries (World Bank 2015).

Notwithstanding these achievements, the country remains beset with challenges of mal-governance, poverty, unemployment, inequality, rising population and dwindling livelihood options, especially in rural areas. The Asian Development Bank (2013) reported that both the agricultural sector and crop growth declined significantly from 1990 to 2010 due to increases in the prices of power, fuel and fertiliser and decreases in the area of arable land, as well as increasing labour supply leading to increased unemployment and underemployment (see also World Bank 2013). Further, diminished livelihood options in rural areas resulted in a widening gap between the demand for and supply of jobs, pushing people to migrate first to cities and later overseas and presently, mostly to the expanding economies of Asia.

To understand the dynamics of remittance income and South-South migration at the migrants' household level, this chapter presents a detailed analysis of migrant and migrant household experiences in a rural village of Bangladesh (here called 'Malaysia Village'[2]) from where rural labourers are migrating, in increasing numbers, to Malaysia. Applying a case study approach to explore migration patterns and livelihoods strategies in Malaysia Village, the study, since early 2011, utilized several data collection methods, including a household survey, in-depth interviews and ethnographic observation in two phases of intensive fieldwork, and ongoing contact with key informants. The chapter will focus upon the dynamics of South-South migration and remittance income in both first-cycle and repeat-cycle migrants'[3] households and in the community as a whole. The chapter will highlight changing patterns of rural livelihoods and the emergence of what we term 'livelihood-induced migration', where one or only some members of the household are compelled to migrate in order to provide or supplement essential income for their whole household. It will focus on the factors that affect the migration decisions and experiences of Malaysia Villagers, as a way of understanding the emergence of such patterns of migration within the Asian region, particularly between Bangladesh and Malaysia. The aim of the chapter is to elucidate the dynamics of migration and remittance income at the migrants' household level and, in turn, to explain how a particular system of limited or bounded bi-cyclical migration and associated patterns of 'migration-induced livelihoods', shaped by remittance incomes have become established in Malaysia Village.

2.   Rural livelihoods, and patterns and trends of international migration in Bangladesh

Of the many drivers of overseas migration from Bangladesh, the foremost force is widespread poverty. The poverty rate in 2014 places Bangladesh as one of the poorest countries, not only in South Asia, but also in the world, next to Sub-Saharan Africa (Asian Development Bank 2015). Bangladesh has significantly reduced its poverty rate from 58.8 percent in 1990 to 35.5 percent in 2010 (Bangladesh Bureau of Statistics 2010) and 24.7 percent in 2014 (Bangladesh Planning Commission 2015). Among the poor, approximately 80 percent live in rural areas, and with few and dwindling livelihood options available in the rural sector, most rural poor opt to migrate (either to urban areas in Bangladesh or abroad) to survive (Kibria 2011).

The impacts of widespread poverty have been further intensified by natural disasters. The country faced more than thirty-three major natural disasters, including cyclones, tsunamis, tidal surges, storms, floods, droughts, and Cyclone Sidr, between 1970 and 2009 (Zimmermann, Glombitza and Rothenberger 2010), making thousands of people homeless, damaging and destroying property, pushing affected people, especially the poor to leave their homes. Moreover, natural disasters have damaged coastal and fresh water resources, changed cropping patterns and reduced productivity, damaged eco-systems and biodiversity and human health, created environmental imbalance and increased forced migration (Paul 2005; International Organisation for Migration 2010; Warner 2010; Black et al. 2011; Dillon, Mueller and Salau 2011; Lein 2011).

Added to these factors, unregulated and poorly functioning rural markets, the lack of an enabling rural investment climate, weak rural institutions that exclude the poor from access to government facilities and lack of state welfare facilities have further exacerbated the decline in rural livelihoods (World Bank 2013). Furthermore, social and economic development programs in Bangladesh have prioritized urban-based activities over the rural. Patterns and rates of economic growth have consistently failed to absorb the growing number of unemployed youth, especially in rural areas, pushing villagers to migrate either to urban areas within the country or, increasingly, to overseas destinations, especially the Middle East and Southeast Asia, where shortages of labour match the occupational skills of a large mass of aspiring migrants, including semi-skilled and unskilled rural workers.

Due to the increasing demand for unskilled and semi-skilled migrant workers in the growing economies of the Middle East and Southeast Asia, the rate of Bangladeshi migration to these destinations has been increasing, and there has been observable change in the outflow of different categories of migrants. Bangladesh Manpower Employment and Training (BMET 2015) reports that migration under the professional category has decreased steadily, migrants under the skilled category has fluctuated, falling dramatically to 33.2 percent from 2001–2005 to 4 percent in the period 2005–2010. At the same time, migration under the semi-skilled and unskilled categories has risen from 5.3 percent from 1976–1980 to 20.3 percent during 2006–2010 and from 47.4 percent to 75.5 percent, respectively, over the same period. In 2011–2015, semi-skilled and less-skilled migrants combined still comprised more than half the total number of migrants. More recent data indicate that both Middle Eastern and Southeast Asian countries continue to demand mainly low-skilled migrants rather than professional and skilled migrants from Bangladesh (BMET 2015).

In terms of remittances, Bangladesh is one of the largest receiving countries in the Asian region, recording continuing and significant increases (as have Pakistan, Sri Lanka and Nepal) in recent years. By 2013, remittances to Bangladesh exceeded 6 percent of GDP and 75 percent of international reserves (World Bank 2015). The lion's share of remittances has come from unskilled and semi-skilled migrants who work in Southeast Asia and the Middle East. As South-North migration is declining and now constitutes a much smaller proportion of total migration than South-South migration, the contribution of North-South remittances to the national economy is considerably less than that of South-South remittances, as illustrated in Figure 6.1.

In the context of these changes, it is important to understand the factors that encourage rural Bangladeshi villagers to travel to the Middle East and Southeast Asia via destinations in the global North, and how regional systems of migration and remittances shape the livelihoods of migrants and migrants' households. Significantly, migration governance arrangements are substantially weaker or less developed within the emerging and rapidly growing systems of South-South (specifically Asia-to-Asia) migration by comparison, in general, with well-established South-North arrangements. Migration to the growing economies of Asia typically entails quite different mechanisms and means of migration, substantially lower costs and a complex of social and cultural factors that play into migration decisions that, at the household and community level, present quite different options for aspiring migrants, compared with those going to high-income countries of the global North.

Those who migrate to the North are mostly permanent migrants. South-South migration usually involves temporary migration and return. Being permanent

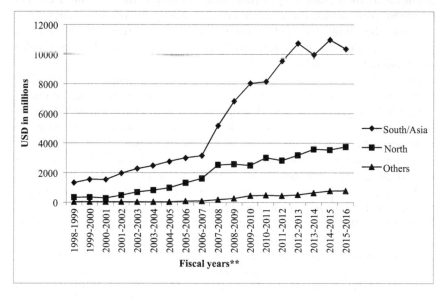

Figure 6.1 Changing patterns of remittances to Bangladesh, 1994–2012*

  * 'South/Asia' destination countries include Bahrain, Kuwait, Oman, Qatar, KSA, UAE,
    Libya, Iran, Hong, Kong, Malaysia, Singapore; 'North' destination countries include Aus-
    tralia, Italy, United States, UK, Japan, Germany.
 ** For fiscal years 2007–2008 and 2008–2009, remittance inflows from Australia (North),
    Hong Kong and South Korea (South) are missing. Remittances from these destination
    countries constituted approximately 0.2 percent, 0.1 percent and 0.3 percent of total remit-
    tances in FY2006–2007 and approximately 0.1 percent, 0.1 percent and 0.2 percent of
    total remittances in FY2009–2010.

Source: Bangladesh Bank (2011), BMET (2013) and Bangladesh Bank (2016)

settlers the former group of migrants typically do not invest their income in
their original country of residence; the latter group remit a very high proportion, if not all their earned income, after expenditure, to their household in
their home countries. To understand the experiences of migrants and their
household members, and the dynamics of migration and remittance income at
the migrants' household level, this chapter presents an analysis of migration
from Malaysia Village as a case of livelihood-induced, South-South migration
in Bangladesh.

3.   Malaysia village: factors affecting
        livelihood-induced migration

Consistent with the general patterns of migration and change noted previously,
the livelihood strategies of households in rural Bangladesh, including Malaysia
Village, have changed significantly over the past twenty years, influenced by
push factors (flood and population growth), pull factors (more wages than in

home country, availability of jobs, ease of entry, low cost of travel and active social networks abroad) as well as motivating and enabling factors (the operations of middlemen and moneylenders, the mobilisation of household resources and amenable household structures) that have led mostly unskilled or semi-skilled villagers to migrate overseas to sustain or improve their livelihoods.

Formerly, the livelihoods of the villagers were concentrated almost exclusively in subsistence agriculture, and supporting industries such as boat transport and the production of household and agricultural requirements. Villagers mainly produced crops for their subsistence and local exchange, including sugarcane, jute and paddy, using traditional methods of cultivation and irrigation. However, over an extended period of some years, flood and drought have threatened and transformed the subsistence economy and led to a decline in local markets, increasing risks and vulnerability, and compelled villagers to seek alternative sources of income, including through migration and remittance. As city labour markets have failed to respond adequately to the burgeoning employment demands of the country as a whole, the unemployed and underemployed of Malaysia Village have opted in greater numbers to seek employment overseas. Population growth and fragmentation of land holdings, caused by the break-up of extended family households into nuclear household arrangements, and the significant decrease per capita in availability of arable land have exacerbated vulnerabilities in rural villages.

In this context, transnational migration from Malaysia Village has grown steadily over the years. The relative ease of obtaining entry visas for travel to Malaysia, and the low cost of travel are significant factors in attracting potential migrants from the village to Malaysia, but it is the motivating, connecting and facilitating role played by middlemen and their networks of operation that has boosted the flow of emigrants, both legal and illegal – more so the latter – since the early 1990s. During this period, there has been a significant increase in the number of middlemen, some of whom are former Bangladesh-Malaysia migrants themselves. Not only are middlemen and former migrants engaged in the migration process in Malaysia Village, and in Dhaka, the principal port of exit from Bangladesh, their networks connect them with transit country based middlemen as well as agents in Malaysia, the destination country.

The web of middlemen networks or 'syndicates of middlemen' (Fee and Rahman 2006; Hugo 2008; Rahman 2012; Ullah 2009) and other formal and informal agents including employers, the law enforcement agencies, and relatives, friends and neighbours of migrants, working at various stages of the migration process have established four main methods by which villagers enter Malaysia. The majority use the 'tourist visa of Thailand' and the 'tourist visa of Malaysia' as their primary means, although some are able to use a 'calling visa' (with employment arranged) or a 'free visa' (without pre-arranged employment) issued by the Malaysian government and initiated by informal networks such as friends and relatives, respectively, both of which are legal and costlier than the former two visas. The role of middlemen in constructing patterns of migration is particularly important for Malaysia Village because, essentially, it is middlemen who have created the pathways for migration to Malaysia. Their activities and operations thus have given form to changing livelihood strategies in migrants' households, albeit the financial capacity and assets (including saleable land) of aspirant migrants is fundamental in decisions to migrate.

The role of moneylenders also has been significant, though it is decreasing because aspiring migrants are able to rely increasingly on the remittances that have been sent by their relatives overseas to avoid high interest rates and protect themselves from the unscrupulous activities of moneylenders. The transference of the facilitating roles of non-relatives, middlemen and moneylenders, to kinship and associative networks in more recent years, has contributed to changing the methods and routes of migration. Migrants who wish to migrate for the first time, whether they have kinship networks or not, mostly use middlemen networks, while second-time visitors or second-generation migrants, using the knowledge gained from their first visit or from close relatives or household members, rely upon kinship networks in most cases and may be able, therefore, to access a 'free visa' or 'calling visa' providing legal entry to Malaysia, although these entail a significant financial cost compared with the other modes of migration.

Under conditions of weak migration governance, all categories of visa holders face some level of economic and/or social exploitation and harassment at the hands of middlemen, moneylenders, employers, law enforcement agencies and other formal and informal actors and agents. Despite a myriad of public and private institutions and organizations emerging to regulate and control labour migration from Bangladesh and the Bangladesh government's promulgation of new migration laws and policies, the governance of international migration and remittances continues to pose challenges, with significant consequences not only for migrant workers but also for the members of their households who remain at home in Bangladesh, and become increasingly reliant upon remittances for income.

On the receiving end, recognizing the importance of labour migration for the Malaysian economy, successive Malaysian governments have introduced laws and policies for managing migration, but these, for the most part, have not been effective in regulating either the conditions of entry or the employment conditions of migrant workers. Migrant workers continue to experience exploitation in relation to recruitment, working conditions, wages, and accommodation (Kaur 2010; Kibria 2011). Such laws and regulations as do exist have been labelled ad hoc, erratic and even chaotic (Devadason and Chan 2014, p. 8), highly politicized, fluid, unpredictable and possessing a 'stop-go' quality (Rudnick 1996, 2009; Kanapathy 2001; Kassim 1998; Yaw 2002; Robertson 2008; Siddiquee 2013). Nonetheless, despite their vulnerable conditions in Malaysia, the majority of migrants do earn an income and their households do receive and use remittance income to limit their income risks and repay debts and over time, with repeated cycles of migration and longer absences, in most cases, accumulate capital funds for investment.

4. Migration, remittances and changing livelihood patterns of migrants' households

The dynamics of remittance income are dependent, in large part, upon the net amount that finally reaches a migrant's household and is available for consumption, and this depends on three major factors: first, the actual amount earned (this refers to any differences between the 'contracted amount' and the amount actually paid, and also between the amount actually received and the net amount after subsistence and other related costs including transaction costs); second, the amount of ongoing repayments of debts incurred to pay for migration-related costs; and third, the amount that is paid to middlemen and other rent seekers, both at home and in Malaysia.

Further, net remittances vary also between first-cycle and repeat-cycle migrants and in relation to the duration of migration. First-cycle migrants spend more on transaction costs and may gain little from migration for a variety of reasons: their ignorance of rules and regulations and of their rights and privileges; their lack of networks in Malaysia; their lack of work experience and language proficiency. Repeat-cycle migrants who have become more conversant with rules and opportunities as well as the networks, working experiences and language proficiency are able to cut down on transaction costs and increase their net income significantly.

For these reasons, there is a significant difference in the utilization of remittance income between the first-cycle and repeat-cycle migrants' households. Overall, remittance income has diversified the income-generating activities of migrant households, and reduced risks and vulnerabilities associated with debt, health and natural disasters, enabled householders to achieve a better balance of spending and saving over time, and created, in some cases, financial capital for the present and foreseeable future. To understand the different dynamics and utilization of remittance income between first-cycle migrants and repeat-cycle migrants' households, this section will draw upon both survey data on first-cycle migrants' households and detailed case study information on repeat-cycle migrants.

In terms of the dynamics of remittances, most first-cycle migrants, while still in Malaysia, are typically in a much worse position than repeat-cycle migrants. Spending remittances income to repay loans, buy (or reclaim) arable land (Mahmood 1991; Rahman 2000; Siddiqui 2001; Joarder and Hasanuzzaman 2008) or invest in business (Siddiqui and Abrar 2003; Hossain, Khan and Short 2013) is common for all groups of migrants, but patterns of spending vary between first-cycle and repeat-cycle migrants, as illustrated in Figure 6.2. Among first-cycle migrants' households, approximately 34 percent of remittance income is used in paying loans they had borrowed from moneylenders or other rent seekers, and approximately a quarter was used to buy (or reclaim) arable land, the most important natural resource for providing a livelihood in Malaysia Village. One-fifth of remittance income is used for other purposes such as food, clothing, education and treatment of household members. First-cycle migrants'

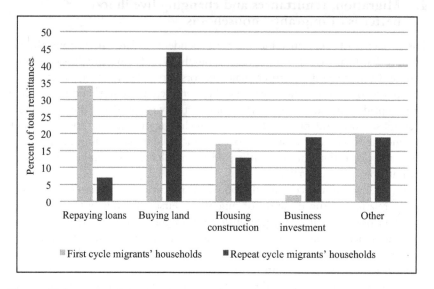

Figure 6.2 Patterns of remittances expenditure among first-cycle and repeat-cycle migrants' households

households reported using only a very small proportion of remittances (approximately 2 percent) for business activity or small-scale enterprises. For first-cycle migrants, repayment of loans borrowed from moneylenders or others in order to cover migration costs was the main expenditure. Only after loans are repaid do migrants begin to earn additional income.

In addition to loan repayments, first-cycle migrants' income also goes toward release of their mortgaged land, and constructing dwellings (cf. UNDP 2009), which contrasts with the type of investments in arable land that repeat-cycle migrants typically are able to make. First-cycle migrants' households in Malaysia Village also reported spending a large proportion of remittances on food, health, education and clothing[4] (cf. Rahman and Fee 2012) but only approximately 1 percent of total remittances for community initiatives, such as donations to mosques, madrasas, welfare activities and charity to the poor (Hossain 2009).

The dynamics of remittance income of repeat-cycle migrants' households is significantly different from that of the first-cycle migrants' households. Repeat-cycle migrants will usually have returned from Malaysia to resettle, permanently, after working nearly six years on average, typically over two cycles of migration. The majority of repeat-cycle migrants resettle in the village, having invested their remittance income in income-generating activities in the village and local market, while a few now live permanently in a nearby city. Most repeat-cycle migrants are in a better position than the first-cycle migrants in terms of income, savings and assets, with their economic, social and personal situation improving as they have built up migration-specific knowledge and local capital in both countries, each time they have gone abroad (Constant and Zimmermann 2011). It is apparent from Figure 6.2 that the repeat-cycle migrants, overall, invested approximately 44 percent of remittance income in buying arable land. Further, they were more than eight times more likely than first-cycle migrants to invest remittance income in businesses. Thus, whereas first-cycle migrants face the problem of repayment of loans that they have borrowed from moneylenders or others to mobilize migration costs, repeat-cycle migrants have been able to engage progressively in investment and capital formation.

The case profiles of repeat-cycle migrants indicate that almost half have returned to their previous occupation, agriculture, for reasons such as illiteracy, lack of business experience, lack of opportunity to use overseas experience or skills acquired and/or limited capital formation through remittance income. In rural areas of Bangladesh, the alternative to agriculture for livelihoods is small-scale business, but due to lack of education as well as due to lack of business knowledge and skills, some will not attempt to run a small business. Further, previous losses experienced in running businesses discourage some from restarting a business; instead they have chosen to buy arable land and engage in agriculture. Fakir is one of the repeat-cycle migrants who preferred to return to agriculture as the basis for sustaining his livelihood.

> Fakir lives with his elderly parents and wife. He has a one-year-old son. Fakir could not continue his studies because his results were poor. His father had a piece of arable land which he gave to Fakir who used it as the basis of his livelihood. He also worked on others' land as a day labourer. It was hard for him to manage three meals daily for his parents. So he decided to go to Malaysia. Before his final departure, he was deceived by an unscrupulous middleman who took BDT40,000 from him but the middleman would not return it as the money was spent for migration purposes, claimed by the middleman. Fakir arranged this money by selling his only land which he received from his father. Later he went to Malaysia with the help of his brother who worked there. During his 14 years as a migrant, Fakir returned home three times. He sent in total BDT800,000 with which he bought a piece of arable land for BDT320,000, built a house worth BDT200,000 and used approximately BDT200,000 for family maintenance. The land is the asset from which he gets paddy and mustard and some other crops which are the main source of income.
>
> (Fakir, 38, illiterate, farming, repeat-cycle migrant)

Cultivable land is one of the important financial and social resources for households, contributing to upward social mobility of migrants and their family members (Islam 2010); it is the most important natural resource that helps to sustain their livelihoods in rural areas because agriculture is still the main livelihood option in Malaysia Village. Therefore, like Fakir, the majority of repeat-cycle migrants ultimately have invested remittance monies in buying agricultural land and have chosen to return to agriculture as their primary means of livelihood. They produce mainly paddy and mustard on the land, to meet their needs, and sell the rest of crops in the local markets and meet other needs such as clothing, education, medical treatment. Thus, in such cases, migrants have improved their economic situation in the village and at the same time they have enhanced their social standing as a result of remittance income and its investment in agriculture.

Another group have returned to their previous occupations in agriculture, not entirely by choice but due to lack of capital, because they have not earned enough income in their time abroad. Some have returned with no money, while others have only just enough to recover the land which they mortgaged to mobilize migration costs. Without sufficient remittance income to generate capital to invest, they are unable to change their livelihood options and they return to their previous occupations, even though they are acutely aware of the vulnerability of the local agricultural economy. The case of Baju illustrates how migration sometimes forces repeat-cycle migrants to return to their previous occupation, making them even more vulnerable than before.

> Having been encouraged by villagers and motivated by a village middleman, Baju decided to go to Malaysia to earn money and reduce his household's income risks and vulnerabilities. As he was poor, he managed his migration costs by selling his only natural resource, arable land (BDT60,000) and borrowed BDT20,000 from a village moneylender. As he faced many problems in Malaysia, he returned home taking only BDT20,000. He then had to sell a piece of land to pay his debt upon his return home.
>
> (Baju 55, illiterate, farming, repeat-cycle migrant)

Baju's story also reveals how migrants can lose their only resource, land, from which they produce crops and maintain their family. Even after returning home, migrants may have to sell a piece of land in order to repay their debts. Some who have other income sources can cope with such conditions but those who have not face severe economic hardship.

Villagers who have enough resources, particularly financial, natural and material resources in Malaysia Village, do not face such major problems, even if they return home from overseas empty-handed, because most of them mobilize migration money from cash or assets other than land, such as social resources or human resources. In addition, after their return, some resume their previous occupations while others change their previous occupations such as small and medium scale businesses in and outside the village.

Sobhan, for example, now runs a small business in the local market, providing a modest livelihood for his family:

> Sobhan passed grade five at the village school. He went to Malaysia twice. During his first visit he returned home from Thailand and that is why his family faced severe financial hardship. He belonged to a poor household in the village before his first visit because he had no land and he worked

on other's land as a day labourer. The money he earned from labouring work in the village was insufficient for his four-member family. After his second visit he reports that he has improved his economic conditions and he now sees himself as belonging to a lower middle class household in the village. This is because he has deposited BDT100,000 in a government bank from where he gets BDT1,000 per month as interest and he has invested BDT151,000 in a small-scale business in the local market after repaying his loan and other household expenses. He buys seasonal crops, stores the crops in a house at the local market and sells the stored crops when the prices rise. He thinks that the money he earns from his business is enough for his family. Sobhan is able to afford the educational expenses of his younger son who is studying in grade 12. He also thinks that he and his family are eating better quality food and wearing better clothes than before. His elder son works in a garment factory and contributes to the family financially.

(Sobhan, 45, grade 5, business, repeat-cycle migrant)

Sobhan is happy with his life because he and his wife, and their sons, daughter-in-law and grandson live together. His major income comes from his business, and in lean times, as he cannot run the business the whole year, his son helps him financially.

Others, like Motiur, who migrated to Malaysia during the first-wave of migration, have earned a significant amount of money, enabling them to invest in income-generating activities, particularly in businesses different from their previous occupations in agriculture and thus substantially reduce income risks and household vulnerabilities.

Motiur's family were not poor because his father had sufficient land to cultivate and sustain the family's livelihood. But he felt ashamed working in agriculture because he studied up to grade nine. As he did not work in the field, he personally faced income risks and vulnerabilities. His father also had a small business in the local market. In order to invest more money in the business Motiur went to Malaysia in 1991, as one of the first-wave migrants. He spent only BDT60,000 for his migration but he sent back BDT1,500,000, the most among all the migrants in Malaysia Village. He has not only changed his social and economic status upwards in society, buying cultivable land in the village and homestead land in town, he also built a house on the land in the town and at the same time he invested BDT300,000 in his timber business in town. He is making a profit and now his total capital is around BDT800,000. He gets crops from village land but his livelihood is mainly derived from his timber business.

(Motiur, 50, grade 9 business, repeat-cycle migrant)

It is clear that migration, in such instances, leads to changes in migrants' occupations that assist them to enhance their livelihoods. Motiur believes that he has reached his dream of being a businessman and living in the town with his family, relating his ambition to send his son and daughter to town to study.

Other repeat-cycle migrants have also returned and established businesses in the village or in the local town, even though they were unemployed and under-employed before migration. Like Sobhan and Motiur, their economic conditions have improved because they have invested money in self-employed activities and thus, even in these cases, migration has contributed to occupational mobility and reduced income vulnerabilities for the household. Maula is one such repeat-cycle migrant.

> Maula failed grade 10 and was underemployed. The propensity for migra-tion in Malaysia Village and the income of migrants motivated him to migrate to Malaysia. He compared himself with the villagers who migrated. He thought that he was more educated than others. If they could earn money, he expected he would earn more than them. So, he made his deci-sion and informed his family. The family agreed because he had discontinued his study. He spent BDT140,000 and went to Malaysia. The remittance income he sent was used for different purposes: Maula sent one of his brothers to Malaysia by spending remittance money; he bought a piece of arable land and invested BDT150,000 in a poultry business in the village; he got training in poultry cultivation in the city. He lives in a joint family and financially supports the whole family. His business capital is increasing day by day, he is making more profit. He hopes that he will extend the business in future.
>
> (Maula, 32, grade 12, poultry farming, repeat-cycle migrant)

Migration of students as labourers is also a common phenomenon in Malaysia Village. The two main factors motivating students to migrate are poverty and the propensity for migration as an income earning strategy. Students or young school-leavers who face poverty are motivated by past migrants and see migra-tion as a viable option, a pattern also documented by Ahmed (2012). Under-standing the economic hardship of their parents, they look to alternative ways of earning an income. One of them, Yakub, who left school to go to Malaysia to work, recounted his story as follows:

> During his childhood, Yakub lost his father. His younger brother had a small business in the local market but the income from business could not sustain their family's livelihoods. When his family faced economic crisis, he was studying in grade 12. As he witnessed the family's severe hardship, he decided to migrate to Malaysia. He was so poor that he acquired BDT46,000 by selling a cow, a piece of land and paddy. Like other migrants, he also faced many social and economic problems in Malaysia. He tackled all the problems and sent home BDT700,000. He invested BDT200,000 in a fertiliser business in the local market. Afterwards, he moved from the fer-tiliser business to a garments business in the sub-district town with two

employees. He has a total capital in his business of BDT1,000,000 but the total value of garments would be more than BDT1,500,000. He pays BDT7,000 per month to his two employees. He earns a considerable amount of money in peak seasons, for example, during any Muslim and Hindu religious ceremonies.

(Yakub, 36, grade 10, garment business, repeat-cycle migrant)

Yakub has significantly changed his economic and social circumstances because he increased his initial capital, bought a piece of land in town and now lives in town with his family. He hopes that he will be able to send his son to a good school. The story of Yakub illustrates how poverty motivates young people to migrate overseas. It also demonstrates how, with perseverance, migrants can reduce their income vulnerability and poverty as well as enhance their social status through the utilization of remittance income and thus sustain their livelihoods (cf. Hadi 1999).

The cases presented here illustrate the considerable variation in the dynamics and uses of financial remittances among migrants' households. Consumption of remittances depends on net income, which is further dependent upon the working and living conditions of migrants in Malaysia, the amount of money spent in Malaysia and returned to households in Bangladesh and the number of visits and the duration of migration. The households of absentee migrants typically use the biggest part of their remittance income to pay their debts, and they do this for considerable periods of time. Only after long periods away and return visits to Malaysia are some migrants able to invest remittance income in agriculture or in businesses in the village, local market and sub-district town and thereby impact on their lives and livelihoods. On the other hand, migrants' absence for long period of time and regular/irregular flow of remittance income influence the social and behavioural dynamics of migrants' household members, an important part of the migration-induced livelihoods that have emerged in Malaysia Village.

5. Migrant absenteeism, remittance income and the dynamics of migrants' households

In addition to the dynamics of remittance income of first-cycle and repeat-cycle migrants' households, the long absence of migrants from home and dependency on remittances has contributed to the rise of a number of social and behavioural problems of left-behind household members, including the development of what is perceived as a 'culture of dependency' among youths in migrants' household, and joblessness. 'Easy money'[5] from remittances is seen by villagers to have contributed, also, to an increase in the dropout rate of migrants' children and other family members from schools and colleges, as well as a range of socially unacceptable behaviours such as smoking and illicit sexual relations among village youths (Hossain et al. 2013). In the absence of husbands and fathers, and due to low levels of literacy among women, an increased burden of household

work, and highly restrictive norms of mobility for women, mothers face significant challenges when young adult sons and daughters deviate from acceptable
norms. Sanwar, one of the repeat-cycle migrants, recounted the story of his
son's dropping out of high school in such circumstances:

> The elder son of Sanwar was a brilliant student who studied in the village
> madrasa. When Sanwar went to Malaysia, his son was free to mix, in and
> outside the village, with friends who were not conforming to social norms.
> Ignoring his mother's advice, the son went here and there with his friends,
> returning home late at night. Sanwar attempted to advise his son from
> Malaysia. As Sanwar was away, his son could ignore both his mother and
> Sanwar. The situation worsened to the point that he did not pass grade
> ten. Sanwar now laments that if he did not go to Malaysia his son would
> have continued to study. He sees this situation as a result of his migration
> and expressed his deep sadness about this.
>
> (Sanwar, 50, grade 9, farmer, repeat-cycle migrant)

It is a difficult experience for parents when their children discontinue their
studies at schools and colleges (Hadi 2001; Hossain et al. 2013). It becomes
more so when children do not conform to social norms and the family loses
status and dignity. Villagers recounted stories about how some migrants' adolescent children, particularly adolescent sons, had fallen in love and married
without their parents' consent, behaviour that villagers see as the result of the
lack of their fathers' guidance and proper socialisation. They related, for example,
the story of Afsar's son:

> Afsar, 55, went to Malaysia in 1995 leaving his only son, a nephew and his
> wife. When he was preparing to migrate, his son was studying in grade 12
> in the village madarasa. Unbeknownst to his parents, he formed a relation-
> ship with a girl in a neighbouring village who also studied in the same
> madrasa. When Afsar was away, one midnight his son went to the girl's
> house, left the village with his girlfriend and went to live in Dhaka where
> nobody traced them for many days. The guardians of the girl lodged a case
> in the court. Both parties spent a considerable amount of money to settle
> the problem. The conflict was so severe that many people of both villages
> became embroiled in the conflict.
>
> (Focus Group Discussion, younger male, age 15–25)

Stories were also told of migrants' younger brothers (who are dependent upon
the migrants) responding, in unacceptable ways, to the regular flow of remittances as well as their relatively unhindered freedom. Yaqub described his
brother's story:

> Yaqub regularly sent a particular amount of money to his younger brother
> who studied in a college which was far from his village. He estimated that

he spent approximately BDT150,000 to support his studies. Nobody knew what he was doing, but later Yaqub heard from people that his brother was not studying and was associating with some bad fellows. He was also informed that his brother may be using prohibited drugs. He expected his brother would get good results but he failed in the examination and did not continue his studies. He thinks that his brother deviated because he had access to a regular flow of money from Yaqub. After ignoring Yaqub's advice, his brother bought a motorbike. Recently, he had an accident and Yaqub spent nearly BDT600,000 for his treatment.

(Yaqub, 36, SSC, business, repeat-cycle migrant)

In addition to the children and siblings of migrants, the wives of some migrants have faced other social challenges including disempowerment and chronic depression (cf. Siddiqui 2001), arising from women being perceived as violating cultural norms. Perceived 'indiscretions' may arise from their increased responsibilities, including shopping in the local market[6] or responding to emergencies such as the illness of household members, because cultural norms limit women's mobility. More serious breaches have occurred when some wives, in the long-term absence of their husbands, have become involved in other relationships, violating fundamental social norms and values and causing severe problems that diminish the social status and prestige of migrants and their household members.

Some migrants, prior to migration, tell their wives to limit their movements unless there is an emergency which forces them to move into to the extended family households of their parents-in-law, contributing to the loss of whatever limited independence they may have enjoyed before their husbands migrated. In the extended family households of their parents-in-law, these left-behind spouses are forced to take on an additional workload and, in the process, often suffer not only physical stress but also emotional indignity (cf. Siddiqui 2001). Household members of nuclear households, particularly the wives of migrants, also endure severe workloads in the absence of their husbands because they have to do not only their own work but also that which their husbands would usually do. One of the most severe impacts of migration is that wives of migrants, during their husbands' long absences, sometimes form extramarital relationships in and outside the family household and, ultimately, family ties may be disrupted or broken through divorce (Afsar, Yunus and Islam 2002). One of the key informants reported one such case that occurred in the village:

Tahmid, a 56-year old man went to Malaysia to recover business losses. He left his parents, wife, son and younger brother. In Afsar's absence, his brother formed an extramarital relationship with his sister-in-law (Afsar's wife). Other family members were aware of the relationship but they hid it to protect their reputation and prestige. After a time, villagers came to know about the relationship. At some stage Afsar was informed. He arranged for his brother to go to Malaysia and then he came home to resolve the situation with his wife and then went to Malaysia again. His wife then became involved in a relationship with Afsar's nephew who studied in Malaysia Village madrasa. Afsar came home again and divorced his wife and sent his nephew to his parent's house. After some time, Asfar and his wife re-married each other.

(Zaman, 34, key informant, school teacher)

The study also found that some returnee migrants, estranged by their long absences and their experience abroad, have formed extramarital relationships that not only have disrupted their own family relationships but also those of others. One of the young villagers narrated a story that illustrated how returned migrants are perceived to be involved in socially unacceptable activities in the village and the breakdown of familial ties.

Polash formed an extramarital relationship with a woman after his return from Malaysia. He used to go to his friend's house in the same village. He and his friend's wife fell in love. His friend could not comprehend the relationship and could not believe his wife's infidelity, until she eventually left his house and went to live with Polash.

(Polash, 35, grade 10, business, repeat-cycle migrant)

Disruption of family ties also occurs as a result of conflict over the control and management of migrant remittance money, contributing in some cases to the breakdown of traditional family and household authority and of extended family ties (cf. Rahman 2009). In extended family households in Bangladesh, the (senior) father is regarded as the traditional head of the family, and thus there is an expectation that he will receive and manage remittance money. However, in some migrant households, the non-observance of this norm (the migrant's spouse or another relative may have been entrusted with this task) has caused much tension and bitterness, especially when parents have spent money for their sons' migration but their sons send money to their wives to manage. Such normative discrepancies are perceived as threatening the customary headship of the household (Rahman 2009) and have led, in some cases, to 'dual headship' in the same household, or splitting of joint families.

When Zahid went to Malaysia, his father arranged all the monies he needed. His father even sold land he received from his father (Zahid's grandfather). After four years Zahid returned home and married. He had no choice in the selection of his bride. He valued his parent's choice. He again went to Malaysia. From his second visit he started to send money home to his wife whereas before his marriage, he sent it to his father's bank account. His parents were shocked. When Zahid again came home, his parents became estranged from Zahid and his wife although Zahid still helps his parents financially.

(Tarif, 60, grade 5, tailor)

The study of Malaysia Village has pointed to a range of economic and social problems associated with migration and reliance upon remittance income that have adversely affected the livelihoods (including social ties and status in the community) of migrants' family members left at home. The majority of migrants' households, particularly those of first-cycle migrants, face high levels of debt over considerable periods of time. The study has also found that first-cycle migrants face acute financial crises, while for repeat-cycle migrants, severe social problems due to prolonged absence from home, become much more significant. The social problems that migrants and their households encounter may diminish their social status and disrupt their social identity. The withdrawal of migrants' children and younger siblings from schools and colleges (cf. Siddiqui 2001), as well as their engagement in socially unacceptable activities, and the tensions and distress that arise from strained marital relations, family breakdown and divorce, rupture social bonds and, over time, increase household vulnerabilities.

6. Conclusions: a limited bi-cyclical pattern of migration and shifting livelihoods

The chapter has focused upon the impacts of migration and remittances (financial and social), and the social dimensions of financial remittance on the lives and livelihood strategies of migrants' households and their community in Malaysia Village, a study village in rural Bangladesh. It has shown how the livelihood strategies of migrants' households have shifted to include new sources of income, leading to the emergence of new and more diverse 'migration-induced' livelihoods. A limited bi-cyclical pattern of South-South migration has now become established in Malaysia Village (see Figure 6.3). Migrants from Malaysia Village typically migrate to Malaysia twice, returning to settle after the second cycle, after calculating both social and economic costs and benefits. The migration-induced livelihood strategies documented here have emerged from a complex of social, economic and political relations operating at household, community, national and global levels. Such conditions (relations and practices) have been shaped very largely by the practices of formal and informal actors and agents who regulate and control migration processes 'on the ground', under conditions of relatively weak governance of migration in and between Bangladesh and Malaysia.

It is evident that villagers who migrate for the first-time, typically for around three years, face a series of social, economic and psychological problems in transit and in Malaysia that have negative financial impacts on them and on their household livelihoods. In the vulnerable working and living conditions migrants experience in Malaysia, first-cycle migrants usually fail to earn enough income to send sufficient money home to sustain their household. If migrants are unable to send money home, the left behind household members may face extreme financial hardship and, at the same time, become socially vulnerable because of their financial circumstances and disrupted household relations (where important household members are absent). Provided that within their

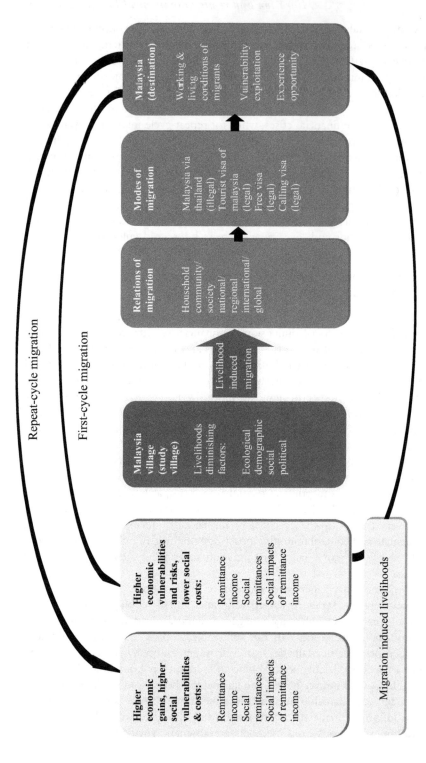

Figure 6.3 'Bi-cyclical' system of labour migration and the relationships among 'livelihood-induced migration' and 'migration-induced livelihood'

first cycle of migration (usually about three years in duration) migrants manage to remit some money, albeit typically only very small amounts, the social costs of migration (and absence from home) can be limited. However, to recover the financial losses incurred in their first-cycle of migration and improve their livelihoods, migrants usually migrate for a second time.

Those who migrate for a second time are able to capitalize on the experiences of first-time migration and usually adopt a different mode of migration from that which they used the first time. Though not all repeat-cycle migrants are able to use a more secure mode of entry, when they arrive in Malaysia they are able to utilize their work experience from their first cycle of migration and their established networks with employers, middlemen and co-workers (migrants with whom they worked). Thus, though working under essentially the same conditions, repeat-cycle migrants face relatively fewer social, economic and personal difficulties in Malaysia compared with their first-time migration. In these circumstances, repeat-cycle migrants are able to reduce costs, earn more income and send more money home. This group of migrants typically acquires some capital, particularly financial capital, investing it for income-earning activities on their return, and are able to improve their livelihoods financially. However, their left behind household members encounter more social problems compared with first-cycle migrants because the absence of the migrant from home for another period of three years has significant impact. Generally, the longer the duration of migration, the more the economic gain but the greater the social cost.

When second-time migrants calculate social costs and benefits and realize that it is hard to maximize economic gains without substantial social costs, they typically refrain from migrating a third time and resettle, sometimes in their former occupations, often in changed circumstances. Rarely do migrants return to Malaysia (or elsewhere) for a third cycle of migration but, in some families and households, the next generation of men have now begun to migrate, drawing upon the experiences of their forebears. As a consequence, a particular system of migration involving a limited number of cycles of migration and return, typically no more than two, has become established, wherein migrants and their household members (resident at home) engage in what is termed, here, 'migration-induced livelihoods', ways of earning income that are highly dependent upon and adjusted around migration (and migrant worker absence) and remittance.

Migration-induced livelihoods, patterns of life and income-producing activities organized around the 'absence' of transnational migrant workers from their households, and remittances, encompass not only conventionally understood productive economic activities of migrants and their household members but also reproductive activities, those activities that sustain and replenish productive capacities, including the cultural and social resources and practices supporting life (livelihood). Livelihood analysis, as conventionally applied, focuses principally upon the economic or productive dimension of 'making a living'; this analysis of migration-induced livelihoods draws attention to the importance of both 'productive' and 'reproductive' dimensions of livelihood (economic, social and

cultural) and points, in particular, to the significant impacts of lengthy separation of these dimensions of livelihood in migrants' households, in the context
of contemporary (temporary) South-South, transnational migration patterns and
the governance of South-South migration in the Asian region.

The study of a particular local system of migration and migration-induced
livelihoods in rural Bangladesh has focused attention not only on the financial
aspects of livelihood-induced migration but also upon the social dimensions of
migration-induced livelihoods. It has focused attention on the complex of relations of production *and* reproduction entailed in migration-induced livelihoods
and, in particular, the extreme form of 'separation' – between work and household relations (production and reproduction) – that constitute the livelihood
patterns that have emerged among migrants' households in Malaysia Village
and elsewhere in poor, rural economies of the global South.

Notes

1 Reported in *The Daily Star* (Bangladesh) of 31/12/2011 on the occasion of a
   speech by Professor Amartya Sen at an event organized by the Centre for Policy
   Dialogue (CPD) to mark the fortieth anniversary of Bangladesh's Independence
   held on 30/12/2011, at the National Museum Auditorium (see http://www.
   thedailystar.net/news-detail-216408). See also Centre for Policy Dialogue (CPD)
   at http://cpd.org.bd/index.php/bangladesh-at-40-achievements-are-many-but-
   more-could-have-been-done/.
2 The study village is a small village situated in the northwest of Bangladesh. As
   the majority of villagers from this village migrate to Malaysia, the village has been
   given the pseudonym 'Malaysia Village' so as not to disclose the original name
   of the study village or the identities of research participants. Pseudonyms are also
   used for all research participants.
3 First-cycle migrants are those migrants who went to Malaysia once, returned
   home and resettled as well as those who went to Malaysia a second time, imme-
   diately after their first visit (approximately three years); repeat-cycle migrants
   are those who went to Malaysia twice and resettled in the village (approximately
   six years).
4 Villagers reported this but, as they were unable to provide accurate estimates of
   these day-to-day expenses, they did not include all when reporting expenditure.
5 Remittance money is called 'easy money' in the village because migrants' children
   receive remittances when they need it, without being aware or mindful of the
   labour involved in obtaining it.
6 Rural women in Bangladesh do not go to the local market to buy and sell goods
   because there is a long custom that it is the duty of males in the household. Due to
   the absence of household heads, the left behind wives face problems shopping in the
   local market, although it is acceptable for them to buy goods from city markets.

References

Afsar, R, Yunus, M, and Islam, AS 2002, *Are Migrants Chasing after the "Golden
   Deer"?: A Study on Cost-benefit Analysis of Overseas Migration by the Bangladeshi
   Labour*, International Organization for Migration (IOM) Regional Office for
   South Asia, and UNDP, Dhaka.

Ahmed, SM 2012, *Migration and Remittances to Migrant Sending Households in Rural Bangladesh*, Master of International Development and Management Thesis, Lund University, Sweden.

Asian Development Bank 2013, *Asian Development Outlook 2013*, Manila, viewed 8 August 2014, <http://www.adb.org/sites/default/files/publication/30205/ado2013_2.pdf>.

Asian Development Bank 2015, *Poverty in Bangladesh*, viewed 12 January 2014, <https://www.adb.org/countries/bangladesh/poverty>.

Bangladesh Bank 2011, *Uses of Remittances in Bangladesh: Future Guidelines*, Bangladesh Bank, Research Division, Head Office, Dhaka, Bangladesh, viewed 28 September 2016, <https://www.bb.org.bd/pub/researchindex.php>.

Bangladesh Bank 2016, *Country-wise Wage Earners' Remittance Inflows (Yearly)*, viewed 26 September 2016, <http://www.ovijogbmet.org/bmet_forms/country wiseremittance.htm>.

Bangladesh Bureau of Statistics 2010, *Report of the Household Income and Expenditure Survey 2010*, viewed 14 June 2013, <http://www.bbs.gov.bd/WebTestApplication/userfiles/Image/LatestReports/HIES-10.pdf>.

Bangladesh Manpower Employment and Training 2013, *Overseas Employment and Remittances from 1976 to 2015*, viewed 21 May 2016, <http://www.bmet.org.bd/BMET/viewStatReport.action?reportnumber=18>.

Bangladesh Manpower Employment and Training 2015, *Category-wise Overseas Migration from 1976–2015*, viewed 21 May 2016, <http://www.bmet.org.bd/BMET/viewStatReport.action?reportnumber=27>

Bangladesh Planning Commission, General Economic Division (GED) 2015, *Millennium Development Goals: Bangladesh Progress Report 2015*, Government of the People's Republic of Bangladesh.

Bashar, K and Khan, H 2007, 'Liberalisation and Growth in Bangladesh: An Empirical Investigation', *Bangladesh Development Studies*, vol. 32, no. 1, pp. 61–76.

Black, R, Adger, WN, Arnell, NW, Dercon, S, Geddes, A, and Thomas, D 2011, 'The Effect of Environmental Change on Human Migration', *Global Environmental Change*, vol. 21, pp. S3–S11.

Constant, AF and Zimmermann, KF 2011, 'Circular and Repeat Migration: Counts of Exits and Years Away from the Host Country', *Population Research and Policy Review*, vol. 30, no. 4, pp. 495–515.

Devadason, ES and Chan, CW 2014, 'Policies and Laws Regulating Migrant Workers in Malaysia: A Critical Appraisal', *Journal of Contemporary Asia*, vol. 44, no. 1, pp. 19–35.

Dillon, A, Mueller, V, and Salau, S 2011, 'Migratory Responses to Agricultural Risk in Northern Nigeria', *American Journal of Agricultural Economics*, vol. 93, pp. 1048–61.

Fee, LK and Rahman, MM 2006, 'International Labour Recruitment: Channelling Bangladeshi Labour to East and South-East Asia', *Asia-Pacific Population Journal*, vol. 21, no. 1, pp. 85–107.

Hadi, A 1999, 'Overseas Migration and the Well-Being of Those Left behind in Rural Communities in Bangladesh,' *Asia-Pacific Population Journal*, vol. 14, no. 1, pp. 43–58.

Hadi, A 2001, 'International Migration and the Change of Women's Position among the Left behind in Rural Bangladesh', *International Journal of Population Geography*, vol. 7, no. 1, pp. 53–61.

Hossain, I 2013, 'Impact of Economic Liberalization Reforms in Bangladesh', *Ritsumeikan Journal of Asia Pacific Studies*, vol. 32, pp. 101–13 .

Hossain, M 2009, 'Overseas Labour Migration: A Nexus between Remittances and Well-being', *Journal of the Institute of Bangladesh Studies*, vol. 32, pp. 97–108.

Hossain, MI, Khan, MA, and Short, P 2013, 'Migration of Bangladeshi Workers to Malaysia: Emerging Lessons of Economic and Social Cost and Benefits at the Migrant, Migrant Household and Community Levels', in M Hossain, T Sarker and M McIntosh (eds), *The Asian Century, Sustainable Growth and Climate Change: Responsible Futures Matter*, Edward Elgar Publishing Ltd, Cheltenham, pp. 200–22.

Hugo, G 2008, 'International Migration in Indonesia and Its Impacts on Regional Development', in TV Naerssen, E Spaan and A Zoomers (eds), *Global Migration and Development*, Routledge, New York, pp. 43–65.

International Organisation for Migration 2010, *Assessing the Evidence: Environment, Climate Change and Migration in Bangladesh*, Regional Office for South Asia, Dhaka, Bangladesh.

Islam, MN 2010, *Strategy Paper for Re-integration of Returnee Migrants*, ILO, Dhaka, viewed 25 January 2012, <http://www.bmet.gov.bd/BMET/resources/Static%20 PDF%20and%20DOC/publication/Strategy%20Pap%20for%20re-integration. pdf>.

Joarder, MAM and Hasanuzzaman, S 2008, 'Migration Decision from Bangladesh: Permanent Versus Temporary', *Asia Europe Journal*, vol. 6, no. 3–4, pp. 531–45.

Kanapathy, V 2001 'International Migration and Labor Market Adjustments in Malaysia: The Role of Foreign Labor Management Policies', *Asia Pacific Migration Journal*, vol. 10, no. 3–4, pp. 429–61.

Kassim, A 1998, 'Profile of Foreign Migrant Workers in Malaysia: Towards Compiling Reliable Statistics', Paper Presented to *Conference on Migrant Workers and the Malaysian Economy*, Malaysian Institute of Economic Research, Kuala Lumpur, May 19–20.

Kaur, A 2010, 'Labour Migration in Southeast Asia: Migration Policies, Labour Exploitation and Regulation', *Journal of the Asia Pacific Economy*, vol. 15 , no. 1, pp. 6–19.

Kibria, N 2011, *Working Hard for the Money: Bangladesh Faces Challenges of Large-scale Labour Migration*, Migration Policy Institute, Washington, viewed 26 December 2011, <http://www.migrationpolicy.org/article/working-hard-money-bangladesh-faces-challenges-large-scale-labor-migration>.

Lein, H 2011, 'Hazards and Forced Migration in Bangladesh', *Norwegian Journal of Geography*, vol. 53, no. 3, pp. 122–7.

Mahmood, RA 1991, 'Bangladeshi Returned Migrants from the Middle East: Process, Achievement and Adjustment', in G Gunatilleke (ed), *Migration to the Arab World: Experience of Returning Migrants*, United Nations University Press, Tokyo, pp. 238–98.

Mahmud, W, Ahmed, S, and Mahajan, S 2008, *Economic Reforms, Growth, and Governance: The Political Economy Aspects of Bangladesh's Development Surprise*, Working Paper No. 22, World Bank, USA.

Paul, BK 2005, 'Evidence against Disaster-induced Migration: The Case of the 2004 Tornado in North-central Bangladesh', *Disasters*, vol. 29, no. 4, pp. 370–85.

Rahman, J and Yusuf, A 2010, 'Economic Growth in Bangladesh: Experience and Policy Priorities', *Journal of Bangladesh Studies*, vol. 12, no. 1, pp. 347–84.

Rahman, MM 2000, 'Emigration and Development: The Case of a Bangladeshi Village', *International Migration*, vol. 38, no. 4, pp. 109–30.

Rahman, MM 2009, 'Temporary Migration and Changing Family Dynamics: Implications for Social Development', *Population, Space and Place*, vol. 15, pp. 161–74.

Rahman, MM 2012, 'Bangladeshi Labour Migration to the Gulf States: Patterns of Recruitment and Processes,' *Canadian Journal of Development Studies*, vol. 33, no. 2, pp. 214–31.

Rahman, MM and Fee, LK 2012, 'Towards a Sociology of Migrant Remittances in Asia: Conceptual and Methodological Challenges', *Journal of Ethnic and Migration Studies*, vol. 38, no. 4, pp. 689–706.

Robertson, PS 2008, *Migrant Workers in Malaysia: Issues, Concerns and Points for Action*, Fair Labour Association, Malaysia, viewed September 2013, <http://digitalcommons.ilr.cornell.edu/cgi/viewcontent.cgi?article=2223&context=globaldocs>.

Rudnick, A 1996, *Foreign Labour in Malaysian Manufacturing: Bangladeshi Workers in the Textile Industry*, INSAN, Malaysia, viewed 3 March 2014, <https://books.google.com.bd/books/about/Foreign_labour_in_Malaysian_manufacturin.html?id=MlTtAAAAMAAJ&redir_esc=y>.

Rudnick, A 2009, *Working Gendered Boundaries: Temporary Migration Experiences of Bangladeshi Women in the Malaysian Export Industry from a Multi-sited Perspective*, Amsterdam University Press, Amsterdam.

Siddiquee, NA 2013, *Public Management and Governance in Malaysia: Trends and Transformations*, Routledge, New York.

Siddiqui, T 2001, *Transcending Boundaries: Labour Migration of Women from Bangladesh*, University Press Limited, Dhaka, Bangladesh.

Siddiqui, T and Abrar, CR 2003, *Migrant Worker Remittances and Micro-finance in Bangladesh*, Working Paper No. 38, Social Finance Programme, ILO, viewed 19 December 2010, <http://ilo.org/wcmsp5/groups/public/—edemp/documents/publication/wcms_117970.pdf>.

Ullah, AKMA 2009, 'Theoretical Rhetoric about Migration Networks: A Case of a Journey of Bangladeshi Workers to Malaysia', *International Migration*, vol. 51, no. 3, pp. 151–68.

United Nations Development Programme (UNDP) 2009, *HIV Vulnerabilities Faced by Women Migrants from Bangladesh to the Arab States*, Gulshan 2, Dhaka, Bangladesh, viewed 5 January 2011, <http://www.undp.org/content/dam/aplaws/publication/en/publications/hiv-aids/hiv-vulnerabilities-faced-by-women-migrants-from-asia-to-the-arab-states/UNDP%20Mobility%20Study.pdf>.

United Nations Development Progranme 2014, 'Human Development Report 2014', *Sustaining Human Progress: Reducing Vulnerabilities and Building Resilience*, viewed 12 March 2015, <http://hdr.undp.org/sites/default/files/hdr14-report-en-1.pdf>.

Warner, K 2010, 'Global Environmental Change and Migration: Governance Challenges,' *Global Environmental Change*, vol. 20, no. 3, pp. 402–13.

World Bank 2013, *Immigration in Malaysia: Assessment of Its Economic Effects, and a Review of the Policy and System*, Human Development Social Protection and Labour Unit, East and Pacific Region, World Bank, viewed 23 June 2014, <http://psu.um.edu.my/images/psu/doc/Recommended%20Reading/Immigration%20in%20Malaysia.pdf>.

World Bank 2015, *Migration and Remittances: Recent Developments and Outlooks*, Migration and Development Brief 24, viewed 8 October 2015, <http://pubdocs. worldbank.org/pubdocs/publicdoc/2015/10/102761445353157305/Migration andDevelopmentBrief25.pdf>.

Yaw, AD (ed) 2002, 'Introduction', in *Migrant Workers in Pacific Asia*, pp. 1–18, Frank Cass Publishers, London.

Zimmermann, MG, Glombitza, K-F, and Rothenberger, B 2010, *Disaster Risk Reduction Programme for Bangladesh*, Swiss Agency for Development and Cooperation SDC, Sweden, Denmark, viewed 11 December 2011, <http://unpan1. un.org/intradoc/groups/public/documents/apcity/unpan050296.pdf>.

7 Socioeconomic impact of South-South migration at household level in Nepal

Amina Maharjan

1. Background[1]

Nepal is one of the least developed countries in the world, with a Human Development Index ranking of 145 out of 188 in 2014 (UNDP 2015). Per capita GDP is low at USD703 (MoF 2014) with annual growth of GDP at 5.1 percent (ADB 2015). Agriculture is still the main economic sector, contributing a third of the country's GDP. However, farming in rural Nepal is mostly subsistence in nature and constrained by weather and structural deficiencies. The performance of the agricultural sector has generally been poor since the 1980s. The yield of most crops has increased marginally or stagnated, whereas population growth has been high. Thus the yield rate in relation to population growth rate has been declining since the 1980s (Paudel and Adhikari 2012). The contribution of the agricultural sector to GDP decreased from 37.4 percent in 2001–2002 to 33.1 percent in 2013–2014 (MoF 2014). The non-agricultural sector consists mainly of manufacturing, construction, wholesale and the retail trade, transport and communication, and real estate and renting activities. Tourism, which rebounded after a decade of armed conflict and the subsequent unstable political situation, still contributes less than 10 percent to GDP and employment (WTTC 2014). This sector has suffered further decline since the Gorkha earthquake of April 25, 2015.

Under the present conditions of low economic growth, labour migration is being used as a major livelihood strategy by many households in Nepal, particularly by farming households in rural areas. International labour migration, which previously consisted mainly of cross-border migration to India, has now diversified to include other destinations. International migration in Nepal can be classified into two main streams – namely, cross-border migration to India and overseas migration to Southeast and Western Asian countries. South-South migration accounts for more than 90 percent of total international migration from Nepal. With the increase in migration and destination diversification, the remittances received by the country have also increased over the years from 11.2 percent of the country's GDP in 2002 to 32.2 percent in 2015 (World Bank 2016).

Labour migration of a household member from rural areas of the country is expected to have an impact on the household's socioeconomic situation, including its human capital, the health condition of its members, food security, household social structure and the psychosocial wellbeing of household members. Although labour migration is an integral part of household livelihood strategies in Nepal, a fact that is now well recognized by researchers and policy makers, research on the impact of labour migration at the household level is limited. This chapter seeks to shed light on the impacts of labour migration using primary data sets, econometric tools, focus group interviews and the personal experience of the author as a practitioner in the field of migration. This chapter considers both main streams of South-South migration from Nepal (cross-border and overseas migration) and examines their impacts on the sending households and communities. South-North migration is intentionally not covered in this chapter, as the extent of such migration is low and the impact of South-North migration is expected to be very different from that of South-South migration.

2.   Objective

The objective of this chapter is to analyse and understand the impact of migration on the socioeconomic situation of migrant-sending households. As the impacts of migration are highly localized and differ according to the type of migration, an effort is made to observe the differences in the main types of migration and the changes over time.

The following research questions are explored:

• Why do people migrate?
• What is the overall impact of migration on households' livelihood situations?
• What is the impact of migration on the economic conditions, food security, health, education and skills, and social structure of households?
• How does the impact of migration differ over time for different migration patterns and for similar migration patterns?

3.   Analytical approach

This study uses household survey data, gathered by the author in the Far Western and Western development regions of Nepal as part of her doctoral research in 2007, as the baseline information (Maharjan 2010). The author draws on this primary data, as well as other research, including grey literature, and her own experience working in the field of migration in Nepal to answer the research questions. Research on the impact of migration at the household level in Nepal, particularly on socioeconomic changes, is rare and geographically disparate. Thus, whenever possible, research conducted in the same geographic region as the author's 2007 survey (i.e. Syangja and Baitadi districts) is studied to observe changes over time. However, where no studies over time have been found, grey literature and the experience of the author are relied upon. The author has also recently conducted a rapid appraisal of communities with a high level of cross-border migration, the results of which are also reflected in the study (Maharjan,

Knerr and Maharjan 2015). Finally, the study also uses secondary data and information sources wherever available and applicable.

This chapter focuses on the difference in the impact of the two streams of migration – namely, cross-border migration to India and international migration to other destinations. For the purposes of this chapter, cross-border migration to India is simply referred as 'cross-border migration' and international migration to other destinations as 'overseas migration'. The household is defined as all persons or the group of people who usually live and eat together and consider their living quarters or the space occupied by them as their usual place of residence. This is the definition used by the Household Budget Survey of Nepal (NRB 2008). The interest of this study is in the impact of migration on a household – the household is, therefore, the basic unit of analysis. The migrant household is defined following Koc and Onan (2004), who extend the definition of household to include not only those persons who are living together, but also those who are presently residing abroad and whose principal commitments and obligations are to that household and who are expected to return to that household in the future after completion of their migration.

4.   South-South migration in Nepal

Labour migration from Nepal began approximately two hundred years ago, with men moving from the hills of Nepal to the city of Lahore in the northern region of the Punjab to work as soldiers in the army of the Sikh King, Ranjit Singh. The popular term 'Lahure', which is used to refer to men working outside the country, was derived from this connection (Seddon 2005). This trend of working in the foreign military continues today. Apart from the military, the establishment of tea estates in Northern India resulted in a high demand for labour, which was partly met by labour migrants from Nepal. The development of the North Indian states, or 'hill stations', also created a demand for Nepalese workers as porters, construction workers and so forth. Therefore, until the early 1980s, labour migration from Nepal was more or less restricted to India as a destination. From the late 1980s onward, however, the destination for labour migrants diversified, with Nepalese migrants beginning to migrate in significant numbers to Southeast Asia and the Far East and, from the mid-1990s onward, westward to the Gulf countries (Seddon 2005).

Patterns and trends of South-South migration in Nepal

In 1981 the destination for more than 90 percent of all migrants was India. This fell to approximately 77 percent in 2001 (Kansakar 2003), with the number of international labour migrants going to destinations other than India increasing dramatically in 1999–2000, a trend that continues to date (Figure 7.1). More than 1,500 people leave Nepal for work in various destinations every day. The most popular destinations are Malaysia, Qatar and Saudi Arabia. Labour migration in Nepal is, therefore, predominantly a South-South phenomenon,

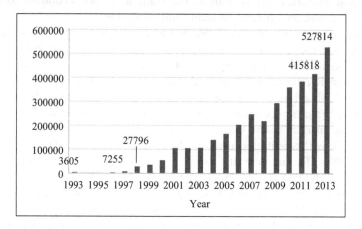

Figure 7.1 International labour migration from Nepal (India not included), 1993–
2013

Source: DoFE (2014)

consisting of two main streams: cross-border migration to India and migration
to Southeast and Western Asia, accounting for more than 90 percent of total
international migration. Migration to the global north is very limited, with most
of these migrants going as students, and is not within the scope of this study.

Although in absolute numbers, international labour migration from Nepal
does not attract global attention, Nepal was ranked third highest globally in
terms of remittances as a share of GDP in 2013 (World Bank 2015). One in
every four households in Nepal has at least one migrant member living abroad
(CBS 2012). The percentage of households receiving remittances increased from
23.4 percent in 1995–1996 to 55.8 percent in 2010–2011, and the average
remittance per recipient household increased from USD262[2] (26.6 percent of
total household income) to USD520 (30.9 percent of total household income)
in the same period (CBS 2011). This clearly indicates the importance of South-
South international labour migration and remittances, not only for the national
economy, but also for the wellbeing of remittance-receiving households.

The extent of international labour migration, as well as the type of migration
stream, differs among the different ecological belts and development regions.
Nepal is divided into three agro-ecological zones (mountains, hills and Tarai)
from north to south, and five development regions (Eastern, Central, Western,
Mid-Western and Far Western) from east to west. There is a high level of
disparity among the three agro-ecological zones and development regions in
terms of development, as well as resource endowment. The hills have a high
population, but low capacity in terms of resource holdings, compared to the
mountains and Tarai. Similarly, the Mid-Western and Far Western development
regions are the most marginalized. These disparities also extend to the selection

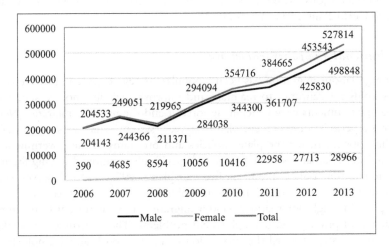

Figure 7.2 International labour migration trend by gender
Source: DoFE (2014)

of migration destination. From the Far Western and Mid-Western development regions, people migrate mostly to India, either as seasonal migrants or circular migrants. However, from the Western, Central and Eastern development regions, people migrate more to overseas destinations for a period of two to three years. Within these regions, people from higher altitudes and lower economic situations migrate predominantly to India, whereas those from middle-income households migrate to the Gulf countries and Malaysia. Those from high-income households migrate to the United States, Europe, Australia, the United Kingdom and Canada.

Migration is also highly gendered, as can be seen from Figure 7.2. International labour migration to destinations other than India is highly male dominated. However, in recent years, the international labour migration of females has been increasing with women accounting for 13 percent of overseas migration (excluding cross-border migration to India) as early as 2011 (DoFE 2014).

Cross-border migrants can be from a wide age group (fifteen to fifty years), while those going to other destinations are mostly aged eighteen to thirty-five years. The Foreign Employment Act 2007 requires Nepali migrants to be at least eighteen years old. Although there is no upper age limit for migrants, it is reported to be difficult to find jobs through overseas migration once the migrant is more than thirty-five years old. Williams et al. (2012) found the average age of Nepali migrant workers in Western Asia to be thirty-two years. While cross-border migration to India can be individual or family migration, almost all migrants to other international destinations migrate individually, leaving their families behind, including their spouse and children (Pun 2013). The majority of Nepali migrant workers are involved in low-skilled work and some in semi-skilled jobs, working as plumbers, electricians, scaffolders, drivers and so on (World Bank 2011; Wasti 2012).

Institutional and policy framework

Although labour migration has been a popular strategy engaged in by Nepalese households for centuries to maintain and improve their livelihoods, successive Nepali governments have generally ignored it and the needs of migrants. Nepal follows a periodic development plan (five-year) system, which acts as the major guiding document for the plans, policies and programs of the government of Nepal. International labour migration was specifically mentioned and highlighted for the first time only in the ninth five-year plan (1997–2002). However, since then, international labour migration has gained attention in all successive plans. The plans highlight international labour migration as an important factor in the reduction of poverty and unemployment problems. The government has taken a number of steps toward the promotion of international labour employment and protection of the rights of its citizens in overseas destinations, including the decentralization of passport issuing authorities, the opening of consulates and labour attachés in major destination countries, and the signing of a memorandum of understanding with major destination countries (e.g. Malaysia, the United Arab Emirates, and Qatar).

The Foreign Labour Act of 1985 was formulated with the aim 'to protect and to provide support in the matters relating to foreign employment'. It aims at controlling and managing foreign employment to 'maintain economic interests and conveniences of the general public'. The act was amended twice (in 1992 and 1998) and has now been replaced by the Foreign Employment Act 2007, which is the main legal basis for international labour migration at present. Unlike its predecessor, the Foreign Employment Act envisages protecting the rights of migrants, as well as regulating the migration process. The Foreign Employment Act contains provisions regarding insurance, the removal of gender-based discrimination against women migrant workers, producing skilled human resources for foreign employment, and making the migration process shorter and more systematic. This act also provides for the establishment of the Foreign Employment Promotion Board, the Foreign Employment Tribunal and labour attachés at Nepali missions in popular destination countries. Currently, the government of Nepal has once again imposed an age limit on women migrant workers seeking domestic work in the Gulf countries. For such work, a female migrant worker must be at least thirty years of age.

Similarly, the government of Nepal has formulated the Foreign Employment Policy 2012 to give direction to the effective management of foreign employment, make the migration process safer and more efficient, and overcome the shortcomings of the prevailing acts and rules (Sijapati and Limbu 2012). Apart from migration governance, this policy also addresses the use of the economic and noneconomic benefits of migration for the country's sustainable economic and social development, which are issues in the migration cycle that were not considered previously.

The Ministry of Labour and Employment is the apex organization responsible for all labour related matters including international labour migration. The Department of Foreign Employment, under the Ministry of Labour and Employment, looks after the main administrative issues relating to international labour migration, including issuing labour permits and the regulation of private sector stakeholders involved in international labour migration. At the destination country, Nepalese missions are primarily responsible for the welfare of Nepali citizens, and in most of the popular destinations, labour attachés have been appointed specially to look into the issues of concern to Nepali labour migrant workers.

The role of civil society (I/NGOs, the media, and informal diaspora associations) cannot be underestimated in the field of migration in Nepal. Civil society has been playing a crucial role in better migration governance and the protection of rights of migrant workers. Their role in reintegration and the use of remittances is limited, but vital.

Major challenges in South-South migration

Cross-border migration to India is almost entirely informally processed, except in the case of formal sector employment, such as in the security forces. There are no legal frameworks or institutions to monitor or regulate this flow of migration. The entire migration process is dependent on social networks that have been active for centuries. There has been little input or support from either the home government or the host-country government in this process, except for small initiatives with limited coverage by NGOs. However, the international labour migration of Nepalese to countries other than India is highly regulated by the government of Nepal. Although there are policies and legal instruments in place, as mentioned in the previous sub-section, this stream of migration also faces a number of challenges. Some of the main problems faced by Nepali migrant workers in the migration process are as follows:[3]

- Inadequate and false information: As the information related to the migration process is mostly only centrally available, it is difficult for potential migrant workers in rural areas of Nepal to access information.[4] Potential migrants are almost entirely reliant on local agents, who themselves are dependent on other agents at the regional level. Thus the information flow through this chain of agents, even when correct, is diluted by the time it reaches the potential migrant worker. As most of the agents involved are motivated by profit, rather than providing correct information, they sell 'dreams' to the migrants rather than the real situation. Thus most migrants complete the whole migration process based on incorrect or misleading information and false promises (Amnesty International 2011). There is hardly ever direct contact between the recruiting agency and the actual migrant worker, giving traffickers and fraudulent persons an opportunity to profit.

- High cost of migration: The government of Nepal has a fixed maximum ceiling for charges for facilitating the migration process by destination (a maximum of NPR70,000 [USD702] for most destinations in the Gulf countries and NPR80,000 [USD802] for Malaysia). However, most migrants pay more than this ceiling.

- High interest rate on loan: Most migrant workers have to take out a loan to finance their migration costs. In the absence of the provision of migration loans by financial institutions, they are reliant on informal moneylenders who charge high interest rates – usually 30 percent per annum. This reduces the return on investment for migrant households.

- Differences between the contract signed in the home country and the work and wages provided in the destination country: Migrant workers are required to sign a work contract in the home country that specifies the area of work and the wages and benefits they are entitled to. However, migrant workers are often forced to sign another contract upon arrival in the country of destination, with different (usually lower) work and pay benefits. This not only reduces their earning capacity, but also negatively affects their mental state, as they feel that they have been cheated and that their migration objectives are hampered.

- Lack of skills: Most migrant workers from Nepal are employed in low-skilled labour work. This kind of work is not only at the very bottom of the work hierarchy, but also pays less and is physically strenuous, impacting on their health in the long term. Also, no matter how many years of experience the migrant has working as a labourer, their chances of earning more are almost non-existent. By contrast, a migrant worker employed as a semi-skilled labourer, with experience, has a strong chance of graduating to work as a skilled labourer. For example, a lot of migrant workers from Nepal who work as helpers in scaffolding work eventually become skilled scaffolders and supervisors. This growth entails not only higher returns, but also better working conditions and less strenuous work.

- Forced retention of labour after completion of contract: A major problem reported by Nepali migrant workers, particularly in Qatar, is the unwillingness of employers to allow migrant workers to return home after completion of their contract.[5] Employers who do let migrant workers leave are sometimes reported as withholding end of employment benefits agreed to in the contract.

- Late or non-payment: This is one of the most common problems reported by migrant workers in the Gulf countries and Malaysia. Among the Gulf countries, late or non-payment is reported to be more rampant in Qatar and less in Saudi Arabia.[6] This problem is also reported by female migrant workers working as domestic help.

- Long working hours: This is particularly reported by female migrant workers working as domestic help in the Gulf countries. There are no defined working hours, thus domestic workers are expected to be available for eighteen to twenty hours a day. Lack of sufficient sleep and rest/recreation is a major complaint by migrants working as domestic help in destination countries, particularly Gulf countries.

- Exploitation and abuse in the workplace: Physical and mental abuse and labour exploitation are also reported by many migrant workers, both male and female. However, the extent of this problem is difficult to ascertain in the absence of systematic research into this issue.
- High number of deaths of migrant workers: There is a high number of deaths of migrant workers in destination countries. The number of deaths reported at the Foreign Employment Promotion Board increased from 90 (87 male, 3 female) in 2008–2009 to 842 (818 male, 24 female) in 2013–2014 (DoFE 2014). The majority of deaths are reported in Malaysia followed by Saudi Arabia and Qatar, which are the most popular destinations for Nepali migrant workers. The main causes of death reported are heart failure, natural causes, traffic accident, suicide and workplace accidents (DoFE 2014).

5. A literature review of the impact of migration on the development of source communities

The impacts of migration in the place of origin are manifold. The most tangible impact of migration is the direct economic impact through remittances. However, remittances also have non-pecuniary consequences, including an impact on health, gender equality, education and even on the social structure of households. Non-remittance related impacts include impacts on the culture and social changes in the origin societies (De Haas 2007).

There has been a longstanding debate about whether migration is beneficial or detrimental to the overall and sustainable development of individual households and nations as a whole. The view of researchers on the impact of migration on development at the place of origin began with an optimistic view, which was replaced by a pessimistic view, eventually giving way to a more pluralistic view (De Haas 2007). The neoclassical view on the impact of migration at the place of origin is highly optimistic. Neoclassists assume that migration leads to a North-South transfer of investment capital and that traditional communities at the place of origin benefit from exposure to modern knowledge and education. Under this view, migrants are considered important agents of change to help developing countries in their economic take-off (De Hass 2007). Migration pessimists, on the other hand, argue that migration leads to underdevelopment instead of development. Supporters of this view believe that migration leads to the depletion of human capital and the breakdown of traditional communities and their economies, leading to non-productive remittance dependent communities (Massey et al. 1993). A more pluralistic view is offered by the New Economics of Labour Migration (NELM), which argues that migration tends to have diverse impacts at different places origins (Ghosh 1992; Taylor 1999) and at various stages of migration (Lucas 1987; Jones 1998).

Migration can have a direct and indirect impact on the sending households and nations (Taylor and Wyatt 1996). The direct impacts are seen through changes in household income, which change consumption and asset accumulation patterns in the sending households. Indirect impacts occur through multiplier effects at the village, meso- and macro-levels.

Direct impact

The New Economics of Labour Migration views migration as a household strategy to improve overall livelihoods in an imperfect credit and risk market. Therefore, migration is expected to help households in smoothing out household consumption and investing in productive activities, such as farming and small businesses. However, the empirical findings on household consumption suggest that the impact is not spread equally across the spectrum of goods and services. Contradictory findings are also reported from different studies. Adams (2005) found, in a study conducted in Guatemala, that migrant households spend more on education, health, and housing and less on food. Similarly, Zarate-Hoyos (2004) reports that Mexican migrant-sending households allocate a larger share of household income to investment and savings than to current consumption and durable goods. In contrast, Orozco (2003) reports that migrant households in Mexico, Nicaragua and El Salvador spend the largest share of their income on food and clothing.

Remittances are the most tangible impact of migration on the sending household (Mendola 2010; Ratha, Mohapatra and Scheja 2011). Remittances are associated with a reduction in poverty, increased household resources devoted to investment and improvements in health and education (Ratha et al. 2011). Labour migration and remittances have been important factors in poverty reduction and improving living standards in Nepal (Shrestha 2004; Lokshin, Bontch-Osmolovski and Glinskaya 2010). Lokshin et al. (2010) studied the impact of work-related migration on poverty in Nepal using data from the Nepal Living Standard Surveys of 1996 (NLSS-I) and 2004 (NLSS-II), conducted by the Nepal Central Bureau of Statistics. The study findings revealed that migration and remittances accounted for a 20 percent decline in poverty in Nepal between 1995 and 2004.

The empirical evidence of the impact of migration on the labour supply of the source household is, again, contradictory. There is a high possibility of the household labour supply decreasing after receiving remittances, as remittances can be used for leisure. Also, there can be a gender-differential impact on household labour supply. Hanson (2005) reports reduced labour supply and increased leisure among households receiving remittances in Mexico and a stronger impact on women than men. Grigorian and Melkonyan (2011) reported, in a study conducted in Armenia based on the 2004 Integrated Living Standards Measurement Survey, that remittance-receiving households worked fewer hours and that remittances were used more to buy leisure. Amuedo-Dorantes and Pozo (2006a) reported an overall reduction in female labour supply among migrant households, but the result for males was the reverse (i.e. the males from migrant households worked more than from non-migrant households). They also reported that males in migrant households allocate their labour supply across various types of employment.

Migration also impacts on the education opportunities of children. Remittances are expected to increase household income, thus increasing the ability of households to cover the cost of education (Cox-Edwards and Ureta 2003, for El Salvador; Hanson and Woodruff 2003, for Mexico; Yang 2008, for the Philippines; Cattaneo 2010, for Albania; Sharma 2013, for Sri Lanka). Thieme and Wyss (2005), in their study in Western Nepal, found that migration and remittances have a positive impact on the education of children. Remittances are also expected to reduce the burden on children to work for household income and thus improve their educational attainment. Mansuri (2006), in an empirical study based on the Pakistan Rural Household Survey 2001–2002, found that migration and the resulting remittances helped increase a child's years of schooling and reduced the work burden on children. Amuedo-Dorantes and Pozo (2006b), in their study in the Dominican Republic, arrived at the finding that migration has a negative impact on the education of children and remittances a positive impact. Migration can also have a disruptive influence on the family, which can negatively impact on the education of children (McKenzie 2006). Children often plan to follow in the footsteps of their elders and sometimes do not see the returns from education, as found in a study in Mexico by McKenzie and Rapoport (2010).

The relationship between migration and the health outcomes of the migrants and their households are expected to be mixed. While migration might expose the migrant to higher health risks (Kahn et al. 2003), the impact on the household members left behind is generally positive (Hildebrant and McKenzie 2005, in Mexico; Lopez-Cordoba 2006, in Botswana; Ponce, Olivié and Onofa 2011, in Ecuador). Sharma (2013), based on a household survey conducted in West Sri Lanka, reported higher health expenditure by migrant households than non-migrant households.

The social and mental/emotional costs of migration are more difficult to assess. Generally, as migration entails the separation of family members for long periods of time, it has negative social costs in terms of loneliness, risk of family breakdown and psychosocial stress (Kahn et al. 2003). The migrant may feel stressed living and working in a geographically, culturally and linguistically different place, while the family members left behind have to deal with the emotional stress of not knowing the situation of the migrant. Advancements in technology, particularly the mobile telephone, have significantly improved communication between migrants and their families, which has improved transnational familial ties (UNDP 2009).

Indirect impact

Indirect impacts are mostly visible at the meso- and macro-levels. At the meso-level, migration not only impacts those households sending migrants, but also non-migrant households through multiplier effects on local incomes, labour and employment. Remittances can provide capital stock to finance investments at the local level, which is of particular importance in the imperfect credit and risk market conditions in rural areas of most developing countries. Remittances can also improve education systems and increase the productivity of the rural agriculture sector through increased investment. In addition, the movement of labour out of the agricultural sector can help solve the problem of unemployment/underemployment.

Conversely, migration can have a negative impact on rural production, as a result of the loss of skilled labour. When remittances are invested in products that have low local multiplier effects, or when they are used to move out of rural areas, migration generally has a negative impact on source communities. At least in the initial phase, migration can lead to increased income inequality in the community, although this affect is expected to reverse as more households become involved in migration (Stark, Taylor and Yitzhaki 1986). Therefore, the extent and nature of the impact of migration on the sending communities is mixed and hotly debated.

In general, as pointed out by Taylor and Martin (2001), migration is likely to have the largest positive impact on the source communities when the loss of human and other capital is the least and when the benefits of migration go to those households that face the greatest constraints on local production and when remittances are spent in such a way that they have the largest local income multiplier effect. As households are at the focus of this research, this chapter focuses on the direct impact of migration on the socioeconomic and social structures of households.

6.   Reasons for international labour migration

Before discussing the impact of international labour migration on the socioeconomic situations of households, it is important to understand the reasons for the migration decision by households. By understanding why households send one or more members for international labour migration, it is easier to measure the impact of international labour migration in terms of its success in achieving the objectives of migration. This section considers the household's decision (reasons and perceived reasons) for international labour migration.

The decision of a household to take up migration as a livelihood strategy is dependent on the household's situation (economic, social and financial). The reasons for migration are also expected to be different for the two streams of migration from Nepal (cross-border migration to India and overseas migration to other countries). The author's survey on migration decisions found that the main reason for migrating is lack of sufficient economic opportunities in the village of origin, which was reported by more than 95 percent of respondent in both streams of migration (Maharjan 2010). The other important reasons reported for overseas migration (reported in Syangja district in the Western Development Region of Nepal) are food insecurity, to improve their livelihood situation, and for better earning opportunities (reported by more than 90 percent of respondents), more respect in the village (reported by more than 80 percent of respondents) and lack of interest in studying or work in the village (reported by about 45 percent of respondents). Similar results were reported by Ale (2004) in Kaski district, which is also in the Western Development Region of Nepal.

However, over time, some changes in the reasons for migration have been observed. As found in a more recent study by Nepal (2013) in Eastern Development Region of Nepal, the majority of migrant households reported saving/capital accumulation (61.4 percent) as the reason for migration, followed by low income locally (37.8 percent), their own education or that of other family members (26.9 percent) and unemployment (20.4 percent). This study was based on household-level data collected in two districts, Jhapa and Sunsari, which have very high levels of overseas migration. Similarly, another study in Central Development Region of Nepal by Maharjan et al. (2015) reports capital accumulation as the main reason for migration, followed by unemployment and the management of household financial constraints. Thus these findings show that, over the years, capital accumulation with the objective of livelihood diversification has become a predominant factor in migration, as compared to food security and lack of economic opportunity.

The reasons for cross-border migration differ from those for overseas migration. In cross-border migration (as represented by Baitadi), food insecurity is reported by approximately 80 percent of respondents, livelihood improvement by approximately 48 percent and conflict by approximately 16 percent. Other reasons, such as better earning opportunities, more respect in society and lack of interest in studying and working, were not reported by many respondents. A similar result was reported by Shahi (2005) in a study in Bajhang district in the Far Western Development Region of Nepal. This variation in perceived reasons for migration clearly indicates the importance of the earning opportunities that the migrants have in the destination country. As most cross-border migrants are involved in low-paying informal sectors, this type of migration is seen as a mere survival strategy. This situation has not changed significantly over the years, as witnessed by the author in her recent visit to pockets of Sindhupalchowk and Nuwakot districts with high levels of migration to India. Even now, migration is undertaken mostly as a survival strategy by cross-border migrants, except those working in the defence sector and formal sectors. However, with the rapid economic growth that India has seen over the years, the wages of migrants have also increased, which helps them accumulate small amounts of savings to build their capital base.

7. Socioeconomic impact of international labour migration

The socioeconomic impact of international labour migration was measured in terms of perceptions and actual changes in various socioeconomic aspects of the migrant households, vis-à-vis non-migrant households. The impact was analysed in terms of the general perception of households of the changes observed in their livelihood situation, as well as any changes in their economic, labour, food security, human resources and health situation. As migration decisions, as well as the impact of migration, are perceived in relative terms to other households, an effort was also made to analyse the changes in the social structure within households and communities, including changes in gender roles and responsibilities. The main findings are reported in this section.

Perception of change in household livelihoods

One very important measure of the impact of international labour migration is the household's perception of changes in their livelihood situation. Households often measure the impact of migration based on their relative performance, as compared to their situation before migration. As perceptions are often used to make (and measure) decisions at the household level, the measuring of perceptions is important in understanding the impact of migration.

The household livelihood situation of migrant households was perceived to have improved by 91 percent of the households involved in overseas migration and by 70 percent of those involved in cross-border migration (Maharjan 2010). These findings clearly show that migration is successfully used by rural households as a livelihood improvement strategy. However, a small proportion of households do not manage to meet their migration objectives, with their livelihood situation remaining the same or deteriorating. Particularly, when overseas migration fails and the household is unable to repay the debt incurred to finance the migration, the household can be pushed deeper into poverty. However, such incidences were reported by only 1 percent of households in the study districts (Maharjan 2010).

Ale (2004) also reported that migration generally leads to improved livelihoods in Kaski district in Nepal. Similarly, Nepal (2013) reported that migration has a positive impact on households' socioeconomic conditions in Eastern Development Region of Nepal, suggesting that the general perception of large-scale cheating by labour migration agents is not warranted. However, this result should be considered with caution as the sample size was small, and the study did not focus on this dimension.

Economic situation

One of the main reasons for migration is not only to earn a better income, but also to reduce a household's risks. Migration is expected to make significant positive impact on the overall economic situation of the migrant household. However, the actual economic benefits of migration depend on the cost of migration, sector of work, skill level of migrant and destination country. Cross-border migration to India is much cheaper than overseas migration. Nepal and India share more than 400 km of open land border, which makes it easy for

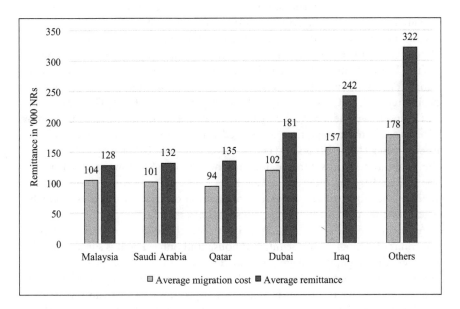

Figure 7.3 Average costs and annual returns of migration by destination
Source: Maharjan (2010)

people from the two countries to cross the border. Also, there is no requirement of official document or permits for Nepali people to work in India and
vice versa. Thus the cost of migration is much lower compared to overseas
migration.

In 2007, the average cost of cross-border migration to India was around
NPR3,000 (USD30) (Maharjan 2010). However, the returns from cross-border
migration varied significantly based on the sector of work from NPR17,702
(USD178) to NPR94,000 (USD943) per annum per household (Maharjan
2010). Similar results were also reported by Ale (2004) and Shahi (2005). This
stream of migration has seen a lot of change since 2007, with the cost of cross-
border migration increasing to NPR7,500 (USD75) and the returns almost
doubling. Even in low-paying jobs (e.g. washing dishes in a restaurant), a migrant
can save a minimum of NPR50,000 (USD502) per annum.[7] There have also
been some positive developments regarding the mode of payment. In 2007, for
most informal sector work, in restaurants/food stalls and construction (two major
sectors of employment for Nepali migrant workers in India), payments were
made on a daily basis in cash and migrant workers had no access to bank accounts.
This made saving difficult. Now workers can open a bank account and their
wages are paid on a monthly basis. But to what extent this change has been
realized and in which sectors of employment is still an open question.

The average cost of overseas migration ranged from NPR94,000–178,000
(USD943–1,785; for a breakdown, see Figure 5.5). This is significantly higher

than the upper ceiling permitted by the government of Nepal. For example, the maximum ceiling for migration to Qatar is NPR70,000 (USD702); however, the survey results show that the average cost of migration to Qatar is NPR94,000 (USD943). Similar findings of higher payment made by migrants are reported by the World Bank (2011). At times, the cost of migration is related to the benefit or salary being offered to the migrant. The cost of migration to countries prohibited by the Government, such as Iraq, are even higher. This has a negative impact on the economic benefits that the migrant worker may enjoy. Moreover, as most migration is financed using informal moneylenders at high interest rates (from 24–36 percent per annum; SaMi 2013b), this also reduces the economic returns for the migrant household. So how much benefit is appropriated by the different stakeholders in the migration process (recruiting agencies, health certificate providers, orientation centres, local agents) and what is left for the migrant worker requires further research.

As mentioned in the sub-section on major challenges, migration becomes economically beneficial to the migrant household only when it is successful – that is, when the migrant manages to find the job and wages as promised in the contract signed prior to departure. However, the overseas migrants often find the job and wages to be less beneficial than promised, which can put them in a vulnerable situation. It is reported that, on average, four to six months of earnings in the country of destination are required to cover the cost of overseas migration (Maharjan et al. 2015). In 2007, average annual remittances by overseas migrants were at NPR128,000–320,000 (USD1,283–3,210) (Maharjan 2010). Arter (2009) and Maharjan et al. (2015) reported average annual remittances of NPR226,158 (USD2,268) and NPR280,260 (USD2,803), respectively. The skill level of the migrant also determines the return. A semi-skilled migrant worker earns 50–100 percent more than a low or unskilled migrant worker.

Other than maximizing household income, migration also helps diversify livelihoods. As shown in the aftermath of the Gorkha earthquake of April 25, 2015, when all other sectors of the economy were negatively impacted, remittances showed positive growth (Rasul et al. 2015), in line with the thesis that remittances tend to act counter-cyclically and increase in times of economic and environmental shocks and conflict (Paulson 2000; Suleri and Savage 2006; Bettin, Presbitero and Spatafora 2014). Migrant households in earthquake-affected areas have been depending on remittances to rebuild their houses, and non-migrant households considering taking up migration to finance reconstruction. Thus an income source de-linked from local economic fluctuations and events improves the livelihood resilience of households. However, to what extent remittances are used to build diversity into livelihoods so that the benefits of migration are sustained over time is hotly debated and needs further research.

Labour situation

The out-migration of a family member reduces the total labour endowment of the household. However, as excess labour and unavailability of sufficient employment opportunities is a major driver of international labour migration (Maharjan 2010), whether or not migration actually results in a critical labour shortage and whether or not it is negative for migrant households and communities are not straightforward questions. Farming is the main economic activity in rural areas and is highly labour intensive. However, the labour requirements for agriculture are not uniform throughout the year, with peak demands during planting and harvesting seasons and lower demands at other times. In addition, farming in rural Nepal is subsistence in nature, with little profit for farmers when labour costs are included in the cost-benefit analysis. Thus, many migrant households forgo farming when the earnings from migration are sufficiently high. In some very high migration areas, the cultivation of land resources is left to the households not involved in migration, with little or no rent charged. Thus the perception of labour shortages is also conditional on how dependent the household is on farm production/incomes.

In the farming sector, to address the labour shortage, mechanization (power tillers) has been adopted in the more accessible areas and areas where farming is more commercial. There has also been an increase in wage rates in the agriculture sector over time, which can also be attributed to labour shortages. Thus the extent and perception of labour shortages is also dependent on the ability of households/communities to adopt technology and hire labour to replace the lost labour. Furthermore, for those poor households that are dependent on daily wages to sustain their livelihoods, increased wages as a result of the loss of labour from the farming sector (constriction of the supply of labour) might actually be positive.

After the earthquake on April 25, 2015, there was increased debate once again about whether Nepal should have policies to promote or discourage international labour migration. The logic behind this debate being that labour is required within the country to rebuild damaged private and public infrastructure. The press reported labour shortages for the construction of temporary shelters and in farming. However, there was no clear understanding of the actual extent of the labour shortages, if any, and if these shortages were for all labour types – namely, low-, semi- and high-skilled labour. In relation to the availability of skilled workers in the construction sector, important questions include how to identify skilled construction workers, including migrant returnees, and if it would be possible to train people for rebuilding or if the increased demand will create internal migration of skilled people. Most importantly, would the new work generated be sufficient to provide employment to all potential migrant workers and returnees, not only to sustain their livelihoods, but also to rebuild the assets lost in the earthquake? These questions, too, need a more detailed analysis in the changing situation post-earthquake.

Food security situation

For the majority of households in rural areas of Nepal, attending to household food security is very important. This is particularly so in the Far and Mid-Western

Table 7.1 Food security measure by migration status and stream in two districts of Nepal

Food security measure	Syangja		Baitadi	
	Migrant	*Non-migrant*	*Migrant*	*Non-migrant*
Perception of food insecurity (number of households)	9	27	44	61
Dietary diversity score	83.98	80.10	70.72	70.99
Per capita household expenditure (NPR)	22,250	13,923	4,757	4,444

Source: Maharjan (2010)

development regions of the country, where food insecurity issues are a regular feature of life. The importance of food security is also reflected in the responses given by surveyed households, being one of the reasons given for household migration (by more than 85 percent of households; Maharjan 2010). Food security was measured using select criteria: the household's own perception of their food security situation, dietary diversity and per capita expenditure on food and non-food goods (see Maharjan 2010 for details on the methods used in calculating these indicators). The results are presented in Table 7.1.

Overall, all measures of household food security indicate that the food security is better among migrant households than non-migrant households for both streams of migration; however, the impact is much higher for overseas migration than cross-border migration. Thus it can be concluded that overseas migration significantly improves household food security, including the quality of food intake. Cross-border migration to India, on the other hand, has a slight positive impact on overall food security, but the remittances are not large enough to impact on the quality of the food intake. Similarly, Nepal (2013) also reported that remittances have a positive influence on household food expenditure. As the earnings (as well as the savings) of migrants in cross-border migration have increased over the years, this is expected to have a positive impact on the food security situation. However, lack of research on this topic means that trends for cross-border migration are difficult to establish.

Education and skills situation

International labour migration is also expected to improve the skills and knowledge of households, particularly the education of children. Migrant workers are exposed to a new environment, new skills and new work culture, which can help in developing their self-confidence. Similarly, the new roles and responsibilities taken up by the spouse of the migrant worker, particularly when it is a nuclear household, help in developing managerial/leadership skills and self-confidence in the spouse. As a study by the Centre for the Study of Labour and Mobility (Sijapati and Subedi 2015) found, often these acquired skills are used by the migrants in further building their livelihoods or as a reintegration strategy when they return home.

One of the main areas of remittance use is the better education of children, which is expected to have a long-term impact on the capacities of the human resources of migrant households. Nearly all (97 percent) of the households surveyed in Syangja and 84 percent in Baitadi perceived that migration has helped to better educate their children (Maharjan 2010). On average, migrant households spend about 61 percent more on the education of their children than non-migrant households in overseas migration households.

The extent of the impact of migration on the education of children differs between the two migration streams. In the case of cross-border migration the impact is much lower or sometimes even negative. Cross-border migration is mostly undertaken by poor segments of society and from poor regions of the country. Thus the priority of households to meet immediate needs far outweighs the need to educate their children. Also, due to their extreme poverty, there is more pressure on the children of these poor households to be involved in household work and to migrate to earn additional income for their household. However, with increased incomes from cross-border migration in recent years, it is expected that migration will have a greater positive impact on the education of their children.

An interaction with a school in a high cross-border migration community in Sindhupalchowk district in July 2015 revealed the complexity of the impact of migration on children's education. The teachers noted that there has been an increase in school enrolment of children from migrant households, but the challenge is with their attendance, as some cross-border migrants take their children with them; thus the children miss almost six months of school each year. Also, the children lose interest in studying as they plan to follow in the footsteps of their parents and therefore consider education irrelevant. However, as the teacher highlighted, with better awareness and higher incomes from migration, more migrant households are paying attention to the education of their children. Thus indications are that, when remittances are high enough, households do prioritize investment in the education of their children.

Health situation

The impact of international labour migration on the health of migrants and their households is quite complex. On the one hand, the poor working and living conditions in the destination workplaces has been an area of huge public and media interest, and has been considered to be the reason for the poor health and high number of deaths of migrant workers (Amnesty International 2011). Cross-border migration is also considered to be a major factor in the widespread incidence of HIV/AIDs in the Far and Mid-Western Development Regions of Nepal.[8] On the other hand, migration is considered to be beneficial to the health of the families left behind. As the results from the impact on the household food security situation suggest, migrant households consume better quality and quantities of food, which has a positive impact on the health situation of the household members. In a country like Nepal, where there is no provision for health coverage by the government, access to health facilities is directly linked to the income of the household (Gartaula, Niehof and Visser 2012). Despite that, migrant households have increased purchasing capacity, giving their members better access to health care and to improving their overall health condition. The survey found annual average household spending on health care to be NPR8,171 (USD82) by migrant households and NPR4,801 (USD48) by non-migrant households in Syangja, and NPR2,937 (USD29) by migrant households and NPR2,237 (USD22) by non-migrant households in Baitadi. Nepal's (2013) study in the Eastern Development Region of Nepal and Maharjan et al.'s (2015) study in central Nepal also reported the significant and positive impact of remittances on health expenditure.

Changes in social structure and psychological impacts

When a migrant leaves the household to work abroad, the roles and responsibilities that the migrant has been undertaking within the household are distributed among other members of the household. Thus migration is expected to influence the workload of the remaining household members. The survey analysed the per capita workload by age category (see Table 7.2). The results show that in Syangja, across age and gender, household members worked more compared to their non-migrant counterparts. However, the findings were the reverse in Baitadi, except for children (Maharjan 2010). It can in general, therefore, be concluded that when migration is successful and it is a capital accumulation strategy, migration results in more leisure time. A similar result was reported by Kaspar (2005) in the Far Western Development Region of Nepal.

As international labour migration in Nepal is predominantly undertaken by young males, this has a significant impact on the household social structure, including gender roles. Nepal is a patriarchal society, in which the male members take the lead as household head in all decisions related to the household. However, when the male household head migrates, in the case of a nuclear family, the wife generally becomes the de facto household head (Kaspar 2005; Nepal 2013). This has implications for gender relations within the household. Women are taking an increasing role in household decision-making processes; however, they are more active in operational decisions than in strategic decisions (Kaspar 2005; Maharjan, Bauer and Knerr 2012). The Population Census 2011 also shows a growth in female-headed households, as well as ownership of land, houses and other assets (CBS 2012).

As migration continues and grows, these changes are not limited to households, but can also be observed at the community level. With more and more men migrating, communities are facing situations requiring structural changes. In terms of the gender division of work in Nepal, three types of activities are

Table 7.2 Average per capita workload on household members by age and gender (in months)

District	HH migration status	Children		Youth		Adult		Old	
		Male	Female	Male	Female	Male	Female	Male	Female
Syangja	Non-migrant	1.9	2.9	2.1	3.8	10.9	13.9	5.8	3.7
	Migrant	0.6	1.3	2.3	3.2	5.7	10.3	3.7	3.7
	Total	1.1	1.8	2.2	3.4	7.8	11.7	4.4	3.7
	T test	3.22***	2.75***	-.429	.752	6.05***	4.33***	1.04	.018
Baitadi	Non-migrant	1.5	1.9	2.9	4.7	13.6	12.4	6.7	3.7
	Migrant	1.0	1.2	3.9	7.5	10.6	13.2	5.5	7.9
	Total	1.3	1.6	3.4	5.9	12.3	12.8	6.0	5.8
	T test	1.71*	2.18**	-1.38	-3.16***	3.74***	-1.15	.82	-2.2**

Note: *** significant at 1 percent; ** significant at 5 percent; * significant at 10 percent.

Source: Maharjan (2010)

considered taboo for women (based on the Hindu belief system): ploughing the field, mending the roof and taking part in a funeral (administering last rites). However, it is increasingly being reported by the media that women are involved in the first two types of work. In the aftermath of the Gorkha earthquake, many women were forced to retrieve galvanized iron sheets from the roofs of destroyed houses to build temporary shelters.[9] For funerals, more and more villages are depending on support from nearby villages. A decade ago, development projects had to take additional measures to ensure the participation of women in project/community work. However, these days, there is higher participation of women in all group activities and there is no need for additional efforts to be made. Thus women's roles are diversifying from reproductive and household-based to conservation and community work.

Migration can have a negative impact on the psychosocial wellbeing of both the migrant and the household members left behind. The migrant has to live in a different environment away from home, which can cause loneliness and emotional stress (Pun 2013). The migrants interviewed by the author in Qatar in 2013 reported spending a significant portion of their earnings on telecommunication with their family at home (QAR100–200 from total monthly earnings of QAR800–1,000). Furthermore, when migrants find that their aspirations for migration are not likely to be realized, it can lead to a high degree of frustration, which increases the risk of suicide. The Department of Foreign Employment reported 306 deaths as a result of suicide in the period 2008–2009 to 2013–2014, and suicide is the third most common cause of death among migrant workers from Nepal (DoFE 2014). Other psychosocial problems[10] associated with migration include

- Marriage breakup as a result of misunderstanding and miscommunication between the spouses involved in migration
- Insecurity on the part of women household members left behind, particularly the wife of the migrant worker in the case of a nuclear family
- The migrant worker missing the emotional and physical bond with their spouse and children
- A feeling of abandonment by the children of the migrant worker, which is much stronger among children when the mother is the migrant.

The psychosocial costs generally increase with the duration of separation (Kahn et al. 2003).

8.   Conclusion and recommendations

International labour migration (cross-border and overseas) is increasingly being used as a major livelihood strategy by rural households in Nepal. This chapter has examined the household-level socioeconomic impact of international migration, both cross-border migration to India and overseas migration to Malaysia and the Gulf countries.

Overseas migration from Nepal is predominantly by men, with women accounting for only approximately 13 percent of total migrants (excluding cross-border migration to India). Most migrants are young adults with low or limited skills. Migration entails certain costs, both economic and social, which vary between the two main streams of migration. The costs are higher for overseas compared to cross-border destinations, but the returns are also higher. However, the higher returns from overseas migration are conditional on having a successful outcome. Migrants face many challenges, such as inadequate and false information about the migration process and benefits, the high cost of migration, high interest rates on loans, differences in actual work contracts and wages from those agreed in the home country, lack of vocational skills, forced retention of workers after completion of their contract, non-payment or late payment of wages, long working hours, exploitation and abuse at the workplace, and high number of deaths of migrant workers. These challenges/problems severely curtail the benefits enjoyed by migrant workers and, at times, can even push migrant households into extreme poverty and vulnerability. Although a legal and institutional framework regulating or governing the migration process and protecting the rights of migrant workers is in place, its implementation has been poor due to various factors, including resource constraints. Migration governance has a significant impact on the rights of migrant workers and the benefits accruing from migration.

Before analysing the impact of migration on the socioeconomic situation of migrant households, this chapter explored their reasons for choosing migration as a livelihood strategy and their perceptions of change in their livelihood situation. The main reason cited by households for choosing migration as a strategy has changed over the years, particularly for overseas migration. Earlier, lack of sufficient economic opportunity and food security concerns were the main reasons; however, more recently, capital accumulation and low-income locally are cited as the main reasons.

In relation to cross-border migration, changes in the reason for migration over time could not be verified due to a lack of recent studies. It still seems to be a survival strategy, rather than a capital accumulation strategy. However, the returns from cross-border migration have increased over the years.

The socioeconomic situation of households was measured in terms of changes in their economic/income situation, education, health, labour use, and household and community social structures, as well as the psychosocial impact of migration. The majority of households perceived improvement in their general livelihood situation to be a result of migration. The findings suggest a complex impact on the household socioeconomic situation, which is dependent on the outcome of the migration and also on the ability of the household to adapt to the changing situation. However, generally, migrant households had on average a higher total annual income and expenditure than non-migrant households. This situation has not changed over time. Increased income has had positive implications for average spending on food security, education, health and leisure time enjoyed by the household members. Migrant households have enjoyed better food security conditions, both in terms of the quality and quantity of food consumed, compared to non-migrant households. However, the extent of these positive impacts on the household's socioeconomic situation has differed between the two streams of migration. In general, overseas migration was much more beneficial and had significantly higher impact on improving the overall socioeconomic situation of the household than cross-border migration. However, with increases in wages in cross-border migration, the benefits have improved significantly from a decade ago.

This chapter also points to some gaps in policy and the overall understanding of migration, which need to be addressed if we are to fully understand the impact of migration. Some of the main gaps to be addressed by research include the following:

- There is very little panel data on migration and its impact at the household level. In the absence of concrete data and research on the topic, it is difficult to establish the impact of migration over time and for the various migration streams. There is a strong need for further research on the different streams of migration and their evolution over time to better understand their impacts on household livelihoods.
- There are institutional and policy frameworks in place for the governance of overseas migration, however, there are none for cross-border migration. As cross-border migration is an important livelihood strategy for the poorest segments of society, a framework for the governance of this type of migration and the protection of the rights of migrant workers would help in reducing poverty.
- The Ministry of Labour and Employment is mandated solely to govern the migration process and protect migrant workers' rights. However, the challenges facing this sector go beyond the mandate of this ministry, making it difficult to solve the problems. Unless there is policy coherence and concerted action across the various government institutions involved, the good governance of migration will remain elusive.
- One of the most highlighted negative consequences of labour migration is the labour shortage in Nepal. However, there is a need to study the actual shortage and the ability of households to cope with this shortage through adoption of new technologies.
- The productive use of remittances for the sustainable development of household livelihoods is particularly under-researched. There is also no clear policy promoting the productive use of remittances for local economic development.
- The social and psychological costs of migration are often overlooked, and there is scant research on this issue. Apart from some work by non-government organization, there are no institutions, policies or strategies dealing with these costs or aiming to reduce them in the future.

There is no question that remittance plays an important role for migrant households as well as for the nation. However, there are still gaps in understanding how to make migration and remittance work for sustainable development of the migrant households, communities and the nation as a whole. It is hoped that this study will inform the policy makers of the impact that migration has on household socioeconomic situations, and guide further research to increase the benefits to migrant households and protect the rights of migrant workers.

Notes

1 This study was partially supported by core funds of ICIMOD contributed by the governments of Afghanistan, Australia, Austria, Bangladesh, Bhutan, China, India, Myanmar, Nepal, Norway, Pakistan, Switzerland and the United Kingdom.
2 Exchange rate on April 2015: USD1 = NPR99.7.
3 This is based on the experience of the author working as a team leader for the Safer Migration Project in Nepal from November 2011 to July 2013. The two main components of this project are the establishment of an information and counselling centre and the establishment of a legal aid clinic. The cases reported to the information centre and legal aid clinic highlight these issues in the governance of overseas migration (SaMi 2013a).
4 A few initiatives, including those of the Safer Migration Project, are trying to decentralize the information flow to reach rural pockets of Nepal.
5 As reported by hundreds of migrant workers interviewed during a week-long visit to Qatar by the author in February 2013 to identify the key problems faced by Nepali migrant workers in destination countries.
6 An observation reported by the migrant organization, Pravasi Nepali Coordination Committee, on their experience of different problems in different destinations.
7 This is based on information collected as part of an International Centre for Integrated Mountain Development (ICIMOD) study 'Migration and the 2015 Gorkha Earthquake Nepal – Effect on Rescue and Relief Processes and Recovery Plans' during June–July 2015, in Sindhupalchowk and Nuwakot districts.
8 http://www.worldbank.org/en/news/feature/2012/07/10/hiv-aids-nepal
9 http://www.myrepublica.com/opinion/item/24346-wrong-conversation.html
10 Based on discussions with forty returnee women migrant workers and interviews with the wives of migrants in 2013.

References

Adams, RHJ 2005, *Remittances, Household Expenditure and Investment in Guatemala*, World Bank Policy Research Working Paper Series 3532, World Bank, Washington, DC.

ADB (Asian Development Bank) 2015, *Asian Development Outlook 2015: Financing Asia's Future Growth*. Asian Development Bank, Philippines.

Ale, LB 2004, *International Labour Migration: A Case Study of Pumdi Bhumdi VDC, Kaski District*, Unpublished MA Thesis, Department of Geography, Tribhuwan University, Kathmandu, Nepal.

Amnesty International 2011, *False Promises: Exploitation and Forced Labour of Nepalese Migrant Workers*, Amnesty International, London.

148   *Amina Maharjan*

Amuedo-Dorantes, C and Pozo, S 2006a, 'Migration, Remittances and Male and Female Employment Patterns', *American Economic Review*, vol. 96, no. 2, pp. 222–6.

Amuedo-Dorantes, C and Pozo, S 2006b, *International Migration, Remittances and the Education of Children: The Dominican Case*, Working Paper, Western Michigan University.

Arter, F 2009, 'Remittances to the Kathmandu Valley and Their Economical Impacts', Master Thesis, Erasmus University, Rotterdam, Netherlands.

Bettin, G, Presbitero, AF, and Spatafora, N 2014, *Remittances and Vulnerability in Developing Countries*, IMF Working Paper WP/14/13, International Monetary Fund.

Cattaneo, C 2010, *Migrants' International Transfer and Educational Expenditure: Empirical Evidence from Albania*, Fondazione Eni Enrico Mattei Working Papers, Paper 391, Berkeley Electronic Press, Berkeley, CA.

CBS (Central Bureau of Statistics) 2011, *Nepal Living Standard Survey 2010/11*, Central Bureau of Statistics, Government of Nepal, Kathmandu.

CBS (Central Bureau of Statistics) 2012, *National Population and Housing Census 2011*, National Planning Commission Secretariat, Government of Nepal, Kathmandu.

Cox-Edwards, A and Ureta, M 2003, 'International Migration, Remittances and Schooling: Evidence from El Salvador', *Journal of Development Economics*, vol. 72, no. 2, pp. 429–61.

De Haas, H 2007, *Remittances, Migration and Social Development – A Concept Review of the Literature*, Social Policy and Development Programme Paper No. 34, UN Research Institute for Social Development, Geneva.

DoFE (Department of Foreign Employment) 2014, *Labour Migration for Employment: A Status Report for Nepal: 2013/14*, Department of Foreign Employment, Ministry of Labour and Employment, Government of Nepal, Kathmandu.

Gartaula, H, Niehof, A, and Visser, L 2012, 'Socio-cultural Dispositions and Well-being of the Women Left behind: A Case of Migrant Households in Nepal', *Social Indicators Research*, vol. 108, no. 3, pp. 401–20.

Ghosh, B 1992, 'Migration-development Interlinkages: Some Specific Issues and Practical Policy Measures', *International Migration*, vol. 30, no. 3–4, pp. 423–56.

Grigorian, DA and Melkonyan, TA 2011, 'Destined to Receive: the Impact of Remittances on Household Decision in Armenia', *Review of Development Economics*, vol. 15, no. 1, pp. 139–53.

Hanson, GH 2005, *Emigration, Labour Supply and Earnings in Mexico*, National Bureau of Economic Research Working Papers No. 11412.

Hanson, GH and Woodruff, C 2003, *Emigration and Educational Attainment in Mexico*, Mimeo, University of California, San Diego.

Hildebrant, N and McKenzie, D 2005, 'The Effects of Migration on Child Health in Mexico', *Economica*, vol. 6, no. 1, pp. 257–89.

Jones, RC 1998, 'Remittances and Inequality: A Question of Migration Stage and Geographical Scale', *Economic Geography*, vol. 74, no. 1, pp. 8–25.

Kahn, K, Collison, M, Tollman, M, Wolff, B, Garenne, M, and Clark, S 2003, *Health Consequences of Migration: Evidence from South Africa's Rural Northeast (Agincourt)*, Paper Prepared for Conference on African Migration in Comparative Perspective, Johannesburg, South Africa, 4–7 June 2003.

Kansakar, VBS 2003, 'International Migration and Citizenship in Nepal', in *Population Monograph of Nepal 2003*, vol. II, National Planning Commission Secretariat, Government of Nepal, Central Bureau of Statistics, Kathmandu, pp. 85–119.

Kaspar, H 2005, '*I Am the Household Head Now!' Gender Aspects of Out-migration for Labour in Nepal*, Nepal Institute of Development Studies, Kathmandu, Nepal.

Koc, I and Onan, I 2004, 'International Migrants' Remittances and Welfare Status of the Left-behind Families in Turkey', *International Migration Review*, vol. 38, no. 1, pp. 78–112.

Lokshin, M, Bontch-Osmolovski, M, and Glinskaya, E 2010, 'Work-related Migration and Poverty Reduction in Nepal', *Review of Development Economics*, vol. 14, pp. 323–32.

Lopez-Cordoba, JE 2006, *Globalization, Migration, and Development: The Role of Mexican Migrant Remittances*, Mimeo, the Inter-American Development Bank, Washington, DC.

Lucas, REB 1987, 'Emigration to South-Africa's Mines', *The American Economic Review*, vol. 77, no. 3, pp. 313–30.

Maharjan, A 2010, 'Labour Out Migration and Its Impact on Farm Families in the Mid Hills of Nepal', in W Doppler and S Bauer (eds), *Farming and Rural Systems Economics*, vol. 113, Margraf Publishers, Weikersheim, Germany.

Maharjan, A, Bauer, S, and Knerr, B 2012, 'Do Rural Women Who Stay behind Benefit from Male Out-migration: A Case Study in the Hills of Nepal', *Gender, Technology and Development*, vol. 16, no. 1, pp. 95–123.

Maharjan, S, Knerr, B, and Maharjan, A 2015, 'Labour Migration as a Household Strategy to Reduce Poverty – A Case in Nepal', Paper Presented at the University of Kassel Germany Alumni Workshop *Research on Migration from Nepal*, Kathmandu, 19–20 March 2015.

Mansuri, G 2006, *Migration, School Attainment and Child Labour: Evidence from Rural Pakistan*, World Bank Policy Research Working Paper 3945, World Bank Publications, Washington, DC.

Massey, DS, Arango, J, Hugo, G, Kouaouci, A, Pellegrino, A, and Taylor, JE 1993, 'Theories of International Migration: A Review and Appraisal', *Population and Development Review*, vol. 19, pp. 431–66.

McKenzie, D 2006, *Beyond Remittances: The Effects of Migration on Mexican Households*, World Bank, <http://siteresources.worldbank.org/DEC/Resources/310436360_200509297001236.pdf>.

McKenzie, DJ and Rapoport, H 2010, 'Can Migration Reduce Educational Attainment? Evidence from Mexico', *Journal of Population Economics*, vol. 24, no. 4, pp. 1331–58.

Mendola, M 2010, 'Rural Out-migration and Economic Development', *Journal of International Development*, vol. 24, no. 1, pp. 102–22.

Ministry of Finance (MoF) 2014, *Economic Survey Fiscal Year 2013/14*, Ministry of Finance, Government of Nepal, Kathmandu.

Nepal, R 2013, *Remittances and Livelihood Strategies: A Case Study in Eastern Nepal*, Kassel University Press, Kassel, Germany.

NRB (Nepal Rastra Bank) 2008, *Household Budget Survey, Nepal (Mid-November 2005-mid-November 2006*, Household Budget Survey Project Office, Nepal Rastra Bank, Kathmandu.

Orozco, M 2003, *Remittances, the Rural Sector, and Policy Options in Latin America*, USAID and BASIS Collaborative Research Support Programme (CRSP).

Paudel, KP and Adhikari, J 2012, *The Local Food System, Livelihoods and Its Political Economy. Food and Agriculture in Nepal: Situation, Policies and Scope*, Study Report, Action Aid Nepal.

Paulson AL 2000, *Insurance Motives for Migration: Evidence from Thailand*, viewed 7 March 2016, <http://www.kellogg.northwestern.edu/faculty/paulson/ftp/thaimig.pdf>.

Ponce, J, Olivié, I, and Onofa, M 2011, 'The Role of International Remittances in Health Outcomes in Ecuador: Prevention and Response to Shocks', *International Migration Review*, vol. 45, no. 3, pp. 727–45.

Pun, R 2013, *Social and Psychological Costs of Labor Migration on Rural Areas of Nepal*, MSc Thesis, Asian Institute of Technology, Thailand.

Rasul, G, Sharma, B, Mishra, B, Neupane, N, Dorji, T, Khadka, M, and Joshi, S 2015, *Strategic Framework for Resilient Livelihoods in Earthquake Affected Areas of Nepal*, ICIMOD Working Paper 2015/6, ICIMOD, Kathmandu.

Ratha, D, Mohapatra, S, and Scheja, E 2011, *Impact of Migration on Economic and Social Development. A Review of Evidence and Emerging Issues*, Policy Research Working Paper 5558, Migration and Remittances Unit and Poverty Reduction and Economic Management Network, World Bank, Washington, DC.

SaMi (Safer Migration Project) 2013a, SaMi – Achievement and Reflections 2011–13, HELVETAS Swiss Intercooperation, Nepal.

SaMi (Safer Migration Project) 2013b, *SaMi – Baseline Survey Report. Safer Migration Project*, HELVETAS Swiss Intercooperation, Nepal.

Seddon, D 2005, *Nepal's Dependence on Exporting Labour*, Country Profile, Migration Information Source, viewed 7 March 2016, <http://www.migrationinformation.org/Feature/display.cfm?id=277>.

Shahi, MB 2005, 'International Labour Migration from Bajhang to India: A Case Study of Lamatola VDC, Bajhang District, Nepal', Unpublished MA Thesis in Geography, Central Department of Geography, Faculty of Humanities and Social Sciences, Tribhuwan University, Kathmandu.

Sharma, MP 2013, 'International Contract-based Migration, Remittances, and Household Well-being in the Western Province of Sri Lanka', *International Migration*, vol. 51, no. s1, pp. 1–33.

Shrestha, B 2004, *Foreign Employment and the Remittance Economy of Nepal: The Nepalese Economy: Towards Building a Strong Economic Nation-state*, Tribhuvan University, Central Department of Economics (CEDECON), Kathmandu.

Sijapati, B and Limbu, A 2012, *Governing Labour Migration in Nepal: An Analysis of Existing Policies and Institutional Mechanisms*, Centre for the Study of Labour and Mobility, Kathmandu, Nepal.

Sijapati, B and Subedi, BP 2015, *Case Study on the Role of Financial and Social Remittances in Supporting Rural Microenterprise Development in Nepal*, Centre for the Study of Labour and Mobility, Social Science Baha, Kathmandu, Nepal.

Stark, O, Taylor, JE, and Yitzhaki, S 1986, 'Remittances and Inequality', *The Economic Journal*, vol. 96, pp. 722–40.

Suleri, AQ and Savage, K 2006, *Remittances in Crises: A Case Study from Pakistan*, A Humanitarian Policy Group Background Paper, Overseas Development Institute, London.

Taylor, JE 1999, 'The New Economics of Labour Migration and the Role of Remittances in the Migration Process', *International Migration*, vol. 37, no. 1, pp. 63–88.

Taylor, JE and Martin, P 2001, 'Human Capital: Migration and Rural Population Change', *Handbook for Agricultural Economics*, vol. 1, part A, pp. 457–511.

Taylor, JE and Wyatt, TJ 1996, 'The Shadow Value of Migrant Remittances, Income and Inequality in a Household-farm Economy', *Journal of Development Studies*, vol. 32, no. 6, pp. 899–912.

Thieme, S and Wyss, S 2005, 'Migration Patterns and Remittance Transfer in Nepal: A Case Study of Sainik Basti in Western Nepal', *International Migration*, vol. 43, no. 5, pp. 59–98.

UNDP (United Nations Development Program) 2009, *Overcoming Barriers: Human Mobility and Development*, United Nations Development Program, New York.

UNDP (United Nations Development Program) 2015, *Human Development Report 2014. Work for Human Development*, United Nations Development Program, New York.

Wasti, K 2012, *Status and Use of Remittances in the Mountains of Nepal*, Unpublished MSc Thesis, Asian Institute of Technology, Thailand.

Williams, NE, Thornton, A, Ghimire, DJ, Young-DeMarco, LC, and Moaddel, M 2012, 'Nepali Migrants to the Gulf Cooperation Council Countries: Behaviors, Plans, and Values,' in M Kamrava and Z Babar (eds), *Migrant Labor in the Persian Gulf*, pp. 155–85, London: Hurst & Co.

World Bank 2011, *Large Scale Migration and Remittance in Nepal: Issues, Challenges, and Opportunities*, World Bank, Washington, DC.

World Bank 2015, *Migration and Remittances: Recent Development and Outlooks. Special Topic: Financing for Development*. Migration and Development Brief 24, World Bank, Washington, DC.

World Bank 2016, *World Development Indicators: Statistical Annex Tables*, Updated 10 August 2016, viewed 26 September 2016, <http://data.worldbank.org/indicator/BX.TRF.PWKR.DT.GD.ZS?locations=NP>.

World Travel and Tourism Council 2014, *Travel and Tourism: Economic Impact 2014, Nepal*, WTTC, London.

Yang, D 2008, 'International Migration, Remittances, and Household Investment: Evidence from Philippine Migrants' Exchange Rate Shocks', *Economic Journal*, vol. 118, pp. 591–630.

Zarate-Hoyos, G 2004, 'Consumption and Remittances in Migrant Households: Towards a Productive Use of Remittances', *Contemporary Economic Policy*, vol. 22, no. 4, pp. 555–65.

8 South to South migration in Asia

Opportunities, challenges and policy implications for the Sustainable Development Goals of the 2030 agenda for sustainable development

Yuko Hamada

1. Introduction[1]

International labour migration presents numerous opportunities and challenges for both sending and receiving countries, migrants and their families. According to the United Nations, in 2015 there were over 244 million international migrants in the world (United Nations 2016a), with 64 percent of this group (157 million) originating from middle-income countries (United Nations 2016b). The International Labour Organization (ILO) estimates 150.3 million of those migrants are migrant workers (ILO 2015) and that 53 percent live in the global North or developed regions, such as North America (76 million) and Europe (54 million). Between 1990 and 2013, the number of international migrants worldwide rose by over 50 percent to over 77 million, and much of this growth occurred between 2000 and 2010 (United Nations 2013). Some 4.6 million migrants were added annually between 2000 and 2010, compared to an average of 2 million per annum during the period 1990–2000 and 3.6 million per annum between 2010 and 2013 (United Nations 2013).

Of the 53 million international migrants added to the North between 1990 and 2013, 42 million (78 percent) were born in the South (United Nations 2013). In the global South or developing regions, migrant population growth results mainly from the South. Compared to South-North movement, South-South migration flows continued to grow and exceed South-North migration in total volume. In 2015, 90.2 million international migrants born in developing countries were living in other countries in the global South, while 85.3 million born in the South lived in countries in the Global North (IOM c2015). A significant common denominator between these diverse migrant populations is the need to acquire financial resources and the desire to channel portions of that to family members.

Remittances are a vital international labour migration product totalling around USD435 billion in 2014, and remaining steady though growth has slowed due to downturns in the economies of major remittance-sending countries (World Bank 2014, 2016). Six of the top ten remittance recipient countries are in Asia: India (USD71 billion), China (USD64 billion), Philippines (USD28 billion), Bangladesh (USD17 billion), Pakistan (USD15 billion) and Vietnam (USD11 billion) (World Bank 2014, p. 4). For some countries, remittances constitute a significant proportion of gross domestic product (GDP). For example, Tajikistan (42 percent), Kyrgyz Republic (32 percent) and Nepal (29 percent) are countries where remittances as a proportion of GDP are among the highest in the world (World Bank 2014, p. 4). For these countries, international migration is currently necessary for economic sustenance as well as growth.

Despite the benefits remittances yield to the economies of countries of origin, they come at a cost measured in personal safety, security and welfare of the migrant workers themselves when they are in the countries of destination. Their working conditions are often challenging and frequently unsafe, and migrant workers have little access to social services such as health care and other public services, including education for their family members. The current weakness in migration governance, labour laws and social protection mechanism for migrants moving within South-South migration corridors contributes to these challenges.

The formal labour migration process remains time-consuming, expensive and complicated. This causes many migrant workers to choose irregular migration channels over the legal channels, increasing the vulnerability of migrant workers. Migrant workers should be accorded the same protection as native workers, but this does not always happen in practice (Article 6 of ILO Convention 143; ILO 1975). However, for many receiving countries, ILO Convention 143 has not catalysed the creation of adequate national policies and practices. The inequalities in protection-related labour market regulations remain a challenge for migrants working within the South-South corridor.

In Asia, due to economic and demographic disparities, as well as geographic and cultural proximities, migrants move to the growing economies that are represented by Newly Industrialized Countries (NICs).[2] Among the NICs, India, Malaysia and Thailand also receive large numbers of foreign workers from other NICs as well as from developing countries in Asia. For instance, Malaysia receives large numbers of foreign workers from Bangladesh, Nepal, Indonesia, Myanmar and India. Thailand is a destination for neighbouring countries such as Myanmar, Cambodia, Lao People's Democratic Republic, as well as Bangladesh and India.

The goal of this chapter is to identify Asia-to-Asia migration policy gaps, especially in relation to the challenges faced by migrant workers, and present suggestions on how the SDGs provide guidance to address these issues. The chapter includes a desk review of various scholars' publications to address the issues of migrant safety, security and income. The chapter also provides an examination of discussions surrounding the SDGs and how these relate to the challenges faced by migrant workers.

The focus in this chapter is on working and living conditions faced by migrant workers in developing Asian destination countries. For those migrants with irregular status, the human security issues are even more serious than those related to safety and security of work and accommodation. Migrant workers frequently lack access to social security, and there are few prospects for job training or skills development, along with little overall job security. Migrant workers seek employment abroad to earn a better income since, in many cases, they receive higher wages than they would receive in their home countries. Migrant workers, however, often face problems such as delayed payment, debt bondage, and confiscation of personal documentation as a result of unethical recruitment and employment practices.

To maximize the gains from migration, it is essential to improve the wellbeing of migrant workers in countries of destination. Ensuring the welfare of migrant workers leads to work efficiency and greater production, whereas human and labour rights violations negatively affect the workers and their families as well as the reputations of labour-receiving countries. In many respects, countries of origin have a better understanding of migration as part of the global development agenda than countries of destination. Countries of origin are developing sustainable ways to utilize migration (and the remittances that result from these migrations) for their own national development goals, and they have a growing understanding regarding the link between migration and development. For many countries of destination, incorporating migration within the global development agenda does not align with their national priorities – migrant workers are considered only a temporary solution to labour shortages to accomplish time-bound tasks. In recognition of this discrepancy, this chapter highlights the message of the Sustainable Development Goals (SDG) of the 2030 Agenda for Sustainable Development[3] regarding the importance of recognizing the positive contribution of migrants to inclusive growth and sustainable development, not only in the countries of origin but also in destination countries. It further discusses the need to capture migration in a regional economic development context rather than being defined as South-South migration, and achieving this will require an enhanced level of cooperation between labour-sending and receiving countries.

If the policies of labour-sending and labour-receiving countries converge and are reflective of the SDG's and relevant conventions, migrants and mobile populations will benefit from an improved standard of physical, mental and social wellbeing, which enables them to contribute more substantially towards the social and economic development of their home communities and host societies (IOM 2013c). As stated by the World Health Organization (WHO), 'addressing the health needs of migrants can improve their health status, avoids stigma and long-term health and social costs, protects global public health, facilitates integration, and contributes to social and economic development' (WHO 2010). Policies tend to emphasize the contribution of migrants through remittance flows rather than focusing efforts on ensuring the wellbeing of migrants during their employment. Addressing both elements is critical to maximizing the effectiveness of migrants' performance and the development outcomes of labour migration.

2. Migration experiences in the context of safety, security and income in countries of destination

South-South migrant workers in Asia are primarily engaged in low-skilled work such as construction, heavy industry, plantations, agriculture, fishing, food processing, forestry and domestic services. Such occupations are so-called 3D jobs – dirty, dangerous and/or difficult (Koser 2010). Due to the nature of work, these jobs are not popular among nationals. They tend to pay relatively low wages with poor employment conditions and have no or little opportunity for skills development or upward mobility.

Even when working in environments with a higher propensity for exploitation, some migrant workers have positive experiences while others are markedly different. The following section provides a desk review of various scholars' publications about migrants' experiences, particularly in relation to migrant safety, security and income, and to highlight policies which improve the conditions of migrant labour.

2.1 Safety of migrant workers

What kind of safety concerns do migrant workers face in the South destination countries, and what impact does migration have on families left behind? There are two primary settings where migrants may face safety concerns: the workplace and living place.

For the workplace, every country has occupational health and safety (OSH) standards. South-South migrant workers are frequently based where OSH standards are poor or not applied to them. Safety levels can significantly differ according to the categories of migrant workers' occupations.

Safety concerns and exposure greatly depend on the work settings and type. For example, construction and farm workers may work long hours in the heat and dust in contrast to domestic workers. Domestic workers normally work in the house, and they often end up working longer hours with minimal rest due to the fact that they live on-site with their bosses. Workers in the agricultural sector, animal husbandry and forestry work are exposed to animals, insecticides, harmful chemical compounds, and dust and heat exposure. For manufacturing and construction workers such as bricklayers, blacksmiths, drivers and plumbers, the risks are associated with the use of construction tools, heavy lifting, handling hazardous chemicals, electrical hazards and fire hazards. Service sector workers tend to face long working hours using sharp objects with minimal rest.

Migrants also often have poor living conditions. Low minimum wages, long working hours and family obligations force workers to minimize their daily expenditures, thereby impacting on their quality of life. IOM's *Fishermen's Report* study conducted in 2007, interviewed migrant fishermen and revealed something of their living conditions:

> Living quarters on fishing boats are extremely cramped, divided into squares
> for the crew, providing enough room to sleep but little space for much

else. No toilets exist on small- or medium-sized fishing boats, and the need to conserve fresh water and food on long trips means both hygiene and nutrition are poor.

(IOM 2011)

In addition to jobs where living quarters are provided, or lack of other alternatives such as those working in the fishing industry, workers are constrained by their wage levels and have to share rented rooms with several other workers. The compounds are often found in close proximity to the industrial parks where infrastructure is undeveloped, where there is a lack adequate security during the evening, and rooms are often unhygienic and lack the design features to prevent flooding during the rainy season (ILO 2012). Moreover, migrant workers have to pay above-average prices for electricity and water, meaning they have less money to spend on other necessities such as health services. These factors leave migrant workers weak, vulnerable to disease, and highly stressed (ILO 2012).

2.2   Security

Safety and security are interconnected. Security is a broad concept, and it has various dimensions. There are two ways of looking at security in countries of destination: 'migration as a security risk' and 'security of migrants'. The securitization of migration was heightened after the 9/11 attacks and subsequent terrorist attacks. Many countries have tightened immigration controls, impacting on the opportunities for migrants seeking employment opportunities abroad (Pinyol-Jiménez 2012). The security issue can be divided into three categories: human security, social security and job security.

2.2.1   Human security

Human security describes the wellbeing of human beings. In the UN General Assembly Resolution 'Follow-up to paragraph 143 on human security of the 2005 World Summit Outcome' on September 10, 2012, human security refers to

> The right of people to live in freedom and dignity, free from poverty and despair. All individuals, in particular, vulnerable people, are entitled to freedom from fear and freedom from want, with an equal opportunity to enjoy all their rights and fully develop their human potential.

(United Nations 2012a)

South-South migration brings specific human security concerns, and two groups which require specific attention are female domestic workers and irregular migrants.

Many women are engaged as domestic workers in developing countries within the South. There are 83,066 migrant domestic workers from Cambodia, Lao People's Democratic Republic, and Myanmar registered with Thai authorities

(ILO 2013b; Huguet 2014). Nepalese women travel to Gulf Cooperation Councils (GCC) countries as domestic workers (Kim 2015). In 2010 there were 310,402 female domestic workers in Kuwait (Thimothy and Sasikumar 2012). Domestic work is considered as an informal sector, where workers often work in a house isolated from others. The experiences of female domestic workers, however, are seldom brought into the broader discussions surrounding human security. Wickramasekara describes the human security issues of women domestic workers as follows:

> Confinement to private homes, poor language skills, insufficient knowledge about their rights, and rules under some migration programs that allow employers to confiscate passports or otherwise control the migrants' ability to stay in the country – all have led to sexual harassment and abuse.
>
> (Wickramasekara 2002)

Many scholars raise similar concerns. For example, Castles and Miller in their *Age of Migration* quote Gumburd, saying that 'women domestic workers are highly vulnerable to exploitation and sexual abuse, and it is difficult to the authorities of their countries of origin to provide protection' (Gumburd 2005; Castles and Miller 2009).

Ratha and Shaw point out that women in South-South migration generally lack access to legal migration channels leading to human security vulnerabilities. Women have unequal access to formal migration channels – because they have less access to information, less education, and because there are fewer established migration routes and networks to serve them, they are highly vulnerable to situations of risk, including trafficking. (Ratha and Shaw 2007). Additionally, female domestic workers are charged high fees by recruitment agencies and often enter into a workplace without prior knowledge of working terms and conditions. The majority of them also have language barriers further isolating them from the society in which they work (ILO 2013b; Huguet 2014).

Human security concerns are linked to irregular migration. According to the ILO's report, irregular migration is believed to be particularly high in India and Pakistan, largely due to cross-border movements from Bangladesh into India and from Afghanistan into Pakistan (Wickramasekara 2011). In addition, there is a high rate of trafficking of women and children across the border from Bangladesh and Nepal into India (Wickramasekara 2011).

As a consequence of utilizing irregular routes, migrant workers are exposed to increased human security concerns while, at the same time, they are less likely to access formal complaint channels. Human trafficking and smuggling are considered a significant problem when it comes to ensuring human security in this region. Often women and young girls are promised lucrative jobs and better lives, only to find themselves becoming victims of trafficking and smuggling at a later stage of the migration process. For example, in the Greater Mekong Sub-region (GMS), all countries have cases of trafficking, but the largest trends can be seen from Lao People's Democratic Republic, Cambodia and Myanmar to Thailand and from Vietnam to Cambodia (Soda 2009; ADB and IOM 2013).

Lastly, human security concerns arise from discrimination or xenophobia toward migrant workers. Many workers suffer from discrimination based on skin colour, cultural differences, and ethnic or national origin, and this manifests itself in racism, xenophobia, intolerance, exclusion, violation of rights and ethnic and religious conflicts, both in the workplace and within society at large (ILO 2007b). Violence toward migrant workers is unacceptably common. In Pakistan, official statistics show that tribal and indigenous people migrating from the tribal areas in the Gulf countries (mainly construction sector) are largely undocumented migrant workers compared to other groups, and this is attributed to their lack of access to official channels of migration and official travel documents (ILO 2007a).

2.2.2   Social security

Social security provides an opportunity for a migrant to access social safety nets. It is a public policy measure aimed to protect members of society from economic and social distress (ILO 2010). Instead of focusing on the traditional notion of national security, social security focuses on the individual; it holds a person-centric approach that ensures human security. The ILO has a dedicated convention for social security, C102 – Social Security (Minimum Standards) Convention, 1952 (No. 102) – which states that 'social security is the protection that society provides to individuals and households to ensure access to health care and to guarantee income security, particularly in cases of old age, unemployment, sickness, invalidity, work injury, maternity or loss of a breadwinner' (ILO 2003). The convention has nine components: medical care, sickness benefit, unemployment benefit, old-age benefit, employment injury benefit, family benefit, maternity benefit, invalidity benefit, survivor's benefit and standards to be complied with by periodic payments (ILO 1952).

Migrant workers undertaking South-South migration in Asia often lack access to social security. There are no standardized social security schemes in many countries of destination for migrant workers; they vary from country to country as well as employer to employer. Prohibitions on the entry of family members and limitations on the reproductive health of migrant workers, for example, are often specified in Memorandums of Understanding (MOU) between countries of origin and destination. Malaysia is a good example, where many migrant workers in plantation industries are insured for occupational health and injuries. However, migrant workers' families do not receive any health insurance or access to other critical services such as education, as many family members are undocumented.

Studies, including those from Migrant Forum in Asia (MFA) and Friedrich-Ebert-Stiftung in Indonesia, the Philippines, Thailand and Singapore, have investigated migrant workers' access to social security. They note that migrant workers may either directly or indirectly be denied access to social protection by their home state or destination country, or they may be employed in informal or other sectors of the economy which make them ineligible for full social protection. In addition, there is often a large gap between migrants having rights to social protection in theory and gaining access to those rights and benefits in practice (MFA and Friedrich-Ebert-Stiftung 2011).

According to an ADB and IOM joint publication, many migrant workers from Cambodia to Thailand complained about limited access to health services, which is especially worrying given the long working hours in unhygienic environments and extreme temperatures (ADB and IOM 2013). The complaints contradict the law which states that migrants registering for a work permit are required to pass a health screening for seven diseases/health conditions (tuberculosis, malaria, elephantiasis/filariasis, syphilis, leprosy, drug addiction/alcoholism and intestinal worms). Once his/her health status is approved, he/she receives a health insurance card that links his/her health insurance benefits to the hospital where he/she underwent the health screening and was registered (Press 2014).

There are three major reasons that is it difficult for migrants and their families to access health services in Thailand, despite there being universal health care for migrant workers. Firstly, migrant workers cannot afford to pay for health services. The cost of modern health systems in Asia is often very high and therefore unaffordable for many migrants (United Nations 2012b). For example, the health examination, which migrants must undergo annually in Thailand, costs Thai Baht (THB) 600,[4] and migrants are also required to pay an annual fee of THB2,200[5] (Press 2014). The fee is often paid in advance by the employer and then deducted from the migrant's wages. For some migrants, this amount might be a burden, especially if employers refuse or delay payment. Secondly, a fear of deportation deters migrants with irregular status from accessing health services. In some instances, documentation to prove regular status has been seized by employers resulting in the same fear (ADB and IOM 2013). Lastly, migrant workers may be hesitant to go to clinics or hospitals, as they cannot speak the language of the destination country. An IOM study assessing the health vulnerability of migrants in Bangladesh, Nepal and Pakistan identified the high costs of health care and language barriers as key reasons that migrants fail to seek appropriate health care while abroad (IOM 2015). Forty-nine percent of Bangladeshi and 32 percent of Pakistani migrant workers found health care unaffordable in destination countries, and consequently many chose to abstain from both treatment and health insurance (IOM 2015).

While migrant workers are often not entitled to social benefits in countries of destination, they also risk losing social benefits from their countries of origin, as many do not pay taxes while working abroad. The ILO describes the conditions of migrant workers with regards to social security as follows:

> They may contribute to social security schemes, either in their home countries or countries of destination, but may not receive any corresponding benefit. They may face constraints in the portability of these rights. Schemes may have long residency requirements, making it difficult for temporary

migrants to claim their benefits, effectively amounting to exclusion from any form of social protection when engaged in temporary or informal work.

(ILO 1952)

This is an issue which needs to be raised by countries of origin. Currently, there are insufficient policies in countries of origin to protect social benefits of migrant workers and their families (at home or abroad).

2.2.3   *Job security*

Many migrant workers in Asia engaged in South-South migration do not have job security. Migrant workers can easily be dismissed and have little opportunity to seek alternative employment after existing contracts end.

There are two ways to determine length and security of employment. One is through a government-to-government or multilateral agreement such as an MOU, and another is through employment contracts. An MOU is often used to manage labour migration between countries and typically describes the period of contracts and limitations of contracts' extension (Victorian Government Solicitor's Office 2015).

Many countries of destination under South-South migration do not plan to bring foreign workers for the long term, and they try to reduce dependence on foreign labour. In the absence of long-term commitments, another way to determine the length and security of employment is through employment contracts. Most employment contracts are short-term (six months to one year) and do not allow changes of employers. This means that migrant workers typically have to stay with the same employer until the contract ends or until they are eligible for a new contract with the same employer or a separate employer. In these conditions, the prospect of migrant workers improving their skills and developing their human resources in countries of destination is very limited.

2.3   *Income*

The income difference in countries under South-South migration is relatively small when compared to South-North migration. It is the availability of employment rather than significantly higher wages in destination countries (NICs), which is the key pull factor. A study conducted by Pearson, Punpuing, Jampaklay, Kittisuksathit and Prohmmo (2006) on the realities of young migrant workers in Thailand found that 89 percent of domestic workers and 38 percent of agricultural workers are paid THB3,000[6] or less per month, and some 41 percent of domestic workers receive THB1,000[7] or less per month, which is less than domestic workers with similar employment and below the Official Poverty Line of Thailand (Development Evaluation and Communication Office 2004).

There are three significant problems that migrant workers face in terms of income within the South-South migration context: delays in or failure to make payments, high migration debt to income ratios and the high costs of remittance.

Many migrant workers often face delays in payment (ILO 2014) and many contracts do not mention when the payment will be made, particularly in the informal sector. Most domestic workers in Thailand, for example, do not even have contracts. Even if they do have contracts, payment terms are often not detailed. It has been reported that Cambodian migrant workers in Thailand often have to accept delayed payment or underpayment of wages (ADB and IOM 2013). It is also difficult to seek legal recourse as many of the workers' travel documents are withheld (ADB and IOM 2013). Without travel documents, the migrant workers are unable to prove their legal status and thus are ineligible for legal support. There are also cases of non-payment. A one-year research study on the level of labour exploitation occurring in four sectors in Thailand – agriculture, domestic work, fishing (fishing boats and fish processing) and manufacturing (textiles) – presented the testimonial of a seventeen-year-old Cambodian female migrant domestic worker who said:

> I worked for two years but never received any payment. I had to work all day. I couldn't go to bed until 2 am, but would then have to get up again at 5 am. I didn't have enough sleep. The employer was evil-minded, not only did he not pay me any money, but he also slapped, hit and pinched me. His wife laughed while he slapped me. She never tried to help. Their three children also hurt me; they were always telling lies to their parents and getting me into trouble.
>
> (Pearson et al. 2006, p. xiv)

It was also reported in the study that migrant workers are often financially sanctioned for 'mistakes' such as taking a sick day off, for damaging stock or equipment or for being tardy. Nearly 50 percent of all workers in the fishing sector received late payment, and 40 percent of them had pay subtracted for mistakes. In manufacturing, these percentages were 25 percent and 15 percent, respectively. Interviews with the workers revealed that these deductions are unsubstantiated. An eighteen-year-old Karen male manufacturing worker reported being charged THB180[8] for each trouser damaged, whereas some of the trousers were so cheap that they only sold for THB50,[9] meaning that they had to pay almost four times the price of a product for their mistake (Pearson et al. 2006).

In addition, many migrant workers are in debt due to high migration costs. Often, international labour migrants have to work several months after arrival just to pay off the debts incurred by the migration process (Hugo 2009). They are charged high fees by recruitment agencies and often enter into a workplace without prior knowledge of working terms and conditions and with significant language barriers (ILO 2013b; Huguet 2014).

Some countries opt not to use private recruitment agencies as a way to reduce the cost of South-South migration. For example, prior to the signing of an MOU between Bangladesh and Malaysia, the recruitment of Bangladeshi workers was an expensive procedure. Now the hiring process is based on government-to-government arrangements designed to improve recruitment in comparison to those operated by private agencies and middlemen. The MOU thus formalized the already existing strong bond between Bangladesh and Malaysia (Bhattacherjee 2013).

Furthermore, net income may be reduced significantly by high remittance fees. An important contributing factor to high remittance prices is a lack of transparency in the market (Schmitz and Endo 2011). It is difficult to compare prices because there are several variables related to financial transfers (Schmitz and Endo 2011). The cost of a remittance transaction typically consists of a fee charged by the service provider and a currency-conversion fee for delivery of remittances in local currency to beneficiaries in another country. Other factors include exclusivity agreements that limit competition and limitations on access to payment systems that allow the service providers to dictate the transaction fees (Schmitz and Endo 2011).

2.4   Policies addressing migrant workers under South-South migration in Asia

Unethical and corrupt recruitment practices place many workers in insecure situations (IOM 2014a). Numerous shortcomings and gaps in the existing international legal framework have led to a lack of protection for migrant workers, especially in the informal sector where workers often face greater disadvantages and discrimination and are usually excluded from social security benefits and legal recourse (ILO 2013c). Unregulated labour markets lacking formal human rights and employment protections in practice, if not also in policy, in countries of destination have made it easier for employers to exploit migrant workers (Cholewinski 2005). Challenges exist, such as the incompatibility of legislation, the lack of national labour administrations' financial resources to develop the protection instruments/social security schemes and the lack of willingness on the part of some destination countries to ensure the protection of labour rights (ILO 2006). Furthermore, unethical and corrupt recruitment practices have exacerbated violations of labour and human rights, increased debt bondage and labour trafficking, and decreased the earnings of labour migrants (IOM 2014b). When migrants leave their home countries in debt, the consequences are that they are forced to take jobs they do not want and are often subject to violations of their labour and human rights (IOM 2014b). These factors have made it difficult for migrant workers to enjoy protection from unsafe work environments, job insecurity and unfair payment.

In Thailand, Malaysia, Lao People's Democratic Republic, Vietnam and Cambodia, Migrant Worker Resource Centres (MRCs) and drop-in centres have been established with the support of trade unions and civil society organizations in the framework of ILO technical cooperation (ILO 2013a). The purpose of the centres is to provide information, counselling and legal assistance to visitors, and to conduct outreach to migrant workers in their communities, churches, dormitories, workplaces and so on. The centres assist female and male migrants in resolving disputes with employers and in lodging complaints with the authorities. They also train migrant community leaders to provide paralegal assistance to migrants. Migrants are also empowered as members of associations, networks and trade unions (ILO 2013a). In Thailand, IOM has developed policy recommendations for relevant ministries and has produced an 'Employer's Package', which contains a handbook and audio-visual resources to educate employers and enable fair and better employment practices, including pregnancy-related rights (IOM 2009). The package provides legal guidance to employers who hire migrant workers in order to enhance their awareness of migrant rights in the workplace (IOM 2009), and there is a special focus on women workers' rights and their health and safety. Regarding maternity rights, a pregnant worker should not be asked to work between 10 p.m. and 6 a.m. or to work overtime or on a holiday. Women workers are entitled to up to ninety days of maternity leave for each pregnancy, and the package notes that employers are not allowed to terminate a woman's employment based on her pregnancy. Furthermore, the package highlights how migrant workers contribute significantly to the Thai economy and therefore deserve equal opportunities and treatment (IOM 2009).

In terms of cooperation between countries of origin and destination, there have been efforts to standardize contracts in order to reflect international standards. For instance, an MOU between Malaysia and Indonesia has a provision requiring employers to sign contracts that specify the rights and obligations of both parties (Hugo 2009). The MOU also prohibits the withholding of workers' wages. Some agreements also specify salaries; for example, in Malaysia, the salary of domestic workers should be between Malaysia Ringgit (RM) 400 and 500[10] (Hugo 2009). Several countries in the region also have policies allowing migrant workers to open bank accounts. A bank account is opened in the name of domestic workers by employers into which their full salary is to be deposited, and employment agencies are banned from taking a share (Hugo 2009).

Both sending and receiving countries need to develop policies to ensure that the sending countries' deployment procedures and receiving countries labour protection laws do not fall short in protecting migrant workers. In recognition of the valuable and contributory role migrants have played, policy development and integration have been emphasized in the Sustainable Development Goals – for example, Goal 8: promote inclusive and sustainable economic growth, employment and decent work for all; and Goal 10: reduce inequality within and among countries. These will be further discussed in the following section (United Nations 2015a).

3. Migration and development: the incorporation of migration agenda within the Sustainable Development Goals (SDGs)

The Millennium Development Goals (MDGs), a framework for development that ended in 2015, focused mainly on national agendas of development with migration mentioned as an important source of development financing. The framework focused much less on the issues of safety, security and income of migrants, especially in the South-South migration context.

Lately, however, global communities have begun to look at linkages between migration and development through the SDG discussions, with an understanding of the important contribution remittances have in the sustainable development of countries of origin. The Rio+20 outcomes initiated an inclusive intergovernmental process to develop SDGs. The final document of the Rio+20 Conference on SDGs, 'The Future We Want', focused on the integration of population trends and projections, including migration, in national, rural and urban development strategies and policies.

As the MDGs formally expired at the end of 2015, the United Nations has established global support for a new international development agenda called 'the 2030 Agenda for Sustainable Development' (IOM 2013a). Guided by the UN Special Representative of the Secretary General for International Migration and Development, Peter Sutherland, this process has captured not only the contributions of migration through remittances to the economic development of countries of origin but also the need to improve the wellbeing of migrants at their destination.

> Making migration part of the world's development strategy will have a meaningful impact on the lives of migrants, affording them greater access to rights and the fruits of their labour . . . it could change public perception of migrants so that they are viewed as a blessing rather than a scourge.
>
> (IOM 2013b)

Migration has long been inadequately reflected in national and local development frameworks and broader sectoral policies (IOM 2013b). Philip Martin, a well-known scholar on migration, says in his chapter on IOM's post-2015 Migration and the United Nations Post-2015 Global Development Framework that migration was not included in the MDGs, as MDGs are an end rather than a means (Martin 2013). This highlights the lack of any target setting on migration and development in the MDGs, despite the fact that migrants faced, and are still facing, high costs and risks (Lönnback 2014). Therefore, it has been seen as essential for the new agenda to set clear targets and mobilize global action to improve the quality of the migration process (Lönnback 2014). IOM expressed clear views on the benefits of the integration of international migration into the 2030 Agenda for Sustainable Development (IOM n.d.), pointing to three key reasons: migrants are agents of development and they deserve to be considered if future development agenda are to be truly inclusive; migration produces tangible development outcomes at household and national level; in unregulated environments, migrants' productivity is too often wasted.

At the forty-sixth session of the UN Statistical Commission, international agencies established the Inter-agency and Expert Group on Sustainable

Table 8.1 SDG targets and selected proposed migration-related indicators

Priority SDG target	Proposed migration-related indicators*
5.2: *Eliminate all forms of violence against all women and girls in the public and private spheres, including trafficking and sexual and other types of exploitation*	Number of victims of human trafficking per 100,000 persons (5.2 and 16.2)
8.8: *Protect labour rights and promote safe and secure working environments of all workers, including migrant workers, particularly women migrants, and those in precarious situations*	Frequency rates of fatal and non-fatal occupational injuries and time lost due to occupational injuries, by sex (disaggregated by migratory status, citizenship status or nativity status)
10.7: *Facilitate orderly, safe, regular and responsible migration and mobility of people, including through implementation of planned and well-managed migration policies*	International Migration Policy Index Recruitment cost born by employee as a percentage of yearly income earned in country of destination (as a secondary indicator)
10.c: *By 2030, reduce to less than 3% the transaction costs of migrant remittances and eliminate remittance corridors with costs higher than 5%*	Remittance costs as a percentage of the amount remitted
16.2: *End abuse, exploitation, trafficking and all forms of violence against and torture of children*	Percentage of refugees and IDPs who have found a durable solution (and indicators proposed for 16.1)

* Since June 2015, the UN IAEG_SDG has regularly updated the meta-data summary of inputs from stakeholders engaged in the consultation process on indicators. Updates are accessible via the IAEG_SDG website at http://unstats.un.org/sdgs/iaeg-sdgs/open-consultation-3/.

Source: UN Inter-agency and Expert Group on SDG Indicators (IAEG-SDG), June 2015

Development Goals (IAEG-SDG) to undertake open consultations and develop an indicator framework for the monitoring of the goals post-2015, and to examine the ways in which international migration can be linked with the SDGs. Of nineteen focus areas, international migration has been linked to five specific SDG priority targets. Table 8.1 lists six proposed indicators of achievements that UN agencies and IOM have linked with the five SDG targets.

These targets and indicators were identified because there is growing evidence showing the significant impact of a multitude of different issues on the wellbeing, dignity and development of migrants and the societies in which they live and come from. All parties engaged in the SDG process recognized that there must be clear measurements to achieve progress. A wide variety of data sources is used, including information from criminal justice systems, various annual reports, databases, migration policy indexes and remittances costs identified through sophisticated formulas. This quantitative process will result in a more transparent way to measure achievement toward these collectively created goals.

4. Summary of issues

South-South migration continues to be a cornerstone of economic growth in new NICs in Asia. NICs are bringing foreign direct investment (FDI) to expand their infrastructure, which requires low-skilled workers on a large-scale. Meanwhile, these countries are concurrently trying to expand primary sectors such as agriculture or fishing. However, more working-age people in NICs tend to choose white collar jobs where they can use their knowledge obtained from higher education to earn higher salaries, which leads to a lack of blue-collar workers in sectors such as agriculture. There are also more opportunities for women in these countries to gain employment in big companies, enabling an increasing number of families in NICs to hire domestic workers from abroad.

Despite the evidence of problems in countries of destination, countries of origin continue to promote their nationals to travel abroad for employment. For a number of countries, remittances often represent a significant share of GDP. Countries of origin establish Migrant Resource Centres to help prepare their citizens for working and living abroad through the provision of information and services for migrants on their rights, legal procedures, risks and documentation required. Many countries of origin in Asia have mandatory pre-departure orientation seminars to provide information to help migrants transition into the new communities and for them to be aware of their rights. Moreover, there is increasing recognition of the importance of broadening the discussion of migration policy to include the integration of migration with development in countries of origin. More nations are working to establish cohesive migration strategies that are embedded in their development goals. Bangladesh, for example, has incorporated migration into their national development goal; the Philippines have taken the lead in promoting investment with remittances; Nepal, Myanmar and Cambodia have migration policies in place to encourage their nationals to go abroad in a safe and orderly manner; and Pakistan provides incentives for migrant workers to remit money through their domestic banks. However, there is not currently enough incentive for countries of destination to systematically incorporate migration into their development planning. Destination countries under South-South migration have maintained a strict stance in keeping their migration policies temporary and primarily without consideration for the permanent (or long-term, temporary) stay of migrants.

Although SDG discussions have promoted the idea of decent work through improved working and living conditions of migrant workers, migrants' conditions currently remain largely in the hands of the governments of countries of destination. Since labour migration is considered a temporary issue of labour demand and supply rather than a developmental issue, it is not prioritized in the national development plans of labour-receiving countries. Hence, it is unlikely that countries of destination will significantly change their policies to improve migrant worker conditions in their countries. They prioritize the development of local labour markets and labour market participation of nationals.

To move forward and improve migrant workers' experiences, both countries of origin and countries of destination need to view migration in the context of SDGs. As noted previously, countries of origin appear to have a better understanding of migration as part of the global development agenda than countries of destination. Countries of origin are finding sustainable ways to utilize migration for national development, rather than merely maintaining a dependency on migration and remittances. In addition to income, countries of origin gain knowledge and experiences that migrants obtain from countries of destination. Countries of origin, however, may suffer from brain drain, the social costs of migration such as children being raised in the absence of parents and negative experiences of migration such as injury, death and exploitation of migrant workers.

For many countries of destination, migration is not part of the development agenda. Although migrant workers are considered a temporary solution to labour shortages, and they may further be reduced due to technology improvements or population policies, many destination countries will remain reliant on migrant workers to sustain their economic growth in the future. SDGs point strongly to the importance of recognizing the positive contribution of migrants for inclusive growth and sustainable development, not only in the countries of origin but also in destination countries (United Nations 2015b), and efforts have been made to recognize migrant workers' socioeconomic contribution toward countries of destination (United Nations 2015b). Some countries of destination have begun to utilize trained migrant workers when they invest abroad. For instance, Korea's Employment Permit System has a 'happy return scheme' that rehires migrant workers who worked in Korea to then work in their countries of origin. In this way, skills and knowledge are transferred to countries of origin, and foreign investment then contributes to sustainable economic development in countries of origin. Countries of destination also benefit from having a workforce familiar with their system of operation.

The concept of South-South migration emerged as a way to promote South-South cooperation for sustainable development, but it is important to ask whether the concept applies to the labour migration systems that have emerged in the Asian region and, if so, how long will the description be valid. It may be more fruitful to think of international migration in the Asian region as contributing to regional growth. Asia is becoming more connected with increased goods and trade crossing multiple borders. There is an increase in people's mobility in the region and regional formations within Asia-to-Asia migration are also changing.

In 2007, ASEAN signed a declaration to protect and promote the rights of migrant workers. The ASEAN Economic Community is moving to promote the mobility of eight professions of highly skilled workers within ASEAN, namely, doctors, dentists, nurses, engineers, architects, accountants, surveyors and tourism professionals (The Government Public Relations Department 2013). In 2014, the South Asian Association for Regional Cooperation (SAARC) announced their commitment to promoting safe migration from the SAARC region to outside of the region (South Asian Association for Regional Cooperation 2014). Currently, there are discussions to establish a declaration similar to Declaration of Protection and Promotion of the Rights of Migrant Workers of ASEAN. Increasingly, government officials are becoming more familiar with international standards that should be applied to migrant workers. Increasing the voice of migrants and civil society organizations that play an important role to promote coordination between citizens and states also adds incentives for governments to improve their policies regarding migrant workers' environments.

As previously highlighted, there needs to be greater cooperation between countries of origin and destination to improve migrant workers' experiences. Currently, there is a lack of global governance on international migration where the numerous shortcomings and gaps in the existing international legal framework result in a lack of protection for migrant workers. The reality of international migration is that countries of destination are in a stronger position than countries of origin, and the two do not share the same agenda. Countries of destination have options to choose from in terms of sources of migrant labour, and unregulated labour markets in countries of destination have made it easier for employers to exploit migrant workers. Countries of origin are in weaker bargaining positions to ensure the rights of their nationals during their employment abroad.

Therefore there is a need to increase the bargaining power of countries of origin. How? Countries of origin can unite and set a standard when sending their nationals abroad. However, to do that, they should not compete with each other but prioritize cooperation to improve their workers' experience in countries of destination. They can aim to standardize salaries, working conditions and social benefits in countries of destination, but this would require a level of collective bargaining and foreign policy alignment currently not in place.

Notes

1 The analysis presented in this chapter represents the view of the author and does not reflect the views of the International Organization for Migration (IOM). The author would like to thank Sanam Rahman, Genevieve Gruss and Nissara Spence (IOM Regional Office for Asia and the Pacific) for editing this chapter. The author would also like to acknowledge Laurent de Bock from IOM Headquarters, for reviewing this chapter.
2 China, Indonesia, India, Philippines, Malaysia and Thailand.
3 World leaders adopted the seventeen Sustainable Development Goals (SDGs) of the 2030 Agenda for Sustainable Development in September 2015 at an historic UN Summit (United Nations 2015a).
4 Equivalent to USD16.60.
5 Equivalent to USD60.86.
6 Equivalent to USD75.
7 Equivalent to USD25.
8 Equivalent to USD4.50.
9 Equivalent to USD1.25.
10 Equivalent to USD96.81–USD121.02.

References

ADB and IOM 2013, *Facilitating Safe Labour Migration in the Greater Mekong Subregion: Issues, Challenges, and Forward-Looking Interventions*, ADB, Manila.

Bhattacherjee, A 2013, *Malaysia: MoU with Bangladesh on Manpower Export*, Institute of Peace and Conflict Studies (IPCS), viewed 10 March 2016, <http://www.ipcs.org/article/southeast-asia/malaysia-mou-with-bangladesh-on-manpower-export-3801.html>.

Castles, S and Miller, MJ 2009, *The Age of Migration*, Guilford Press, New York.

Cholewinski, R 2005, *Protecting Migrant Workers in a Globalized World*, Migration Policy Institute, viewed 10 March 2016, <http://www.migrationpolicy.org/article/protecting-migrant-workers-globalized-world>.

Development Evaluation and Communication Office 2004, 'NESDB Moved Poverty Line to 1,163 Baht, the Number of the Poor up to 8.8 Million', *Monthly Report on National Economic and Social Development*.

The Government Public Relations Department 2013, *Thai Engineers and Architects Prepare for ASEAN Free Flow of Skilled Labor*, viewed 15 March 2016, <http://thailand.prd.go.th/ewt_news.php?nid=656&filename=index>.

Gumburd, MR 2005, '"Lentils There, Lentils Here!" Sri Lankan Domestic Workers in the Middle East', in S Huang, BS Yeoh and AN Rahman, *Asian Women as Transnational Domestic Workers*, Marshall Cavendish Academic, Singapore, pp. 92–114.

Hugo, G 2009, 'Best Practice in Temporary Labour Migration for Development: A Perspective from Asia and the Pacific', *International Migration*, vol. 47, no. 5, pp. 23–74.

Huguet, JW 2014, *Thailand Migration Report 2014*, United Nations Thematic Working Group on Migration in Thailand, Bangkok.

ILO 1952, *C102 – Social Security (Minimum Standards) Convention, 1952 (No. 102)*, International Labour Organization, viewed 29 September 2016, <http://www.ilo.org/dyn/normlex/en/f?p=NORMLEXPUB:12100:0::NO::P12100_ILO_CODE:C102>.

ILO 1975, *C143 – Migrant Workers (Supplementary Provisions) Convention, 1975 (No. 143)*, ILO, viewed 29 September 2016, <http://www.ilo.org/dyn/normlex/en/f?p=1000:12100:0::NO::P12100_ILO_CODE:C143#A6>.

ILO 2003, *Facts on Social Security*, International Labour Organization, viewed 10 March 2015, <http://www.ilo.org/wcmsp5/groups/public/---dgreports/---dcomm/documents/publication/wcms_067588.pdf>.

ILO 2006, *ILO Multilateral Framework on Labour Migration: Non-binding Principles and Guidelines for a Rights-based Approach to Labour Migration*, ILO, Geneva.

ILO 2007a, *Discrimination at Work in Asia*, viewed 10 December 2015, <http://www.ilo.org/wcmsp5/groups/public/@ed_norm/@declaration/documents/publication/wcms_decl_fs_89_en.pdf>.

ILO 2007b, *Towards a Strategy for Trade Unions in the Fight against Racial Discrimination and Xenophobia*, ILO, viewed 10 December 2015, <http://www.ilo.org/declaration/events/WCMS_099522/lang--en/index.htm>.

ILO 2010, *World Social Security Report 2010/11: Providing Coverage in Times of Crisis and Beyond*, ILO, Geneva.

ILO 2012, *Action-oriented Research on Gender Equality and the Working and Living Conditions of Garment Factory Workers in Cambodia*, ILO, Geneva.

ILO 2013a, *Background Paper: Progress on the Implementation of the Recommendations Adopted at the 3rd and 4th ASEAN Forum on Migrant Labour*, ILO, Geneva.

ILO 2013b, 'Legal Background Note: National Legislation Regarding Working Conditions for Domestic Workers in Asia', *Asian Knowledge-Sharing Forum: Realizing Decent Work for Domestic Workers*, ILO, Bangkok.

ILO 2013c, 'Social Protection for Low-Skilled Migrant Workers and Their Families', *Migrant Forum in Asia*, viewed 15 January 2016, <http://www.ilo.org/dyn/migpractice/docs/137/PB7.pdf>.

ILO 2014, *REPRESENTATION (article 24) – QATAR – C029 – (Lodged: 2013 – Report: 2014)*, ILO, Geneva.

ILO 2015, *ILO Global Estimates on Migrant Workers*, ILO, Geneva.

IOM n.d., *2030 Agenda for Sustainable Development*, viewed 29 September 2016, <https://unobserver.iom.int/2030-agenda-sustainable-development>.

IOM 2009, *Working to Prevent and Address Violence against Women Migrant Workers*, ILO, Geneva.

IOM 2011, *Trafficking of Fishermen in Thailand*, IOM, Bangkok.

IOM 2013a, *IOM Position on the Post-2015 United Nations Development Agenda*, ILO, Geneva.

IOM 2013b, *2013 United Nations General Assembly High Level Dialogue on International Migration and Development IOM Position Paper*, ILO, Geneva.

IOM 2013c, *Migration Health: Healthy Migrants in Healthy Communities*, viewed 19 January 2015, <http://health.iom.int/>.

IOM 2014a, *About Ethical Recruitment*, International Recruitment Integrity System, viewed 1 April 2016, <https://iris.iom.int/about-ethical-recruitment>.

IOM 2014b, *Unethical Recruitment and the Exploitation of Migrant Workers*, viewed 10 March 2016, <http://iris.iom.int/sites/default/files/document/IRIS_Brochure-March-5th-2014.pdf>.

IOM c2015, *Global Migration Trends 2015 Factsheet*, viewed 1 April 2016, <http://iomgmdac.org/global-trends-2015-factsheet/>.

IOM 2015, *Migrant Health an Increasingly Important Policy Concern for Asia*, IOM, viewed 15 January 2016, <http://www.iom.int/news/migrant-health-increasingly-important-policy-concern-asia>.

Kim, TE 2015, *Nepali Migrants Watch Recovery from Afar, Some Prevented from Going Home*, Al Jazeera America, viewed 10 June 2016, <http://america.aljazeera.com/articles/2015/4/30/nepali-migrant-workers.html>.

Koser, K 2010, 'Introduction: International Migration and Global Governance', *Global Governance*, vol. 16, pp. 301–15, viewed 23 August 2014, <http://www.thefreelibrary.com/Introduction:internationalmigrationandglobalGovernance.-a0237050213>.

Lönnback, LJ 2014, *Integrating Migration into the Post-2015 United Nations Development Agenda*, International Organization for Migration and Migration Policy Institute, Bangkok.

Martin, PL 2013, 'Labour Migration and Development Indicators', in International Organization for Migration (IOM) (ed), *Migration and the United Nations Post-2015 Global Development Framework*, International Organization for Migration (IOM), Geneva, pp. 67–92.

MFA and Friedrich-Ebert-Stiftung 2011, *Migrant Worker's Rights to Social Protection in ASEAN: Case Studies of Indonesia, Philippines, Singapore and Thailand*, Prepared by Mahidol Migration Centre, Institute for Population and Social Research,

Mahidol University, Thailand for Migrant Forum Asia (MFA) and Frieddrich-Ebert-Stiftung, Office for Regional Cooperation, Singapore, viewed 29 September 2016, <http://www.fes-asia.org/media/publication/2012_MigrantWorkers RightsToSocialProtectionInASEAN_Hall.pdf>.

Pearson, E, Punpuing, S, Jampaklay, A, Kittisuksathit, S, and Prohmmo, A 2006, *The Mekong Challenge: Underpaid, Overworked and Overlooked: The Realities of Young Migrant Workers in Thailand,* International Labour Organization (ILO), Geneva.

Pinyol-Jiménez, G 2012, 'The Migration-Security Nexus in Short: Instruments and Actions in the European Union', *Amsterdam Law Forum,* vol. 4, no. 1, pp. 36–57.

Press, B 2014, *New Health Insurance for Migrant Workers Facing Challenges,* Prevention of HIV AIDs among Migrant Workers in Thailand, viewed 15 March 2016, <http://www.phamit.org/hilight-detail.php?lang=en&id=12>.

Ratha, D and Shaw, W 2007, *South-South Migration and Remittances,* Migration Policy Institute, viewed 8 January 2015, <http://www.migrationpolicy.org/article/ south-south-migration-and-remittances/>.

Schmitz, K and Endo, I 2011, *Lowering the Cost of Sending Money Home,* International Monetary Fund, viewed 15 January 2016, <https://www.imf.org/external/ pubs/ft/fandd/2011/06/pdf/picture.pdf>.

Soda, F 2009, *Migration in the Greater Mekong Subregion,* Asian Development Bank, Manila.

South Asian Association for Regional Cooperation 2014, *18th SAARC Summit Declaration,* viewed 15 April 2016, <http://www.saarc-sec.org/press-releases/ 18th-SAARC-Summit-Declaration/121/>.

Thimothy, R and Sasikumar, SK 2012, *Migration of Women Workers from South Asia to the Gulf,* V.V. Giri National Labour Institute, NOIDA and UN Women South Asia Sub Regional Office, New Delhi.

United Nations 2012a, *Resolution Adopted by the General Assembly on 10 September 2012,* General Assembly of the United Nations, viewed 3 March 2015, <http:// www.un.org/en/ga/search/view_doc.asp?symbol=%20A/RES/66/290>.

United Nations 2012b, *Situation Report on International Migration in South and South-West Asia,* United Nations, Bangkok.

United Nations 2013, *232 Million International Migrants Living Abroad Worldwide–New,* viewed 31 July 2014, <http://www.un.org/en/development/desa/population/ migration/publications/wallchart/docs/wallchart2013.pdf>.

United Nations 2015a, *Sustainable Development Goals,* United Nations, viewed 15 February 2016, <http://www.un.org/sustainabledevelopment/sustainable-development-goals/>.

United Nations 2015b, *Transforming Our World: The 2030 Agenda for Sustainable Development,* United Nations, New York.

United Nations 2016a, *244 Million International Migrants Living Abroad Worldwide, New UN Statistics Reveal,* Sustainable Development Goals, viewed 29 September 2016, <http://www.un.org/sustainabledevelopment/blog/2016/01/244-million-international-migrants-living-abroad-worldwide-new-un-statistics-reveal/>.

United Nations 2016b, *International Migration Report 2015,* United Nations, New York.

United Nations Inter-agency and Expert Group on SDG Indicators 2015, *Meta-data for Proposed Indicators: Rationale and Method of Computation: June 2015,* Inter-agency and Expert Group on SDG Indicators, New York.

Victorian Government Solicitor's Office 2015, *Memoranda of Understanding*, viewed 1 January 2016, <http://vgso.vic.gov.au/content/memoranda-understanding>.

WHO 2010, *Health of Migrants-The Way Forward: Report of a Global Consultation*, WHO, France.

Wickramasekara, P 2002, *Asian Labour Migration. Issues and Challenges in an Era of Globalisation*, International Labour Organization, Geneva.

Wickramasekara, P 2011, *Labour Migration in South Asia: A Review of Issues, Policies and Practices*, ILO, Geneva.

World Bank 2014, *Migration and Development Brief 23: Recent Developments and Outlook. Special Topic: Forced Migration*, World Bank, Washington, DC.

World Bank 2016, *Migration and Development Brief 26: Recent Developments and Outlook*, World Bank, Washington, DC.

9 Migration governance
Global national interface

Habibul Haque Khondker

1. Introduction

The main focus of the chapter is the governance of labour migration, with specific attention to the growing phenomenon of South-South migration. South-North migration involves mainly the migration of professionals, including scientists, doctors, engineers and academics, and concerns long-term relocation, where issues of integration, retaining cultural identity, the rights of migrants and migrant participation as equal citizens are of less concern. The reason for this is the framework of governance within which migrants in the North are covered, constitutionally, by the tenets of human and other democratic rights. In addition to the extent of the governance framework, especially the regulatory framework, that guides migrant rights and their welfare in the receiving countries, integration for migrants, in such circumstances, means better human relations between employers and employees and an amicable relationship between the citizens of the host countries and the non-citizen, migrant workers. South-South migration, however, involves migration of less skilled (predominantly semi-skilled) workers, mostly on a temporary basis and under conditions of minimum rights entailing numerous challenges. Furthermore, with regard to the linkage between receiving and sending countries, South-South migration typically entails conditions such that, at the end of a contract period, temporary migrants will return to the sending countries, their homeland or repeat the process to a third country. The relationship is purely transactional. Yet, as chapters in this volume attest, South-South migration throws up a new set of empirical problems and theoretical challenges, especially those that relate to migration governance.

Recent trends in migration include substantial growth in South-South migration (migration between developing countries) such that the scale of South-South migration now is greater than migration from the South to high-income countries in the North. Some of the countries in the South are both labour-receiving as well as labour-sending countries. Economic forces continue to dominate international migration. Both the working classes as well as the professional classes are driven by the same economic motive. While for the professional class there are more choices, the choice for the working class is constrained by a variety of factors. Sometimes, the line that separates migrants from refuges or asylum seekers becomes blurred, especially when it comes to working class migrants. In 2010, refugees and asylum seekers made up 16.3 million, or 8 percent, of international migrants (World Bank 2011, p. x). In recent years that number has grown. This is an important issue from the point of view of governance but falls outside the scope of this chapter.

South-South migration and issues of migration governance are analysed in this chapter in relation to three interconnected domains – those pertaining to the sending country, the receiving country and the international domain – as well as the ways these three domains intersect with each other. After this brief introduction, the chapter addresses the conceptual issues within which we problematize the theoretical difficulties of migration governance, especially global governance, and then explores the phenomenon of South-South migration in Asia. It then presents, as a case study, the Bangladesh–United Arab Emirates (UAE) migration corridor that has developed over the past decade. While the main focus in this section is migration governance involving the UAE and Bangladesh, it also dwells on the migration governance in the Arabian Gulf region, exploring the relationships between labour-sending countries of South and Southeast Asia and the Arabian Gulf states, as the receiving region, within a framework of multilateral discussions and consultations. This chapter examines various existing institutions and processes at the global and international level that guide and regulate migration processes, including the Colombo framework launched in 2003 and the Abu Dhabi Dialogue in 2008. In the concluding sections we try to elucidate governance, global governance and migration governance as we discuss the evolution of migration governance from bilateral to multilateral processes and from management to diplomacy.

2.   Global-national interface: a theoretical prelude

Mobility is seen as a distinctive feature of modern society. Mobility of labour and capital are the hallmarks of capitalist globalization (Sassen 1990). Mobility, a defining feature of the contemporary world, has been conceptualized at various levels and forms and its pervasiveness has made the very contours of society uncertain (Urry 2000; Cresswell 2006; Urry 2007; Elliot and Urry 2010). In fact, human mobility is nothing new. Human history is the history of human migration, which, for much of human history, was unregulated and went unnoticed. Regulated migration is a product of the emergence of state systems with demarcated boundaries. Colonial migration was regulated and controlled. The needs of colonial powers shipped people from one set of colonies to the other. In the contemporary world, as globalization has led to an increase in the number of people and countries (nation states) involved in the processes of migration (Castles and Miller 2003), the uneven forces of globalization have bought the state back in. Globalization processes are intrinsically uneven in both their form and effect. One of the contradictions of globalization is the free-flow of capital and restricted movement of labour. With the advancing march of globalization, the world has become increasingly bordered and fenced (Turner and Khondker 2010), and the state has become more salient in the control and regulation of people's movements. The relationship between globalization and the state has taken a new turn, and the state has become a key actor governing globalization.

Some enthusiastic proponents of globalization have seriously underrated the variety and adaptability of state capacities, overstating the extent and novelty of transnational movements and the power of transnational corporations. In the euphoria of discussions on globalization, writers such as Ohmae (1990) announced the coming of a 'borderless world'. Ironically, when such celebratory remarks on the so-called borderless world were being made, walls were being erected in many parts of the world to restrict the movement of people. In the twentieth century the world has become more bordered than at any other time in the past. We live, now, in a state-centred world, and the state remains a vital institution at the service of globalization. The state decides who comes in and who goes out. The state has ultimate control over citizenship and migration, permanent or temporary, and these have implications for migration processes, migrant welfare, safety, security, income and remittance. However, since there is a hierarchy of states, both political as well as economic, they have unequal bargaining power, especially between the less developed sending countries and the economically stronger and more politically powerful receiving countries, indicating that a global framework for migration governance is key to ensuring equity and justice in migration processes and in outcomes of migration.

Apart from the normative aspects of interstate relations under conditions of asymmetric power relations, there is also a problem of unequal state capacity in terms of governance. Some of the migrant-sending countries fail in their obligations to protect the interests of their citizens due to an inefficient and disjointed structure of governance that seriously lacks accountability and transparency. Migrant workers often suffer from the poor governance of the sending country as well as the destination countries.

3. Temporary contractual migration in the context of migration governance: a conceptual framework

The main concepts used here are 'temporary labour migration' and 'governance'. Both migration and governance are popular concepts. However, whereas some agreed upon definitions are available for migration, governance as a concept suffers from ambiguity. Migration is defined as the movement of a person or persons from one geographical unit to another across an administrative or political border, with the intention of settling permanently or temporarily in a place other than their place of birth. There are different categories of migrants: refugees, displaced persons, irregular migrants, as well as economic migrants. The main difference between refugees and migrants is individual autonomy or choice.

When people are forced to migrate against their free will, we can define the situation as forced migration. Human trafficking is the most coercive form of forced migration. In the present paper, the focus is on temporary labour migration where migrants go to their destinations for a limited period with the intention of returning to their countries of origin. Labour migration is commonly defined as a cross-border movement for the purpose of employment in a foreign country (IOM 2011), through legal or irregular means, facilitated or otherwise.

The concept of governance has entered the development discourse since the 1990s. A gradual shift from binary state-centred versus market-based development led to the discussion of governance as a more pragmatic concept. Governance is the process of governing in a comprehensive sense involving multiple, interacting actors and institutions; thus it is more inclusive. By governance, we do not mean government and its functions; governance has a wider meaning that focuses on the process as well as the institutional matrix. In addition to the government, other actors such as the private sector, civic society and international nongovernmental organizations (INGO), among others, come to play a role. Thus governance brings multiple stakeholders into play. National or local governments are in charge of formulating policies which may or may not involve consultation with other organizations or sectors of society, but the implementation of those policies is contingent on the cooperation of the public and other institutional actors in the society.

The shift toward a focus upon governance was noticeable in the discussion of International Relations following the decline of the Cold War and bi-polarization in the early 1990s (Rosenau and Cziempel 1992; Rosenau 1995). In positing a model of 'global governance' in the twenty-first century, Rosenau (1995) did not rule out the continued role of the state or interstate systems such as the United Nations; he emphasized the role of the non-state actors. In the context of the growing significance of an interconnected globalized economy, emergence of trans-border epidemics such as AIDS, environmental crises and the rise of transnational nongovernmental movements, the transformation of the role of the state as the sole authority of governance was changing. A growing body of literature in law and public administration introduced the idea of 'new governance', as distinct from traditional governance, or governing which modified the traditional role of the government. Abbot and Snidal (2009) identified four such changes in the role of the state.

> In New Governance, the state: (1) incorporates a *decentralized* range of actors and institutions, both public and private, into the regulatory system, as by negotiating standards with firms, encouraging and supervising self-regulation, or sponsoring voluntary management systems; (2) relies on this range of actors for regulatory *expertise*; (3) modifies its regulatory responsibilities to emphasize *orchestration* of public and private actors and institutions rather than direct promulgation and enforcement of rules;

and (4) utilizes '*soft law*' to complement or substitute for mandatory 'hard law'.

(Abbot and Snidal 2009, p. 509)

The complexities increase, however, when the concept of governance is transposed to the global level. Betts (2011) recognizes that global governance is 'a murky and often poorly defined term' and seeks to clarify it.

A working definition of global governance can be taken to be the 'norms, rules, principles and decision-making procedures that regulate the behavior of states (and other transnational actors)'. Govern*ance* distinguishes itself from govern*ment* insofar as there is no single authoritative rule-maker. . . . What makes governance 'global' is not the 'level' at which it is identified – whether bilateral, regional, transnational, or supranational – but rather the fact that it is constraining or constitutive of the behavior of states (and transnational actors).

(Betts 2011)

John Gerard Ruggie adds:

Governance refers to the systems of authoritative norms, rules, institutions, and practices by means of which any collectivity, from the local to the global, manages its common affairs. *Global governance* is generally defined as an instance of govern*ance* in the absence of govern*ment*. There is no government at the global level. But there is governance, of variable effectiveness.

(Ruggie 2014, p. 5)

Replacing a state-centric approach, global governance depends on a polycentric approach where states draw upon the expertise of relevant actors to promote an 'orchestrated' strategy. Drawing upon Lobel (2004) and Abbott and Snidal (2009) have developed the idea of orchestration as an aspect of governance. 'Orchestration' involves engaging intermediaries between the global economic systems and the fragmented state systems. The main dilemma of global migration governance is that cross-national migration is not matched by a transnational structure of governance. The interface of global migration and national governance is the nub of the problem. Had there been a world state as envisioned by Morgantheu (Speer 1968), global migration governance would not be a difficult proposition. No such world or global government exists. Moreover, the idea of a world state or world government generates the fear of an Orwellian statist society. Hence the problem remains. However, as the discourse on governance has emphasized time and again, governance need not be top down or vertical and authoritarian, it could also be bottom up, horizontal and democratic. More conceptual innovation is in order to grasp migration governance at the regional and global level so that it can deal with the nuances of labour migration, even temporary or circular migration.

4.   Evolution of global migration governance

It is now widely recognized that, when properly managed, temporary contractual labour mobility may benefit both the countries of origin and destination as well as improve the wellbeing of temporary contractual workers. Labour mobility can be an important means of facilitating the development of economies as well as of individual human beings. The huge trans-border movement of people has a variety of implications depending on the countries the migrants are in, the duration of their stay, their own educational background and other demographic variables.

According to Alexander Betts, in the wake of the discussions and debates at the International Conference on Population and Development (ICPD) in Cairo in 1994, at the request of former UN Secretary General Kofi Annan (1997–2006), Michael Doyle examined the international institutions that existed in relation to migration. The 'Doyle Report', completed in 2002, recommended further reflection, leading to the creation of the Global Commission on International Migration (GCIM), which ran between 2003 and 2005, to assess in greater detail the nature of the issue and possible institutional responses. The GCIM's recommendations, in turn, led Kofi Annan to appoint a Special Representative on Migration and Development and to convene a UN High-Level Dialogue on Migration and Development in 2006, at which states openly reflected for the first time on the appropriate location for multilateral debate on migration. Given opposition from Northern states to the creation of a UN-based debate on migration, a new forum, the Global Forum on Migration and Development (GFMD), was created in 2007 and has subsequently held annual informal dialogues (Betts 2011).

There has been a gradual evolution of the discourse of formalizing and regulating migration from 'managing migration' (Ghosh 2000) through migration governance (Betts 2010; Newland 2010) to what I consider to be migration diplomacy. Of course, the latter can be subsumed under global migration governance, yet an autonomous development is evident in the growing importance of bilateral and multilateral negotiations on labour migration. Apart from academic debate and the initiatives of organizations such as the International Organization for Migration, Betts points to religious organizations such as the International Catholic Migration Commission (ICMC), which convened an initiative called 'Conversations on the Global Governance of Migration' in 2009, bringing together a range of stakeholders from the policy and academic worlds to debate global migration governance (Betts 2011). A growing debate on the global governance of migration can be a prelude to concrete steps and formulation of policies and the emergence of appropriate institutions. Alexander Betts correctly points out that although a number of international organizations, such as the International Organization for Migration (IOM), the United Nations Population Fund (UNFPA), the United Nations Department of Economic and Social Affairs (UNDESA) and the United Nations Institute for Training and Research (UNITAR), have official mandates to deal with aspects of migration, the ultimate responsibility and decision-making powers remain in the hands of nation states. States remain the primary actors in migration governance (Betts 2011).

The sovereignty of the state would not be threatened in a new framework of global governance where the state has been a partner with both a large number of international organizations and nongovernmental organizations, both at the local as well as the transnational levels. In fact, a growing global consensus can persuade even the most recalcitrant state to abide by the norms shared by the global community. Here, transnational interstate organizations, such as the United Nations, the International Labor Organization (ILO) or the International Organization for Migration (IOM), need to play a more active role. The IOM initiated an International Dialogue on Migration through which it aimed 'to contribute to a better understanding of migration and to strengthen cooperative mechanisms between governments to comprehensively and effectively address migration issues' (Newland 2010, p. 332). The International Labour Organization (ILO), one of the oldest international organizations, made migration the theme of the 2004 International Labour Conference. In the first decade of the twenty-first century, the United Nations has been more engaged with the issues of global migration governance. By bringing together fifteen UN or UN affiliate organizations in 2006, a Global Migration Group (GMG) was set up under the auspices of the United Nations. When the ILO became the chair by rotation in 2014, it actively promoted the decent work agenda and fair migration policies at the national, regional and global levels. This change of focus is reflected in the inclusion of migrants and migration in the post-2015 agenda of the United Nations – namely, post-Millennium Development, Sustainable Development. The GMG also promotes wider application of international policies and standards relating to migration and greater coordination with governments and other relevant stakeholders (ILO 2014).

At the same time, recognition that global migration governance is relatively incoherent has contributed to the emergence of a debate on the international institutional framework governing international migration. The inclusion of migration in the UN's post-MDG call for Sustainable Development Goals (SDGs) signals a new focus on the importance of migration as a strategy for improvement of wellbeing and reduction of social inequality. However, the experiences of much of the twentieth century and the first decade and a half of the twenty-first century have also exposed the risks of migration and the vulnerability of migrants. Unregulated and informal migration often exposes the migrants to exploitation, human rights violations and death. Slavery and bonded labour are expressions of unsupervised cross-border migration that make many vulnerable. To ensure the safety and security of the migrants, migration governance or managed migration is an effort to provide the migrants all the help they need. Facilitation and safety of the migrants is an important aspect of fair migration. Hence, the SDG target 10.7 is focused on 'orderly, safe regular and responsible migration and mobility of people, including through the implementation of planned and well-managed migration policies'.

In the following section, we will explore the evolution of the discourse of migration governance from bilateral and regional to multilateral and global levels by reference to the particular case of the Bangladesh-UAE migration corridor. Improvement in the governance of temporary labour migration can be of great benefit both for the stakeholders involved – namely, the labour-receiving country, the labour-sending countries and also the contract labourers, with the UAE government assuming leadership in this regard. By initiating the Abu Dhabi Dialogue in January 2008 in partnership with the International Organization for Migration (IOM), the UAE government sought to position itself favourably vis-à-vis the international community. This initiative included all the major stakeholders: representatives of the labour-sending countries and labour-receiving countries, international nongovernmental organizations such as Human Rights Watch and intergovernmental organizations such as the International Organization for Migration (IOM) and International Labour Organization (ILO).

5.   Bangladesh-UAE migration corridor

Some Bangladeshis came to the UAE before the birth of either Bangladesh or the UAE in 1971. They came as professionals or petty traders. Following the visit of Bangladeshi founding leader Sheik Mujibur Rahman to the UAE in 1974, Bengal Development Corporation, a Bangladeshi construction company launched by Jahurul Islam, a prominent Bangladeshi entrepreneur, came to the UAE the same year (interview with Mohamed Khaled Yar,[1] 2016). Bengal Development Corporation built some of the early public housing, five thousand units or villas in Al Wathba outside of Abu Dhabi and a 90-kilometre road from Abu Dhabi to the western region. The majority of the workers of this company came from Bangladesh, thereby launching the movement of Bangladeshi labour migration to the UAE. In 1976 the Bureau of Manpower, Employment and Training (BMET) was established. The Emigration Ordinance was passed in 1982, followed by the establishment of the Bangladesh Overseas Employment Services Ltd (BOESL) in 1984. The Ministry of Expatriate Welfare was set up in 2001, with the Overseas Employment policy being formulated in 2006. As the number of overseas workers increased, new institutions were set up. An Expatriate Welfare Bank Act was passed in 2010 and the Bank was launched the following year. The Overseas Migrant Workers Act was ratified in 2013.

Over the past three decades, Bangladesh has emerged as a major labour-exporting country alongside India and the Philippines. It is estimated that around eight million Bangladeshis (about 5 percent of the total population of Bangladesh) live and work outside Bangladesh. In the mid-1970s, the UAE attracted a large expatriate workforce in the wake of oil price hikes, and a steady migration of labour to the UAE from Bangladesh began in the mid- to late 1970s. For the most part, labour migration from Bangladesh has taken place without much direct governmental support. The near laissez-faire quality of migration has had advantages as well as disadvantages. Many migrants who have

Table 9.1 Top remittance-receiving countries, 2014, as percentage of GDP

Rank	Country	Percentage of GDP
1.	Tajikistan	41.7
2.	Kyrgyz Republic	30.3
3.	Nepal	29.2
4.	Tonga	27.9
5.	Armenia	17.9
6.	Samoa	17.6
7.	West Bank and Gaza	17.1
8.	Lebanon	16.2
9.	Jordan	10.3
10.	Philippines	10.0

Source: World Bank (2016a, p. 30)

left Bangladesh have arranged for work overseas with the help of their relatives and friends. Both family and village networks played a key role in the migration of Bangladeshis to the UAE. The trickle of migrants in the mid-1970s, directed to a handful of countries, became a flood of millions by the end of the 1990s. Between 1976 and 2014, the number of Bangladeshi overseas migrants reached nine million (Siddiqui 2016). In 2015, Bangladeshi workers were working in 146 countries worldwide, and Bangladesh received remittances of over USD15.8 billion (World Bank 2016a), equivalent to approximately 8 percent of the country's GDP in that year (World Bank 2016b). For a country with limited exportable goods other than readymade garments, this is not an insignificant amount and places Bangladesh among the top ten remittance-receiving countries in terms of the amount recorded. The increasing trend in remittance income is a global phenomenon. Table 9.1 indicates the significance of remittances, as a proportion of GDP, for the top ten countries.

As migration of labour becomes a lucrative source of foreign exchange for the country and as the government gets involved in the process, both as a promoter and regulator, the subject of migration governance becomes salient. Meanwhile, as the number of migrant workers, or temporary contract workers as they are called in the UAE, has touched record levels, migrant population numbers in some regions and localities have grown to outnumber citizens. The migrant/citizen ratio in the UAE is one of the most skewed in the world, and the government of the UAE has voiced some concerns.

The UAE receives temporary contract workers from a large number of countries in the global South. Along with several South and Southeast Asian countries, Bangladesh has been a labour-sending country that has supplied migrant labour as well as skilled personnel with various skills to the UAE. Rapid infrastructural and socioeconomic developments in the UAE, combined with its demographic realities, led to reliance on temporary contract workers from labour-surplus Asian countries. While temporary migrant workers play an important role in the UAE's economy, through their remittances they also play a major role in the respective national economies of the sending countries.

An estimated 700,000 Bangladeshis now work in the UAE, dominating the construction and other labour-intensive industries, although the flow of Bangladeshi workers has been stemmed since 2012 when the number of visas for prospective Bangladeshi workers were reduced, except for domestic workers. Despite the significance of these workers for the national economies of both the UAE and Bangladesh, the employment conditions of Bangladeshi workers in the UAE often remain precarious. In a detailed empirical study (Khondker and Madi 2012), it was found that, because of their low level of education, Bangladeshi workers earn less than other groups of workers from South Asia (Pakistan and India) and Southeast Asia (Philippines). There are, however, two sides to the story. The large number of Bangladeshi workers and their contributions to the building of infrastructure are significant, yet Bangladeshi migrant workers have also earned some notoriety for their alleged law-avoidance behaviours in the host county. One of the problems for the host country has been the illegal presence of tens of thousands of workers of all nationalities, among which Bangladeshis are a prominent group. Migration governance, with special reference to the UAE, calls for a consideration of how the interests of labour-sending countries can be harmonized with those of labour-receiving countries.

Over the years, the UAE has received bad press internationally for the dismal conditions of the workers in the country (Human Rights Watch 2006, 2009). Yet, improvement in the conditions failed to receive much attention. Contrary to international perception, the living conditions of temporary migrant workers in the UAE in recent years have improved considerably. In a study conducted in the UAE Khondker and Madi (2012) found that more than 70 percent of the workers consider their accommodation adequate or very good. Of the remaining 30 percent, 20 percent think it is less than adequate, but only 9 percent consider it very poor (see Table 9.2).

Table 9.2 Percentage of responses on the quality of living facilities

Quality of living facilities	Percent (N = 619)
Very good	15.5
Adequate	54.9
Less than adequate	20.0
Very poor	8.9
Total	100.0

Khondker and Madi also found that most of the Bangladeshi migrants surveyed had moved to the UAE because of connections with family, friends or people from their own villages. While such connections provide some protection and security, they are no guarantee for a decent job or a job that matches migrants' skills. There is a preponderance of casual and low-skilled work among the Bangladeshi workers in the UAE and as the host government is pushing for more skills in a push to improve and increase productivity, low-skilled workers are consequently disadvantaged. Khalid Koser has suggested that one of the reasons for irregular migration is restricted immigration policies (Koser 2010, p. 307). It is apparent that some Bangladeshi workers are forced to become irregular, as they remain heavily indebted back home due to exorbitant charges they are forced to pay to agents and sub-agents. So the problem of irregular migration has roots in both receiving and sending countries.

In response to this twin set of pressures, a culture of strategic non-compliance has emerged among Bangladeshi workers. In the course of our research, we met workers who were irregular workers in Oman who had crossed into the UAE illegally, because they knew from reports of irregular migrant workers in Oman that the punishment in the UAE is less severe than in Oman (Khondker and Madi 2012). Unwittingly, by doing this, they swell the statistics of irregular migrants in the UAE, ultimately, with adverse effects on them.

In another kind of response, labour protests increased following the construction boom in the early 2000s in Dubai. Most of those incidents occurred over delayed or irregular payment of wages (*Gulf News* May 30, 2004, cited in Khondker 2010, p. 207). However, following the implementation of a Wage Protection System (WPS), which requires that the employers of migrant workers must pay the monthly salary of the workers directly to their bank accounts, with serious consequences for employer non-compliance, such protests have almost disappeared. In a research study led by the author (Khondker and Madi 2012) it was revealed that the majority of workers identified the WPS as the most important step to their benefit in the UAE, along with the related improvements in temporary workers' health insurance and housing (see Table 9.3).

Table 9.3 Workers' assessment of improvements in the UAE

	Frequency	*Percentage*
Bank payment (wage protection scheme)	340	54.9
Better housing	56	9.0
Health insurance	60	9.7
Labour court	20	3.2
Other	105	17.0
Safety	34	5.5
Total	619	100.0

Table 9.4 Overseas employment of female workers from Bangladesh in 2015

Destination country	Number of female migrant workers
United Arab Emirates	24,307
Jordan	21,776
Kingdom of Saudi Arabia	20,952
Oman	16,980
Lebanon	8,782
Mauritius	1,339
Bahrain	403
Hong Kong	300
Singapore	114
Other (Cyprus, Malaysia, Brunei, etc.)	117
Total	103,718

Source: Compiled by the author using data obtained from the Bangladesh Ministry of Employment and Trade (BMET), http://mail.bmet.gov.bd.

In the wake of these changes and an unofficial UAE restriction on Bangladeshi labour visas that came into effect in September 2012, Bangladeshi labour migration to the UAE dropped. Most of the migrant workers to the UAE from Bangladesh in recent years have been female domestic workers who have chosen the UAE as their main destination, followed by Saudi Arabia, Jordan and Lebanon (see Table 9.4).

Around the same time, in 2012, following months of negotiations, Bangladesh signed a government-to-government agreement with Malaysia. In theory this was a milestone on the path to decent and fair migration, intended to regulate (and hence reduce) the cost of migration for the Bangladeshi worker. While this initiative was able to cut out the highly exploiting 'manpower agencies' in Bangladesh and their counterparts in Malaysia who acted as middlemen, the number of migrant workers dropped to an abysmal low, which created a widespread resentment, especially among the recruiting companies. In the first quarter of 2013, a meagre two hundred workers were sent to Malaysia under the new agreement. While in principle it seems to be a sound idea, at this stage the government of Bangladesh lacks the institutional capacity to negotiate large-scale labour mobility. This is a good example of a well-intentioned policy producing a negative outcome. After years of bickering, a two-track policy of allowing both government-to-government and business-to-business agreements was signed, and a deal was signed with the Malaysian minister in Dhaka. Even before the proverbial ink was dry, the Malaysian interior minister declared that Malaysia would not allow any foreign migrant workers to migrate. This illustrates some of the complexities of migration governance. There was a lack of inter-ministerial coordination, causing a good deal of embarrassment to Bangladesh.

The Bangladeshi government has been able to display selective effectiveness. In a coordinated effort, the Bangladeshi government successfully repatriated 38,000 stranded Bangladeshi workers from Libya during the social turmoil that overthrew the old regime. The Bangladeshi government, it appears, is better at crisis management than routine work. The process lacks transparency. Most of the migrant workers lack reliable information about the countries they are about to move to for work. They are often kept in the dark regarding the contents of the labour contract. They remain hostages at the hands of the manpower agents. I interviewed Meherunnesa (not her real name), an eighteen-year old Bangladeshi girl on her way to Jordan to work as a domestic worker. When I asked her, on a flight from Dhaka to Abu Dhabi in January 2016, how old she was, her answer was twenty-five, the official minimum age required for a Bangladeshi woman to travel overseas for work. When I asked her to give me her real age, she admitted it was eighteen. She was heading for Jordan without knowing where Jordan was. She kept repeatedly asking, 'Bhai (brother), will they give me my salary at the end of the month? I need that 16,000 Taka (USD200) to send home for the upkeep of my family'. She repeated the question, 'Will they pay me regularly?' Meherunnesa asked me, 'Is this plane going to Jordan?' She was never told, it turned out, that she would be required to change planes at Abu Dhabi airport. I coached her all the way from opening the airline food to buttering the bread to the very basic practices that a village girl is completely unfamiliar with.

Meherunnesa's story may not be all that atypical. She is the eldest of the three children. Her father is mentally unstable (she used the word 'pagol', meaning mad in Bengali) and is unable to work. Her mother works as an odd job hand in the village but her income is not adequate. For the survival of her family she has no other recourse but to work. Meherunnesa has completed primary level education. She is confident, friendly and seemingly innocent about the dangers that may lurk. At Abu Dhabi airport, I made sure that she went to the right boarding gate for her flight to Amman. The agent in her village made her trip possible. There has been a growing demand for Bangladeshi female domestic workers in the Middle East and in the Arab Gulf region. The employers pay for the travel cost of the intended domestic help and also a small fee to the employment agency. While interviewing a manpower agent in Dhaka, it was revealed that the profit margin in sending a domestic worker is only a couple of hundred dollars, since the employer bears the cost. Usually, the processing of the domestic workers is left with the sub-agents who remain unaccountable to the government. The informality involved in this arrangement can sometimes be detrimental to the migrant worker, yet this is the only avenue available. At the same time, the sub-agent who lives in the locality is someone who she will trust, rather than a stranger in the city.

Meherunnesa's case illustrates several weaknesses of the system. First, she was not given adequate information. The training and orientation she received was inadequate. If a migrant worker embarks on a journey without knowing her destination, except the name of the country, this reveals serious institutional weaknesses, including the pre-orientation training. In another case, in the departure lounge of the Abu Dhabi airport, we met a household worker who was returning to Bangladesh after working for several months without being paid. She did not contact the Labour attaché of the Bangladesh embassy, about which she had no information. Although work to establish a database of workers is now underway, a majority of the workers are not aware of this. The relationship between the overseas workers and the embassy is limited to consular work (i.e. renewal of passports and related matters). The only important development worth mentioning is the introduction of a life insurance policy for the Bangladeshi domestic workers of AED42,000, for which the one-off AED200 premium is paid by the employer (*The National, UAE,* April 23, 2016). The insurance coverage of the Bangladeshi domestic workers has been an important step implemented since September 2015. Close to 100,000 Bangladeshi domestic workers are currently in employment in the UAE (interview with the Labour Counsellor, Bangladesh Embassy).[2] The new labour law of 2016 also made it easier for the foreign workers to lodge complains for non-payment of salaries and benefits and other violations of the contract, but this did not benefit domestic workers. The labour section is unable to provide any substantial legal help to the overseas workers who need such help due to lack of adequate resources. In the UAE, the overseas workers in the non-household sectors are entitled to get assistance from the labour court. However, since the domestic workers are not recognized as formal workers, they are unable to access the labour court. They often remain outside the radar of the formal organizations. Work contracts and visas for prospective domestic workers are arranged by the employers in the UAE. Since domestic workers are still provided with visas, an increasing number of domestic workers tend to come to the UAE and other Arab states in the region, as shown in Table 9.4.

In terms of strengths, Bangladesh has passed necessary legislation to facilitate overseas migration. A number of institutions involved in providing training exist and they facilitate migration by providing bank loans. In terms of innovations, introduction of smart cards issued to the outgoing workers has been an important achievement. Domestic workers are also provided pre-departure training and minimum language training. These programs need constant monitoring and quality enhancement. Yet the government lacks the capacity and business acumen to explore new markets for Bangladeshi labour, which could be explored in collaboration with private organizations. In this regard, private-public cooperation can open new doors. In protecting the rights of the migrants in the destination country as well as in the home country, the government needs to work closely with the nongovernmental organizations involved in securing the rights of the migrant workers. The lack of institutional capacity in Bangladesh is not restricted to migration governance, as the existing civil service structure lacks a focus on professionalism. Bangladesh does not have a cadre of professionals dedicated to the issues of labour and labour migration. But more importantly, Bangladesh needs an institutional overhaul; a change of mind-set and the creation of a culture of citizen-focused governance where the dignity of the workers and long-term national development must be the focal concerns.

5. Contextualizing migration governance in the Gulf states

I now turn my focus on issues of migration and their harmonization needs and challenges, and the possibilities for multi-tier governance at global, national and local levels. I explore migration governance by considering whether the interests of labour-sending countries can be harmonized with those of labour-receiving countries and, again, consider the UAE, a labour-receiving country, and Bangladesh, a labour-sending country, as cases in point.

As noted previously, rapid infrastructural and socioeconomic developments in the UAE, combined with its demographic realities, have led to a reliance on temporary contract workers from various labour-surplus Asian countries. The resulting demographic imbalance in the labour force has led the UAE, along with other top labour-receiving countries of South Asian, Bangladeshi labour, such as Saudi Arabia, Kuwait and Qatar, to now seriously implement policies geared toward reducing their dependence on foreign labour. In some countries, including the UAE, foreigners constitute nearly 80 percent of the labour force. For Kuwait, this figure is nearly 70 percent, and for Qatar, it is 86.5 percent. This demographic imbalance is increasingly dominating public discourses in the Arabian Gulf countries. Programs such as 'Saudization' (Nitaqat) and 'Qatarization' are in place. Nitaqat or Saudization, for example, set a quota for companies to hire Saudi citizens. In Saudi Arabia, banks that employ 500 or more employees are required to hire at least 49 percent Saudi citizens; in Public Schools, the quota is 19 percent (*Arab News* February 22, 2016). The main objectives of such programs are to reduce local unemployment and to increase self-reliance. Yet the global need for a skilled workforce is likely to continue.

To analyse this phenomenon, I use politico-economic theories of world-system analysis and globalization theories to add to the notion of good practices of global governance. In that sense, this chapter takes an interdisciplinary approach, drawing insights from public administration, international relations (IR), and sociology.

Betts raises some interesting questions on migration governance by making a distinction between perspectives of the sending states and the receiving states (Betts 2010). In this vein, it may also be asked whether we look at the governance from the perspective of the dominant groups, the state, the employers, the recruiting agents on the one hand and the subaltern's perspective on the other – namely, the perspective of the workers themselves.

Foreign workers account for more than 88.5 percent of UAE residents, many of them poor migrant workers. Immigration sponsorship laws allowed employers

Table 9.5 UAE's total population and estimates of the proportion
of non-nationals in census years

Census year	UAE population	Proportion of non-nationals
2010	8.3 million	88.5
2005	4.0 million	79.9
1995	2.5 million	75.6
1985	1.5 million	71.3
1980	1.0 million	72.1
1975	0.5 million	63.9

Source: De Bel-Air (2015, p. 8)

to recruit large numbers of foreign workers. However, in recent years, the
Middle East as a region has seen a spike in youth unemployment with it reaching as high as 25 percent. Even in the UAE, although the figures are not nearly
as high as in the region, there has been a rise in unemployment levels among
the local population. Whereas allowing temporary contractual work in the UAE
has been profitable for businesses, the steady increase in migrant population
over the decades and growing unemployment among citizens has created a
certain amount of unease. In fact, a dilemma between economic interests and
political consequences has arisen over the question of temporary contract
workers.

Given the large proportion of non-national workers and due to a combination
of factors such as international criticisms and the domestic needs for productivity
enhancement, the government of the UAE has pioneered a number of innovations to improve the conditions of the non-national workers. One of the persistent problems about which the workers routinely complained was wages. This
resulted in industrial actions by the workers on occasions, so the UAE government announced a policy known as the Wage Protection System (WPS) in
January 2008, whereby the employers were obliged to pay the workers the
agreed upon wage on time through bank transfer. The policy was implemented
in May 2009 as some of the companies needed time to adjust. Initially, 500,000
workers were covered by the WPS (WAM 26 May 2009).

The Wage Protection System was launched in phases: in the first three months
it targeted companies with over one hundred workers; it aimed to cover companies with fifteen to ninety-nine workers in the first six months; after nine
months, small companies with fewer than fifteen workers would come under
this scheme (UAE Ministry of Human Resources and Emiratisation n.d.).

A similar Wage Protection Program (WPP) is in place in Saudi Arabia, admin-
istered by the Ministry of Labour and Social Development. Under that scheme,
the ministry monitors whether the workers are paid the agreed upon wages by
the respective employing companies. Yet, in 2016 a major company[3] defaulted

on paying salaries to a large number of workers for nine months, leading to a crisis that resulted in the intervention of the Saudi King. According to the Wage Protection Program, if workers are not paid for three months, they can transfer their sponsorship to other employers and they can sue the employers (*Saudi Gazette* August 9, 2016). These recourses seem hardly adequate. If the companies default in the payment of wages, the government would not pay the companies. The Saudi case illustrates that even with the best of policies, failures in the implementation of the policies cannot be ruled out.

Migration in the Gulf states is of purely temporary nature as the UAE Minister of Labor made very clear in his presentation at the United Nations in 2006:

> the UAE has put a set of laws and regulations ensuring that guest workers in the country are temporary, not permanent immigrants; they do not leave their countries to immigrate and live permanently in the UAE, but come according to temporary work contracts to perform specific jobs, after which they return home. Such arrangement has been made according to mechanisms and procedures based on terms agreed on by countries exporting and importing labor, and are ratified by the international migration organization.
>
> (Al-Kaabi 2006)

The minister asserted that

> [given] the important role expatriate labor plays in stimulating the economy, the State has stated laws and regulations to regulate entry, residence and work of foreign workers in the country, ensuring the protection of their rights in accordance with national laws and international treaties on labor and human rights.

The Minister stated that the UAE has ratified nine international treaties on working hours, compulsory labour, inspection of work in industry and trading, night work for women, equal wages for males and females, banning compulsory labour and minimum age for labour, discrimination in employment and occupation, and ending child labour (Al-Kaabi 2006). However, one writer has pointed out that the UAE is not a signatory to 'The 1990 UN Convention on the Protection of the Rights of All Migrant Workers and Members of Their Families' (Mahdavi 2011, p. 51). This has direct bearings on domestic workers. One of the difficulties in the migration governance in the UAE is that employment of household or domestic workers falls outside the ambit of the Ministry of Labor, renamed the Ministry of Human Resources and Emiratization. Domestic employment and the workers involved in this sector fall under the Ministry of Interior. Household workers remain outside the purview of wage protection and other measures offered by the ministry in charge of labour.

The Minister of Labor in the UAE, HE Saqr Ghobash, presented a number of critically important ideas to protect the interests of the migrant workers at the

UN Informal Thematic Debate on Migration and Development. In his address on Improving International Cooperation on Migration and Development, the Minister clearly identified the cost of migration, or, recruitment cost. Such high cost, according to Ghobash, may offset the gain from overseas workers. To ratio nalize the cost of migration, governments in the countries of origin need to pass appropriate legislation and ensure enforcement. According to the Minister,

> Workers need to be empowered to exercise their rights to: informed consent to migrate, fair and transparent recruitment practices, transparent enforceable contracts, protected wages, benefits and end-of-service compensation, and decent work conditions.
>
> (Ghobash 2011, p. 2)

The Minister also emphasized the need to arrange loans and pre-departure information and orientation programs. At the same time, the Minister emphasized the need for consultation and collaboration between the origin and the destination countries in the multilateral framework of the Colombo Process and Abu Dhabi Dialogue.

6.   Migration governance to migration diplomacy

Since migration governance involves relations between multiple state actors and international non-state actors, migration governance leads to migration diplomacy. More intergovernmental initiatives are needed in harmonizing the interests of labour-sending countries with those of labour-receiving countries. There are challenges to such harmonization in an asymmetrical world. The real test is to overcome those challenges through good governance and development diplomacy.

The key problem is to harmonize the interests of the labour-sending countries with those of labour-receiving countries. Their interests are different but they are complementary. In this analysis, I focus on the complementarity of interests rather than their disharmony. As the world is asymmetrical and unequal, not all the nations have the same level of bargaining power. We are living in a highly asymmetrical world. The relative wealth of nations is manifested in the differences in per capita income. In 2015, according to the World Bank's Annual Development Report, the UAE had a per capita gross national income (GNI) of USD70,570, compared to Bangladesh's per capita GNI of USD3,550 (see Table 9.6). The two countries are in an asymmetric economic position. Exportable labour as a 'commodity' does not offer much bargaining power for Bangladesh; there are other countries waiting to export labour. In South Asia, Nepal and Burma are both keen to export labour, and, in fact, the number of migrant workers from Nepal is rising. The UAE has also diversified the sources of labour in recent years.

Although a proactive diplomacy and improvement of relations will help, the asymmetrical relations will continue to put the labour-sending countries at a

Table 9.6 Comparison of per capita income of the source and receiving countries

Source country	GDP per capita 2015 in USD	GNI (PPP) 2015 in USD
Afghanistan	590.3	1,990
Nepal	732.3	2,500
Bangladesh	1,211.7	3,550
Pakistan	1,429	5,350
India	1,581.6	6,020
Philippines	2,899.4	8,900
Sri Lanka	3,926.2	11,480
Destination country		
Oman	15,645.1	37,340
Saudi Arabia	20,481.7	54,730
Bahrain	23,395.7	39,140
Kuwait	28,984.6	79,970
UAE	40,438.4	70,570
Qatar	74,667.2	140,720

Source: Compiled by the author from World Bank country indicators published at http://data.worldbank.org/indicator/NY.GDP.MKTP.CD.

disadvantage. For the receiving countries, the goal of diversification of the economy will entail an improvement in migration governance so that it can ensure immigration of skilled and highly skilled workers who can help achieve their stated goals. Improvement in the governance of temporary labour migration can be of great benefit both for the stakeholders involved – namely, the labour-receiving country and the labour-sending countries and also the contract labourers. In January 2008 the UAE government took the lead in this regard by initiating the Abu Dhabi Dialogue in partnership with the International Organization for Migration (IOM). This initiative included all the major stakeholders: representatives of labour-sending countries and labour-receiving countries; international nongovernmental organizations, such as Human Rights Watch; and intergovernmental organizations, such as the IOM and International Labour Organization.

As we discuss the harmonization of interests of the two sets of countries, we need to find a complementarity of interests between them in pursuing their respective national interests. A win–win situation is possible for both, provided the negotiations are successfully conducted and the resulting policies implemented. For example, skill development is of crucial importance for both the labour-sending and labour-receiving countries. Since the employment at this point is of a temporary nature, the skilled-workers would eventually return to their home countries with added experience and, if deployed properly, can contribute to the development of their own countries. Source countries must appreciate the importance of human resource development and how their own economies can benefit in the long-run and not treat export of labour as a temporary, quick fix solution to their unemployment problem.

While governance reforms in both labour-sending as well as labour-receiving countries is of urgent need, sending countries should move toward long-term thinking. Governance reforms, according to Dani Rodrik, include 'reducing corruption, improving the rule of law, increasing the accountability and effectiveness of public institutions, and enhancing access and voice of the citizenry' (Rodrik 2008). By reducing corruption, the quality of governance in Bangladesh can be vastly improved. However, following Rodrik's caveat, rather than using governance in a broad sense, one has to contextualize and attempt to introduce governance reforms in specific institutions.

In the light of IOM's migration governance index, an index to measure the performance of migration governance needs to be developed as a priority. Institutional capacity remains weak because of the lack of professionalism of the officials in charge of migration management. For example, there is a paucity of reliable data on the number of Bangladeshi overseas workers. The Bureau of Manpower, Employment and Training has data on cumulative and a monthly or annual breakdown of the number of workers overseas, based on the exit document. However, since there is no record of returnee workers, those numbers remain incomplete. Apart from improving the counting of migrant workers, the services to the migrant workers can be improved at three levels of the migration process.

Studies are needed to examine both the short-term and the long-term consequences of such high rates of migration for both the labour-sending and labour-receiving countries. One of the challenges is the ability of the labour-sending countries to develop human resources appropriate for national development, as they remain dependent on only exportable skills. A re-examination of development planning and future trends of labour migration in view of sustainable national development is urgently needed. As the number of women migrant professionals and workers is increasing, comparative research is needed on migrant women from Southeast and South Asia and the various social, economic and cultural ramifications. Here, too, a bilateral – even multilateral – approach involving labour-receiving and labour-sending countries would be more effective to ensure the security and dignity of temporary contractual workers.

7. From the Colombo process to Abu Dhabi Dialogue

In response to calls from several Asian labour-sending countries, the Ministerial Consultation for Asian Labour Sending Countries was held in 2003 in Colombo, Sri Lanka. The ten states initially represented – Bangladesh, China, India, Indonesia, Nepal, Pakistan, the Philippines, Sri Lanka, Thailand and Vietnam – made recommendations for the effective management of overseas employment programs and agreed to regular follow-up meetings. Since the meeting, the member states of the 'Colombo Process' have met in Manila, Bali and Dhaka in 2004, 2005 and 2011, respectively, to review and monitor the implementation of previous recommendations and identify areas for future action.

Since 2003, the Colombo Process has been an important initiative to coordinate the policies of labour-sending countries. Labour-sending countries began to talk about what they could do collectively, which led to the start of the Colombo process in 2003. Initially, the ten participating states were Bangladesh, China, India, Indonesia, Nepal, Pakistan, the Philippines, Sri Lanka, Thailand and Vietnam. In the first meeting, the representatives of these countries made recommendations for the effective management of overseas-employment programs and agreed to regular follow-up meetings. Then, in 2004, the representatives of the labour-sending countries met in Manila. They met in Bali in 2005 when, for the first time, they also invited officials from labour-receiving countries. In 2011, the fourth meeting of the Colombo process took place in Dhaka. The theme of the Fourth Colombo Process meeting was 'Migration with Dignity'. Apart from the Asian migrant-sending countries, representatives of the migrant-receiving countries took part in the Bali and Dhaka meetings. The Ministerial Consultations in Bali and in Dhaka were enriched by the participation of several countries of destination: Australia, Bahrain, European Union, Italy, Kuwait, Malaysia, Qatar, Korea, Saudi Arabia, South Korea, Switzerland, United Arab Emirates and the United States. As the Colombo Process evolved with each Ministerial Consultation, new members and partners have joined and the Consultations have expanded in scope.[4]

In January 2008, at the Abu Dhabi Dialogue in partnership with International Organization for Migration (IOM), all the major stakeholders were present: representatives of the labour-sending countries and labour-receiving countries, international nongovernmental organizations such as Human Rights Watch, and intergovernmental organizations such as IOM and International Labour Organization. However, to harmonize the policies of the labour-sending countries with those of labour-receiving countries, this process should be continued. In fact, the Abu Dhabi Dialogue provides an excellent model for creating a multilateral platform involving all the stakeholders. The Abu Dhabi Dialogue, held in May 2016, focused a great deal of attention on the protection of the rights of the workers as well as the promotion of their interests. At the Abu Dhabi Dialogue, Mubarak Al Daheri, the Undersecretary of the Ministry of Human Resources and Emiratization, UAE said, 'We want to end negative practices that the labour force may be subjected to and want to establish a high level of transparency in recruitment practices' (*Gulf News* May 11, 2016). The UAE officials highlighted the need to strengthen cooperation between labour importing and exporting countries of Asia. Dr. Omar Al Nuaimi, another official, also underscored the need to protect 'the rights of the workforce, especially the lower end of workers from the unskilled and semi-skilled category' (*Gulf News* May 11, 2016).

The mobility of workers received special attention. Mobility of workers not only increases labour market efficiency; it provides an incentive to the workers to enhance their skill level and wages with positive outcomes for productivity. The new labour policy of the UAE government, announced in January 2016, made it easier for the workers to leave a job after six months of work. The new labour law also made the employment contract more transparent, with contract papers available in eleven languages. In addition to Arabic and English, the other approved languages are Bengali, Chinese, Dari, Hindi, Malayalam, Nepalese, Sri Lankan, Tamil and Urdu. In addition to labour mobility, the new law also paid a great deal of attention to ethical recruitment, skill development and career mobility of the workers. From the NGO sector, the Migrant Forum of Asia (MFA) was invited to address the Abu Dhabi Dialogue. William Gois of MFA emphasized fair and ethical recruitment and articulated the need to protect the migrants from the rapacious recruiting agents who charge them exorbitant fees. For Gois, it is a case of uneven power relations where migrant workers are powerless. In order to improve the situation, the power differential has to change. His call for a living wage for the migrant workers also received attention.

Several participants agreed that proper application of information technology will increase transparency. Technology can also reduce information asymmetry, a condition that places the migrant workers at a disadvantage. The government of India, under the Ministry of Rural Development, has taken the lead in creating a database of rural workers at various levels to help improve access to the labour market. India also has a Ministry of Skill Development and Entrepreneurship dedicated to skill development. The Indian Ministry of External Affairs has implemented a system called eMigrate, where a distinction is made between Emigration Check Not Required (ECNR; mostly educated, professionals and skilled labour) and Emigration Check Required (ECR), which tracks the less or uneducated workers who receive special attention to protect them against fraudulent employment agencies and exploitation (interview with Indian Labour Attaché, Abu Dhabi, April 20, 2016). The portal of eMigrate requires overseas employers to register by providing full details of their company profile. Similarly, employment agencies are also required to register by providing detailed information about their company, including the backgrounds of their management. All the stakeholders involved in the recruitment of the Indian workers are on the same page, enabling the Indian government to monitor and take action against potential fraudulent practices.

Saudi Arabia's Ministry of Labour and Social Development has also devised a portal titled MUSANED for the recruitment of domestic labour. It is intended that both employer and employee data would be stored in this portal. This system for recruiting domestic help would screen out blacklisted employers or those with record of defaults in payments. It would also exclude employees with criminal records or health issues. On an experimental basis, Saudi Arabia has launched this system in partnership with Bangladesh, according to the Saudi representative at the Abu Dhabi Dialogue. This portal is equipped with smartphone applications which would facilitate E-visa, E-contract and E-recruiting, ensuring transparency. This system has great potential and can be replicated in other cases. Discussions have focussed on the present challenges and assessed the improvements made since the last Abu Dhabi Dialogue in 2008. Although information technology is not a panacea, it can play an important role in reducing, if not removing, information asymmetry.

8. Conclusions

A well-governed society must address itself to the reduction of human suffering and vulnerabilities that the citizens face. Most of the stable nation states are geared to reduce suffering and enhance wellbeing of their citizens. Migrants often fall between the interstices of the nation states. The home countries that are ultimately responsible for their protection and welfare are too weak to provide those services; however, the host countries may provide minimum attention to the condition of the non-citizens as they prioritize the welfare of their own citizens. It is the lack of appropriate institutional frameworks that result in the vulnerability of the migrant workers in the host countries of the Gulf region.

International agencies such as ILO and IOM can provide important sources of information and data and remind the national governments of their obligations. But other than this, very little can be accomplished by international agencies. IOM is developing a migration governance index (MGI) and will test their indices on fifteen pilot countries: Bahrain, Bangladesh, Canada, Costa Rica, Germany, Ghana, Italy, Mexico, Moldova, Morocco, South Africa, South Korea, Sweden, the Philippines and Turkey (The Economist Intelligence Unit 2016).

The Global Migration Data Analysis Centre (GMDAC) recognizes the positive contribution of migrants to economic growth; commits to eradicating forced labour and human trafficking, and to end child labour; calls for the empowerment of vulnerable groups, including refugees, internally displaced persons and migrants; calls for access by all, including migrants, to life-long learning opportunities; and highlights the impact of humanitarian crises and forced displacement of people to make way for development projects. Of the United Nations' seventeen sustainable development goals, several are relevant to the condition of the migrant workers – for example, Goal 5, Gender equality (5.2 Trafficking of women and children); Goal 8, Employment and decent work (8.7 End modern slavery including trafficking; 8.8 Migrant worker rights); Goal 10, Reduce inequality (10.7 Orderly migration through well-managed policies; 10.c Migrant remittances); and Goal 16, Peaceful and Inclusive societies (16.2 Trafficking of children) (United Nations n.d.). Member states of the United Nations need to pay heed to these goals to ensure their commitment to sustainable global development is achieved, which is in the interests of all.

To improve governance, a clearer understanding of the best practices in each of the labour-sending countries, as well as learning from each other's experiences, is of utmost importance. This chapter examined various existing institutions and processes at the global and/or international level that oversee migration processes under the initiative of the United Nations and the regional efforts that began with the Colombo process in 2003. It is also of utmost importance for the improvement of governance to have a clearer understanding of the best practices in each of the labour-sending countries and to learn from each other's experiences. A commitment to recognize the rights of wellbeing of the migrant workers is also necessary. Although a range of legislation is in place to ensure safe and ethical migration, a concerted effort is still lacking in the effective implementation of those policies. Migration is still within the jurisdiction of national governance. Yet to improve the effectiveness of migration governance that entails ensuring safe migration, protecting the dignity and wellbeing of the migrants, and ensuring their safe-return to the source countries, all three tiers of governance – global, national and local – need to be made efficient, coordinated and accountable.

Notes

1 Mohamed Khaled Yar was one of the early migrants to Abu Dhabi. He came to the United Arab Emirates in June 1975 and worked until his retirement in 2016 (interview conducted on August 3, 2016).
2 In an interview conducted with Arman U. Chowdhury, the Labour Councillor of Bangladesh Embassy in the UAE on August 6, 2016, the estimated figure was shared. Chowdhury also made a case for the advantages of the insurance scheme for the domestic workers, which had been in place in Dubai since 2012. Because of bureaucratic tardiness, the insurance policy was not followed up in Abu Dhabi. While Abu Dhabi, the capital of the UAE, is the location of the Bangladesh Embassy where at this point two labour councillors are at work. In Dubai there is a Consular Office supported by a Labour councillor (interview conducted on July 30, 2016).
3 Saudi Oger Ltd.
4 More detailed information about the Colombo Process can be viewed at http://www.colomboprocess.org/about-the-colombo-process.

References

Abbot, KW and Snidal, D 2009, 'Strengthening International Regulation through Transnational New Governance: Overcoming the Orchestration Deficit', *Vanderbilt Journal of Transnational Law*, vol. 42, no. 2, pp. 501–78.
Al-Kaabi, AA 2006, *Statement Made at the UN General Assembly's High-Level Dialogue on International Migration and Development*, viewed 19 August 2016, <www.un.org/webcast/migration/pdfs/united_arab_emirates-e.pdf>.
Arab News, Jeddah 2016, 'New "Fairer" Saudization Rules Come into Force', viewed 19 August 2016, <http://www.arabnews.com/saudi-arabia/news/709166>.
Betts, A 2010, *Migration Governance: Alternative Futures*, Background Paper, *World Migration Report 2010*, IOM, Geneva.
Betts, A 2011, 'Introduction: Global Migration Governance', in A Betts (ed), *Global Migration Governance*, pp. 1–33, Oxford University Press, Oxford. Published to Oxford Scholarship Online: 11 January doi:10.1093/acprof:oso/9780199 600458.001.0001.

Castles, S and Miller, M 2003, *The Age of Migration: International Population Movements in the Modern World*, Guilford Publications, New York.

Cresswell, T 2006, *On the Move: Mobility in the Modern Western World*, Routledge, New York and London.

De Bel-Air, F 2015 *Demography, Migration, and the Labour Market in the UAE*, Explanatory Note No. 7/2015, Gulf Labour Market and Migration (GLMM) programme of the Migration Policy Center (MPC) and the Gulf Research Center (GRC), viewed 19 August, <http://cadmus.eui.eu/handle/1814/36375>.

The Economist Intelligence Unit 2016, *Measuring Well-governed Migration: The 2016 Migration Governance Index*, The Economist Intelligence Unit, London.

Elliot, A and Urry, J 2010, *Mobile Lives*, Routledge, London and New York.

Ghobash, Saqr HE 2011, *Address at the UN Informal Thematic Debate on Migration and Development: Panel 2 Improving International Cooperation on Migration and Development.* United Nations, New York, viewed 19 August 2016, <www.u.org/en/ga/president/65/initiatives/Migration/Mr.%20Saqr%20Ghobash%20_Eng_.pdf>.

Ghosh, B (ed) 2000, *Managing Migration: Time for a New International Regime?*, Oxford University Press, Oxford.

Gulf News 2016, Workers in UAE May Soon Get Freedom to Move between Jobs, May 11, 2016, viewed 10 October 2016, <http://gulfnews.com/news/uae/government/workers-in-uae-may-soon-get-freedom-to-move-between-jobs-1.1825376>.

Human Rights Watch 2006, *Building Towers, Exploiting Workers: Exploitation of Migrant Construction Workers in the United Arab Emirates*, Human Rights Watch, New York.

Human Rights Watch 2009, *The Island of Happiness: Exploitation of Migrant Workers in the Saadiyat Island*, Human Rights Watch, New York.

International Labour Organization 2014, *ILO and the Global Migration Group: Improving Global Migration Governance*, viewed 14 July 2016, <http://www.ilo.org/global/topics/labour-migration/WCMS_241411/lang – en/index.htm>.

International Organization for Migration (IOM) 2011, *Glossary on Migration*, 2nd edn, International Migration Law, no. 25, IOM, Geneva.

Khondker, HH 2010, 'Wanted But Not Welcome: Social Determinants of Labor Migration in the UAE', in JN Pieterse and HH Khondker (eds), *21st Century Globalization: Perspectives from the Gulf,* Zayed University Press, Abu Dhabi and Dubai, pp. 205–33.

Khondker, HH and Madi, M 2012, *Contract Workers in the UAE* (Unpublished Paper), Department of Humanities and Social Sciences, Zayed University, Abu Dhabi.

Koser, K 2010, 'Introduction: International Migration and Global governance', *Global Governance*, vol. 16, pp. 301–15.

Lobel, O 2004, 'The Renew Deal: The Fall of Regulation and the Rise of Governance in Contemporary Legal Thought', *Minnesota Law Review*, vol. 89, p. 262.

Mahdavi, Pardis 2011, *Gridlock: Labor, Migration, and Human Trafficking in Dubai*, Stanford University Press, Stanford, CA.

The National, UAE 2016, 'Bangladeshi Housemaids in UAE Get Mandatory Insurance Policy', 23 April 2016, viewed 19 August 2016, <http://www.thenational.ae/uae/bangladeshi-housemaids-in-uae-get-mandatory-insurance-policy>.

Newland, K 2010, 'The Governance of International Migration: Mechanisms, Processes, and Institutions', *Global Governance*, vol. 16, pp. 331–43.

Ohmae, K 1990, *The Borderless World*, Harper Business, New York.

Rodrik, D 2008, 'Getting Governance Right', viewed 20 June 2016, <https.//www.project-syndicate.org/commentary/getting-governance-right?barrier=true>.

Rosenau, JN 1995, 'Governance in the Twenty-first Century', *Global Governance*, vol. 1, pp. 13–43.

Rosenau, JN and Cziempel, E (eds) 1992, *Governance without Government: Order and Change in World Politics*, Cambridge University Press, Cambridge.

Ruggie, JG 2014, 'Global Governance and "New Governance Theory": Lessons from Business and Human Rights', *Global Governance*, vol. 20, pp. 5–17.

Sassen, S 1990, *The Mobility of Labor and Capital: A Study in International Investment and Labor Flow*, Cambridge University Press, Cambridge.

Saudi Gazette 2016, 'Saudi King Salman Orders Protection of Workers' Rights', 9 August 2016.

Siddiqui, T 2016, 'International Labour Migration and Remittance', in A Riaz and S Rahman (eds), *Routledge Handbook of Contemporary Bangladesh*, Routledge, New York, pp. 197–206.

Speer, II, J 1968, 'Hans Morganthau and the World State', *World Politics*, vol. 20, no. 2, pp. 207–27.

Turner, B and Khondker, H 2010, *Globalization: East and West*, Sage, London.

UAE Ministry of Human Resources and Emiratisation n.d., *2015 Worker Welfare Report*, viewed 10 October 2016, <http://www.mohre.gov.ae/MOLWebsite/en/home.aspx>

United Nations n.d., *Sustainable Development Goals: 17 Goals to Transform Our World*, viewed 20 June 2016, <http://www.un.org/sustainabledevelopment/sustainable-development-goals/>.

Urry, J 2000, *Sociology beyond Societies: Mobilities for the Twenty-first Century*, Routledge, London.

Urry, J 2007, *Mobilities*, Polity Press, Cambridge.

WAM, Emirates News Agency, UAE 2009, 'MOL and CB Launch Wage Protection System', 26 May 2009.

World Bank 2011, *Migration and Remittances Factbook*, 2nd edn, Washington, DC.

World Bank 2016a, *Migration and Remittances Factbook*, 3rd edn, Washington, DC.

World Bank 2016b, *World Bank, Country Report, Bangladesh*, viewed 10 October 2016, <http://data.worldbank.org/country/bangladesh>.

Index

Millennium Development Goals 80, 99, 164; number of international migrants according to 2, 12, 74, 152; Population Fund 178; Post-2015 Global Development Framework 164; Protocol to Prevent, Suppress, and Punish Trafficking in Persons, Especially Women and Children 56; resolution on human security 156; role of 176; Special Representative on Migration and Development 178; Sustainable Development Goals 8, 9, 154, 163–5, 179, 195–6
United States 76
unregistered migrants 43–4

Vietnam: Anti Human Trafficking Law 56; in Asia-to-Asia migration waves 19; background as migrant-sending country 34, 36; human trafficking in 158; Migrant Worker Resource Centres and drop-in centres 162; National Plan of Action on Human Trafficking 56; remittance income 40, 75; remittances 153
Voluntary Income Enhancement (VIE) migrants 54–5, 64–5, 71
voluntary migration 16–17

Wage Protection System (WPS) 183, 188–9
wellbeing 144
work contracts 130, 161, 163, 185, 194
World Bank (WB) 1, 18
World Health Organization (WHO) 154
World Justice Project Rule of Law Index 23, 25

Yingluck Shinawatra 56